Winging It in the North

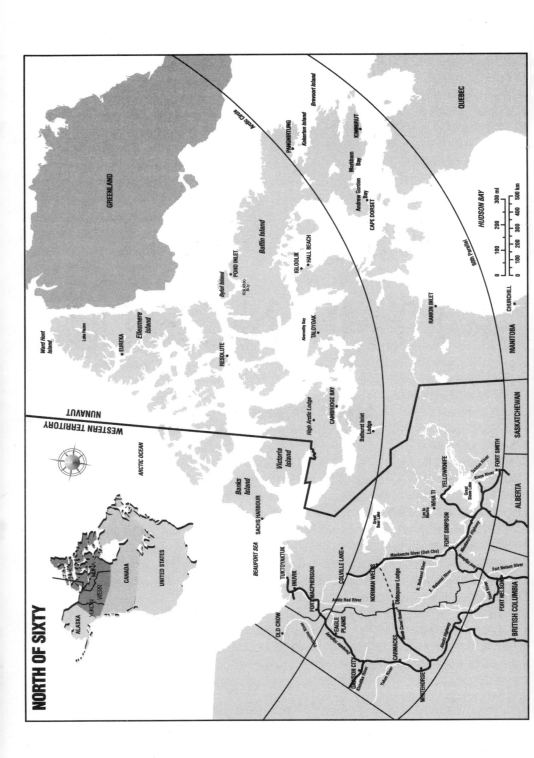

WINGING IT
IN THE NORTH

Lyn Hancock

OOLICHAN BOOKS
LANTZVILLE, BRITISH COLUMBIA, CANADA
1996

Canadian Cataloguing in Publication Data
Hancock, Lyn, (date)
  Winging it in the north

  ISBN 0-88982-159-3

  1. Hancock, Lyn, (date) 2. Canada, Northern—Biography. 3. Canada,
Northern—Description and travel. I. Title.
FC3963.1.H36A3 1996   971.9'03'092   C96-910646-7
F1090.5.H36 1996

Oolichan Books acknowledges the support received for its publishing program from the Canada Council's Block Grants program, the British Columbia Ministry of Small Business, Tourism and Culture, and the Department of Canadian Heritage.

Cover photo courtesy of Lyn Hancock.
Maps by Keith Wilson, West Coast Imaging & Design.

Published by
Oolichan Books
P.O. Box 10
Lantzville, British Columbia
Canada V0R 2H0

Printed in Canada

With much love
to Doris and Ted Taylor,
my Mum and Dad,
who gave me wings

Acknowledgements

HOW DO I THANK THE HUNDREDS—no, the thousands—of people who have helped me write these stories during my thirty-eight years of wandering?

I'm indebted to the bush pilots who squeezed me in as they delivered packages and picked up passengers in some of the wildest places on the planet; the strangers who let me hitch rides on their scows, skidoos, and pickup trucks; the outfitters who shared their love of the land and its adventures; the scientists who took me with them to dig permafrost or tag polar bears; the hunters and fishermen who let me tag along on their once-in-a-lifetime trips; the elders who invited me into tents and cabins to share their memories and tea; the kids who tugged at my arms to take me to their favourite places; and to those strangers, now friends, who put me up and then put up with cameras and ceaseless conversation (yes, Bill Lyall of Cambridge Bay, I *am* a noisy seagull, but thanks for having me back).

Their names are scribbled in notebooks and on countless scraps of paper, and sometimes their faces don't instantly come to mind, but their kindnesses are remembered and their spirit is indelibly printed in my heart. *Mahsi cho, qujannamiik.* Thank you.

The North can be a difficult, expensive place to get around, and most people up here do it at government or industry expense. I have been fortunate on many occasions to trade words and images for seats on planes, which are like buses in these roadless landscapes. Thank you First Air, Ptarmigan Airways, NWT Air, Canadian Airlines, Buffalo Airways, Aklak Air, Simpson Air, Wolverine Air, South Nahanni Airways, Kenn Borek Air, Trans North Air, North-Wright Air, Air Tindi, Liard Air, and BHP. I am grateful, too, to Nissan (Datsun) and Subaru for trusting your vehicles to me for trips on roads that were more like tracks in those pioneering days.

Thank you to the newspapers and magazines in which some of the material in *Winging It in the North* has previously been published. These include: *Above and Beyond, Up Here, Northwest Explorer, The Globe and Mail, Los Angeles Times, Chatelaine, Edmonton Journal, West Australian, Western People, News North, Alaska, BC Outdoors, Canadian Geographic, Hunter's Quest, Victoria Times Colonist,* and *Skyword.* I am indebted also to my longtime buddy, Ivy Pye, who generously shared her journal and her refreshing point of view.

Dene and Inuit did not have a written language, and not yet is there a standard orthography to which everybody agrees, although movement towards one has begun. Different communities use different spellings for the same word. In choosing the spellings for this book, I have relied on many people for advice. I wish to thank especially Peter Ernerk, Norman Keenainak, and Sarah Leonardis. I hope my compromises are accepted.

Thank you, Canada Council and NWT Arts Council, for your own generous contributions to my efforts—through my books, photographs, and lectures—to tell the world about this vast but little-known part of Canada. Are your ears still ringing from my joyous reaction when you phoned me with news of my grant?

Thank you, Government of the Northwest Territories and Government of the Yukon, for your unwavering faith in me as an ambassador for the North and for the many times over nearly three decades that you have smoothed my path.

And for sharing my vision, matching my enthusiasm with unfailing encouragement, and above all, having the courage to let me tell my stories as they happened, I will always be grateful to Rhonda

Bailey and Ursula Vaira of Oolichan Books, the little publishing house by the sea in Lantzville, British Columbia. Far from the centres of Toronto and New York, I found a publisher who understands that north is a landscape of the soul.

—Lyn Hancock, 1996

The North can be a difficult, expensive place to get around, and most people up here do it at government or industry expense. I have been fortunate on many occasions to trade words and images for seats on planes, which are like buses in these roadless landscapes. Thank you First Air, Ptarmigan Airways, NWT Air, Canadian Airlines, Buffalo Airways, Aklak Air, Simpson Air, Wolverine Air, South Nahanni Airways, Kenn Borek Air, Trans North Air, North-Wright Air, Air Tindi, Liard Air, and BHP. I am grateful, too, to Nissan (Datsun) and Subaru for trusting your vehicles to me for trips on roads that were more like tracks in those pioneering days.

Thank you to the newspapers and magazines in which some of the material in *Winging It in the North* has previously been published. These include: *Above and Beyond, Up Here, Northwest Explorer, The Globe and Mail, Los Angeles Times, Chatelaine, Edmonton Journal, West Australian, Western People, News North, Alaska, BC Outdoors, Canadian Geographic, Hunter's Quest, Victoria Times Colonist,* and *Skyword.* I am indebted also to my longtime buddy, Ivy Pye, who generously shared her journal and her refreshing point of view.

Dene and Inuit did not have a written language, and not yet is there a standard orthography to which everybody agrees, although movement towards one has begun. Different communities use different spellings for the same word. In choosing the spellings for this book, I have relied on many people for advice. I wish to thank especially Peter Ernerk, Norman Keenainak, and Sarah Leonardis. I hope my compromises are accepted.

Thank you, Canada Council and NWT Arts Council, for your own generous contributions to my efforts—through my books, photographs, and lectures—to tell the world about this vast but little-known part of Canada. Are your ears still ringing from my joyous reaction when you phoned me with news of my grant?

Thank you, Government of the Northwest Territories and Government of the Yukon, for your unwavering faith in me as an ambassador for the North and for the many times over nearly three decades that you have smoothed my path.

And for sharing my vision, matching my enthusiasm with unfailing encouragement, and above all, having the courage to let me tell my stories as they happened, I will always be grateful to Rhonda

Bailey and Ursula Vaira of Oolichan Books, the little publishing house by the sea in Lantzville, British Columbia. Far from the centres of Toronto and New York, I found a publisher who understands that north is a landscape of the soul.

—Lyn Hancock, 1996

Contents

Foreword

I FIRST MET LYN HANCOCK IN 1972. It was at some community hall in the far reaches of the Arctic; I don't remember exactly where. I was the information director for the territorial government in those days and was on a tour with Stu Hodgson, the infamous Commissioner of the NWT who ruled this vast region like a benevolent dictator.

Lyn, meanwhile, was in the midst of one of her adventures. She was trying to cross the Northwest Passage in a rubber boat, hoping to make a name for herself from this and other Arctic exploits. I didn't think much of her plan at the time and Lyn likes to remind me of that fact. Well, sorry I doubted you, Lyn. You were right and I was wrong.

I left the territorial government in 1975 and went on to become the publisher of *Above and Beyond*, a magazine about the North. Lyn became a valued contributor. She is without question the most experienced Arctic travel writer on the scene today. Her work has appeared in many popular publications such as *Canadian Geographic, Alaska,* and *The Globe and Mail*. I'm happy she had time to write for me.

Lyn is a true adventurer. You'll see that for yourself as you digest these pages. She's also fearless—you'll see that side of her, too. But most of all, Lyn is a navigator who has found paths into secret corners of the North. With an entertaining, highly personal writing style and superb photographs, she throws light into places most of us will never see. Without Lyn's work, the North would be a greater mystery to many people than it already is.

Thanks, Lyn. I won't doubt you next time.

—Jake Ootes, Northern Publisher and MLA Yellowknife Centre, September 25, 1996.

Introduction

WINGING IT IN THE NORTH is an autobiographical record of one woman's extraordinary experiences "North of Sixty" over the past twenty-five years.

The Arctic is my homeland and there is no other place like it on earth. It is a landscape of immense beauty and has one of the coldest climates in the world. Inuit and other aboriginal peoples have adapted and survived in this environment for thousands of years. In Lyn Hancock's stories, we see how people live in harmony with the northern environment.

People who have made the North their home in recent years, or simply visited it, will identify especially with the stories told in *Winging It in the North*, but Lyn's stories are popular with indigenous people too. She describes events as they actually happen and in an interesting way. Despite their harsh environment, Inuit appreciate good fun and Lyn can make people laugh. She can also laugh at herself, such as the time she appeared on the cover of a magazine—covered in nothing but mud.

I first met Lyn twenty-five years ago when she went caribou hunting on Banks Island with my grandmother Susie Tiktalik, my Aunt

Edith, and my cousin Bella. We called her "the Girl in the Yellow Hat" and that hat became one of her trademarks. Lyn came in the summer, but stayed for the fall. I loaned her my parka so she wouldn't freeze! This was the beginning of Lyn Hancock's affection for the North and its peoples. She has been an ambassador for the North ever since.

Through Lyn's account of her personal experiences in a land where travel is not easy and where one has to be flexible, readers will learn of the changes that have occurred up here during the last two or three decades. They will learn what life is like now in the North.

—Rosemarie Kuptana
(President, Inuit Circumpolar Conference
and formerly President, Inuit Tapirisat of Canada),
October 4, 1996

Winging It: A Way Of Life

WHEN I WAS EIGHT YEARS OLD and growing up in Fremantle, Western Australia, I started saving to see the world. Born on the bottom end of the globe, I had no desire then to see the top. Like most Aussie travellers at the time, I dreamed of being at the centre. I longed to know London, Paris, Athens, Rome—I planned to immerse myself in ancient civilizations.

When my parents insisted I see some of Australia before taking off to see the world, I found our organized bus tour too confining, and I left it daily to find my own way—much to the embarrassment of my mother who was left alone to explain her daughter, especially when I didn't show up at the end of the day. Usually, the passengers would find me in the bush on some fencepost where I was waiting to flag down the bus. Later, on another organized tour, this time with dozens of fellow teachers squeezed into a giant live-aboard bus, I often abandoned my companions for days at a time to seek unbeaten tracks.

Most West Aussie travellers went to Europe by the customary route of the day—by sea across the Indian Ocean and around the Cape of Good Hope to England. I started out with my peers, but, in a year when Africa was awash in bloody riots due to apartheid and independence, when people were booked three years ahead in efforts to flee a continent in political upheaval, I suddenly had the urge to leave the ship in Cape Town to hitchhike to Cairo. I had to beg the captain to let me do it in those uncertain times. I can't explain such a sudden detour from my childhood plans. Simply, Africa loomed in front of me, history was passing me by, and I had to be there, not just read about it in the newspapers.

In Durban, I dropped into the tourist department to book a tour and learned it wouldn't be available for another two weeks. I started chatting to the operator and ended up being hired as the tour guide for a group of inland Afrikaaners on their Dream Holiday in Durban-by-the-Sea. In preparation, I spent those two weeks taking daily tours of the local attractions for free.

Another day in Africa when clouds on Table Mountain stopped me climbing to the top, I whiled away a morning watching Parliament debate emergency regulations at a time when nine policemen had just been killed by crowds on the street and black South Africans were burning down government buildings in their villages. This was my first experience of any legislative assembly, and in these tense times I was amazed by the seemingly lackadaisical behaviour of the ruling party, the only side I could see from my seat above them in the Visitors' Gallery. I leaned forward on the ledge in front of me and jotted down notes of the scene in my diary. One member, tie askew, was lounging back in his seat reading a magazine. Two were chatting as if at a club party. Another was passing chocolates.

I grinned and licked my lips. "Good?" I asked in mime. The chocolate man gestured back, "Do you want some?" I nodded. Within minutes, the door to the gallery opened behind me and a curly-haired black boy presented me with a whole box of chocolates. The accompanying card read, "With the compliments of the Honourable Member for Witswatersrand." I thanked the page, waved the chocolates in the air and smiled a thank you to the member below. What an event for this day's diary! There would be more.

As I couldn't speak Afrikaans, I couldn't take an intelligent interest in the parliamentary proceedings. I was content to spend the next few minutes jotting down random thoughts on the contrast between my serious expectations of what a parliament in crisis should be doing and what seemed actually to be happening. I looked down to see the man with the chocolates trying to get my attention. He was shaking his head. "No, no," he seemed to be saying. "Don't write. Put your notebook away. Place your hands on the ledge in front of you so we can see what you are doing."

Suddenly, I realized what he must be thinking. Perhaps I had a bomb. Perhaps I was about to blow up Parliament. Not long before, someone HAD tried to blow up the Prime Minister, and he was at that very moment in a South African hospital recovering from the wounds. In the current climate of the country, I should have been apprehensive, if not plain scared. Instead, I laughed. The idea of me, an innocent tourist, playing Guy Fawkes was too ludicrous for words. Those, I could see by the now serious expression on my chocolate man's face, would have to come later.

I felt ridiculous, sitting there in the gallery of South Africa's Parliament Building, holding up my arms like a criminal. For me, being unable to write or talk with my hands is like being in jail. Fortunately, my imprisonment did not last long. Half an hour later, the door behind me opened again, and I was confronted by half a dozen members of the ruling Nationalist Party. They looked grim.

"Are you a reporter?" asked the portly, balding one.

"No, I'm a schoolteacher," I replied, startled. The ship's captain was right. My curiosity, my yen to explore, and my desire for a personal experience of world history would surely get me into trouble.

"Why then, were you writing?" he continued, still grim.

I tried to explain. Just then, another man joined the group at the door. It was my chocolate man, the Honourable Member for Witswatersrand.

"Would you join us for a tour of the buildings and then afternoon tea in the Members' Lounge?" he asked graciously with a nod to the others.

I relaxed and relished the next hour. It seemed incredible that I should come in off the street from an aborted hike up a mountain to luck in to a personalized tour of parliament with enough members in tow to cause a bell to be rung later in the chambers for lack of a quorum to continue the nation's business.

I didn't seem so lucky afterwards when, cake and tea finished, I sat at the elegant table—one lone woman surrounded by a dozen men—and was interrogated on Australia's White Australia Policy. Their consensus was that Australia's record in race relations was just as good (or as bad) as South Africa's, so why should apartheid be getting all the flack. I got the impression these parliamentarians wanted me to get their message to the world.

Lighthearted banter was impossible. As the afternoon wore on, I felt I was being held ransom for the sins of two countries, Australia and New Zealand, towards their aboriginal inhabitants. There was a glint of fanaticism in the eyes around that table. I was beginning to wonder if or when I was going to be released as my interrogators tried to make up their minds whether I was a reporter or tourist.

And then the mood changed. To my amazement, each one offered me a trip to his constituency. I spent the next weeks being taken around South Africa as an honoured guest. They must have wondered at this weird Australian. I would be on my way to a new town to meet their limousine and get there on a baker's cart. I would be invited to meet the Prime Minister and ask to be taken to the zoo.

One of my hostesses took me to a meeting designed to bolster South Africa's white population by encouraging more babies. Another gave his black servants a holiday weekend to show me that his family was fully able to serve themselves, including the cow on the kitchen stove. The cow was carved into neat chunks, a leg in this pot, a head in another—culture shock for one raised on thin slices of my mother's Sunday roast. My chocolate man invited me to the university to chat to a class about Australia. The hour over, I walked out of the room to be confronted by another class coming in for my next chat—and then another and another in hourly intervals after that. I took part in a play and had to learn my role in Afrikaans. By the time I was ready to continue my trek up the continent, I had been invited to work for the government of South Africa anywhere in the world.

But that empty map kept pulling me northwards. Stalking crocodiles in the Caprivi Strip. Backing from rhinos in Hluhluwe Park. Fleeing elephants in Zambezi. Getting in—and out of—a harem in Zanzibar. Caught in crossfire in Port Said.

After a Belgian diplomat begged me to wade into a Congo bloodbath in order to rescue his Mercedes (he was afraid he would be shot if he did it himself) and then drive the car back north to his home in Belgium, a new acquaintance wrote to warn my mother she should get me back south to my own home instead.

It wasn't a good month for my mother. A few weeks earlier, she'd got the news that, on my way to deliver to a doctor samples from a sick baby on a remote tobacco farm in Rhodesia, I'd rolled my hosts' car. The tribesman I flagged down at the T-junction nodded vigorously when I asked if left was the correct direction. Trouble was, he nodded the same way when I pointed questioningly to the right. My guardian angel must have been sleeping or playing her harp. Within seconds, the road around the corner ran out and I slammed into a sandhill. I made a bloody exit through the window but was otherwise unhurt. I can't say the same for the car.

My pattern of being seduced by the moment continued when I arrived in Europe. I abandoned my carefully planned itinerary and followed where opportunity beckoned. At this time, my destinations were civilized even if often the methods of getting to them were not. For the next two years, I found adventure in studying at the Royal Academy, teaching in London's East End, and when my parents came to check, spending a year with them driving around Europe in what was probably the world's first recreational vehicle, a cramped Dormobile van. I slept in the roof.

I had no particular reason for going to Canada except to earn money for a trip back by ship to Perth, Western Australia. I planned to embark in Vancouver, and after a six-week voyage across the Pacific, arrive home at 5:00 P.M. on Christmas Eve. However, on the eve of my departure, while I was working as a very inexperienced waitress in a coffeeshop close to the University of British Columbia, graduate student David Hancock asked me out on a date.

"Sorry," I said emphatically. "This is my last weekend in Canada and I'm flying to an island in a friend's float plane." In those years, I had never even seen a float plane, let alone been up in one. And I had never before known anyone who owned a whole island. David was not impressed. "How would you like to come in my float plane to my island—and count eagles?"

Surely that was too coincidental to be true. I didn't believe him for a moment. Still, the idea did seem intriguing for what would probably be the final adventure of my life. Two days later, I was bumping around Barkley Sound on a nightmare flight over eagle nests when David proposed. I cancelled my ticket on the ship, removed my luggage from the cabin on the very day of departure, and we flew home to Australia instead. We were married at Christmas, returned to Canada in the New Year, and as the wife of a biologist I found myself mothering sea lions by Easter.

Eight years later, I was travelling to the roof of the world with my husband to film wildlife in northern British Columbia, Yukon, and Alaska; and two years after that, to the Northwest Territories to prepare for a trip across the Northwest Passage in a small rubber boat. I remember thinking that this could be a good a way to die, but the thought didn't prevent me from being a dutiful wife.

In Yellowknife, we learned that the ice was not expected to break up for another month, so instead of flying to the Arctic Ocean, we made a spur-of-the-moment decision to boat there instead—a thousand miles by way of the Mackenzie River. We hoped that by the time we reached the Beaufort Sea, the ice would surely have broken and we would have water underneath us. Characteristically, we had planned our journey across the Northwest Passage for a year. We planned our journey down the Mackenzie in an hour.

A few months later, our Northwest Passage expedition was aborted, and eventually David and I were divorced. He returned south to civilization but I remained in the North. It was a long way from Australia, it was not yet my permanent home, but the North had begun to cast its spell.

Since then, I have wandered across the country alone with packsack, notebook, and cameras, "going with the flow" as people say today. I call this way of life "winging it" because people up here hop on a plane the way people elsewhere hop on a bus. But there have been almost as many times I have hopped a boat, a skidoo, a four-wheeler, or a dogteam.

I have winged around the North in other ways as well. It's an "if and but" land up here where weather and lifestyles dictate activities and strict schedules are impossible. I have to make the most of every moment. This book is a collection of some of those moments. Certainly, none of them were planned.

I remember the time I was innocently birdwatching from a barge puttering down Bathurst Inlet when I got a garbled message by bush radio: "You're invited to paddle the Rapids of the Drowned on the Slave River at Fort Smith with Jacques Rabbit van Pelican Pelt, October 13th." Considering that in October on a subarctic river I'd more likely be ice-skating than paddling, I thanked the bush pilot politely for relaying the request and went back to birdwatching. I had planned to spend October Down Under on an outback safari; I did not want to go down under the Rapids of the Drowned in any season.

It took only a moment next day at the Yellowknife airport to change my mind. A friend happened to tell me that the rafting trip would begin just two days later, August 13 not October 13. I scurried to the ticket counter and changed my routing to Fort Smith and the Rapids of the Drowned.

Over the next three days rafting the Slave River, there were certainly short bursts of heart-thumping, adrenalin-pumping excitement, but there were also long periods of rowing on flat water among tranquil rock gardens. Due to the expertise of my guides, I was never in serious danger of becoming a victim of the Rapids of the Drowned (as were the early voyageurs when they discovered this historic route).

Not so the day I got talking casually to a stranger at a bus stop at Mile 300 of the Alaska Highway in British Columbia and accepted an invitation to his trapline. Dependent this time on my own resources, I very nearly did drown while swimming the wild, wide Fort Nelson River in spring flood.

And then there was the day on the Alaska Highway at Mile 200 when I accepted an invitation to join a party of German tourists on a boat trip down the Toad, another spring-flooded river like the Fort Nelson. The skipper must have gotten his signals crossed; the non-English-speaking passengers all crowded to the wrong side of the boat, it turned over in the raging waters, and we all got tossed in the Toad. My first thoughts were to rescue my still-floating camera case, but after trying to swim after it through the driftwood and tangled debris, I was soon persuaded otherwise by the powerful current. I managed to grab a sweeper from the eroded banks and rescued myself instead.

One by one, the crew and passengers crawled out of the river, and we got a fire going to ward off hypothermia. The group chose me to hike six miles to the Alaska Highway for help. It was dark, well after midnight, and for hours not a single vehicle responded to my bedraggled entreaties to stop. Eventually, I cast caution to the wind and threw myself in the path of every oncoming light. The lights, the cars, and the big trucks all swerved to avoid me, and I chickened to the side each time to escape oblivion.

Finally, one car stopped. It was fully loaded, even to the tires on its roof, and except for gas stops, it was being driven non-stop from Alaska to New York. Nevertheless, the family squeezed me in on their knees and dropped me off at the nearest lodge. I woke up the lodge owner in the middle of the night, seconded his truck, and we drove back up the highway to rescue my shipwrecked companions.

Characteristically, in this winging through the North, I have often planned one thing but ended up doing another. Like the time I joined a group for a boat ride on the South Nahanni River. I thought I was a guest but the guide handed me a wash basin of freshly killed moose and informed me I was the cook.

And the time I scrounged a ride strapped to the groceries on a plane going from Inuvik in the Northwest Territories to Old Crow in the Yukon. The partying—and airsick—passengers were on their way home from celebrating Northern Games in Inuvik and thought I was the flight attendant. I spent the flight strapping and unstrapping myself in and out of my grocery box seat, running up and down the aisle to find places for "strawberry bags," ferrying messages between passengers, finding out arrival times from the cockpit, and explaining that no, I didn't know where the drinks were stored. When we arrived in Old Crow, the passengers were nonplussed. I got off the plane with them but I didn't get back on board. Was I going to stay? And where? they were probably wondering.

I put up my tent on the high sandy banks of the Porcupine River, but that night, Edith Josie, famed for her columns of daily life in Old Crow ("Here are the News"), invited me to her one-room log cabin for a supper of moose. I was touched when she served me a can of mandarins. Such foods are luxuries in Old Crow, where all groceries must come in by plane. I never regretted my sudden surprise job as a flight attendant nor the people I met as a result of it. Winging it has brought me to many happy and unexpected discoveries.

My mother taught me not to talk to strangers but rarely have I heeded this advice. Striking up sudden conversations has led me to some intriguing and out-of-the-way places. When the geologist sitting next to me during breakfast at the hotel in Pond Inlet learned that I was born in his own home town in Australia, he invited me for a helicopter flight over Bylot Island while he fossicked for rocks. Better still, when he needed to stay put at an interesting deposit, he instructed his pilot to fly me around Bylot Island. Having my own chopper pilot—even for an hour—was a dream come true for this northern wanderer.

Another time I was sitting on my bags by the airstrip at Norman Wells wondering what to do next when a gaggle of happy-go-lucky fishermen gathered around me. They were waiting for a chartered plane to take them fishing at Colville Lake. They were amazed that I wasn't travelling on a tight schedule with an organized itinerary as they were, and I was amazed they didn't know anything about their destination.

Colville Lake at that time was a picture postcard place, the only all-log community in Canada, a real Shangri-la with no electricity, no running water nor inside plumbing, no cars, no telephones, and no roads. Even now, there are few amenities in this tiny community of fifty-two people begun in 1962 by Oblate priest, painter, and pilot, Father Bern Will Brown. Except perhaps for Bathurst Inlet, Colville Lake is still the most traditional community in Canada.

"Why don't you come with us on the plane to Colville Lake?" asked one of the anglers. "You can tell us about the country on the way and fly back with the pilot on his return trip."

On that first visit to Colville Lake I had only five minutes standing on the dock in front of the shiny and immaculate log church, the log mission buildings, and a two-storey log museum while the fishermen unloaded their gear and met their Dene guides. I spent the minutes chatting to Bern Will Brown, who by then had left the formal priesthood and was married to Margaret, an Inuvialuk from the Mackenzie Delta.

"Come back for a longer visit," Bern said as the pilot signalled me to go. It was fifteen years before I got back to Colville Lake and then only for an hour.

This visit was a winter one which began at my front door in Fort Simpson. I hitched a ride on one of those massive Matco trucks that ply the ice road along the Mackenzie River. After an exciting forty-eight-hour bone-crunching, rib-wracking, rash-giving ride to Norman Wells, I decided not to continue for another three days cross-country on a Delta 3 all-terrain cat train delivering bulk fuel supplies to Colville Lake. I confess I jumped a plane.

"I can stay only an hour," the pilot warned. "I'm dropping off mail and groceries, that's all."

It was 1993, a year of change in Colville Lake, when electricity, power poles, and a power plant had come to the community, when stick-frame houses were beginning to replace homogeneous log cabins, when household appliances, video sets, computers, and microwave ovens had begun to replace sewing materials and trapping supplies as incoming freight. There was even talk of telephones and cable TV.

Nevertheless, Colville Lake is still the kind of place where class is dismissed when caribou are seen from the window, where pupils rush out to shoot and skin them and are back in their desks within the hour.

It was an embarrassingly short visit, but I had to "do" Colville Lake at a similar rate. As soon as we landed on skis on the frozen lake in front of the Co-op store, the pilot unloaded the mail and groceries onto the ice and the Co-op manager whisked me away by snowmobile for an hour-short tour of the town. First to the new one-room log school to meet the teacher and a few of the kids who were cutting up caribou, then to the rest of the Brown Compound, which consisted of the church, the museum and art gallery, Bern and Margaret's low-ceilinged, heat-efficient house, several guest cottages, the dog kennels, the caribou totem pole, the teacherage, and the nursing station.

Apologetically, I declined tea and breathlessly whizzed around taking pictures of Bern at his easel painting the view of the lake through his window, Margaret with some of her superb pure-bred white huskies, the Browns' famous outhouse in which I believe many famous people have sat, and anything else in between. I clicked off hasty shots with the colour camera, the black and white camera, the print camera; I tossed the video camera to the patient pilot. I am blessed, most of the time, with forbearing companions.

Colville Lake was like a deserted Disneyland; it had an unreal, dreamlike appearance. And then, like a Disneyland train, the Matco cat train with its annual load of fuel came weaving among the buildings after a two-day journey from Norman Wells. I could have stayed and gone back on the cat, I could have stayed at the teacherage and taught at the school—there are still places in this world where such informalities are possible—but there were other opportunities lurking in the hinterland. Perhaps a snowmobile trip along the Canol Trail. Perhaps a helicopter ride through Dodo Canyon. Reluctantly, I climbed into the Cessna and flew back to Norman Wells.

I hope it won't be another fifteen years before I can return to Colville Lake, and when I do, I am determined I will stay longer than five minutes or an hour. Perhaps I'll bump into another bunch of anglers . . . and this time I'll have a lot more to tell.

I have been lucky winging through the vast northland. I have been fortunate to meet the right people at just the right time. The North is still a flexible place where split decisions can be made and plans can be changed.

I nearly didn't get to Kekerten, the site of an old whaling station on Baffin Island, thirty miles south of Pangnirtung. That year, ice in Pang Fiord persisted till mid-August and blocked boats trying to deliver construction materials for the new historic park on Kekerten. When I arrived in Pangnirtung on my third attempt that summer to get to Kekerten, the overcrowded Auyuittuq Hotel was putting overflow guests in the lounge and laundry, and most of the guides and outfitters were away either caribou hunting or repairing their boats. Then came Moe.

To my surprise, Moe Keenainak, the tourism information officer, was at the airport within five minutes of my call. "You can stay at my place, meet Ann Keenleyside, the physical anthropologist who's just come back from reconstructing artifacts and grave sites on Kekerten, and Jaco Qaqasik will take you to the island at high tide tomorrow afternoon."

Simple, once we survived the journey to Moe's house on a tiny trike weighted down with Moe and his baby daughter, and me with my cumbersome packsack and camera bag. Simple, once the wind abated a bit and my Inuit guide successfully crashed through the waves and threaded through house-high icebergs to reach Kekerten Island. Simple, except that the people that I came to see, landscape architect Roel Teunissen and the team of Inuit contractors who had been building the site for three weeks, were already packed up and in their boats for the journey back to Pang for supplies when Jaco and I arrived. I pictured myself abandoned for an undetermined time on a deserted island where polar bears were sighted regularly, left with a guidebook but a guide who couldn't speak English (and I couldn't speak Inuktitut).

Roel, who had been living in a tent for three weeks, saw my predicament. He had one foot in the boat on his way to showers, a soft bed, clean clothes, and phone calls to his girlfriend. He wavered. He unpacked. He stayed to guide me around Kekerten.

Between 1857 and the mid-1920s, this low rocky island was home to American, Scottish, and Inuit whalers as they hunted whales and seals, cut up carcasses, boiled blubber, rendered oil, built sheds and sod houses—lived and died. "Watch where you walk," said Roel. "Try to stay on the boardwalk or the flagstones. There are literally thousands of artifacts you could be crunching underfoot."

With Roel as my interpreter, I wandered along the boardwalk photographing the big iron settling tanks, the stones that marked the walls of the biscuit house, the baleen storehouse, the whaling gear storehouse, the piles of barrel hoops, the remains of Inuit houses. Ann had located about eighty-five graves, reconstructed the skeletons in the correct anatomical positions, roped the boxes together with sisal to show how they used to look, and weighted them with stones on top. Bodies were either placed in barrels, the same ones whale oil had been packed in, or in boxes built from wooden planks from ships, food crates, seamen's chests, or rifle containers.

Taking advantage of the beautiful low-level light that bathed the rolling, rocky island in warmth and colour, we headed across the tundra to a windswept ridge a couple of miles east of the main displays. I wanted to take pictures of the whalers' graveyard at sunset. "It's a powerful site," said Roel reverently.

When I woke up next morning in a cold tent to wind and rain, I felt a little of the rigours of the arctic that the whalers faced. The Kekerten poster tacked to the tent flap depicted men in tiny rowboats against the towering tail of a whale as they fought icy seas and monstrous waves. Outside my tent, the harbour was filled with grey, fog-curled icebergs stranded at low tide among the bold, white-striped black rocks and densely draped seaweed. It was dismal but fascinating.

Suddenly, the sun broke through the fog, gilded the icebergs, burnished the seaweed, and shimmered the sea to blue again. Waves lapped at the beautifully weathered timbers, momentarily bringing them to life again. With the sun now producing glorious images at every turn, I could have stayed another day. The whalers are ghosts, their artifacts fragments, but the spirit of the place is alive.

But Jaco and Roel were anxious to go. Reluctantly, I followed them to the boat. An hour and a half later, after an exquisite trip on an impeccable sea, we were back in Pang.

In that year (1987) three elderly Inuit remembered Kekerten in its heyday: Nutaraq, the eldest at 100, Qatsu about 95, and Etoangat 86. "Could you take me to see Etoangat?" I asked Moe when he picked me up from the boat. He smiled enigmatically and shrugged in a way that made me abandon further conversation. Disappointed, but knowing better than to pursue the topic, I went for a last stroll through the town instead and then headed to the airport terminal.

In Pangnirtung, a village enclosed within the steep arms of Pang Fiord, the airstrip was in the middle of town. Some people dare to get to the airport by crossing the runway but I decided to walk around.

"Want to see Etoangat?" said a voice suddenly behind me. It was Moe on his trike. "You didn't think I'd let you leave town without visiting him, did you?"

Yes, I did. But there was no time to cleave through cross-cultural communication. I hauled myself on board his machine, he hugged my pack, and we sped off in a cloud of dust to Etoangat's place. The legendary Etoangat was carving an exquisite ivory dogteam at the kitchen table.

How do you interview an elder on a life spanning the stone to the laser age when your plane is due to land any moment? Fortunately for me, Etoangat was a gem. He wanted to talk, and I felt immediate rapport. We sat together at the window, Etoangat straight-backed in his chair, Moe interpreting, and me trying to pose hasty, stimulating questions, scribbling phrases for answers and taking pictures. So many memories for this man who was born in Kekerten eighty-six years ago. Which first?

His dad a whaleboat captain for the Americans till they left and the Scots turned their station into a sealskin house . . . living in a *qammaq* . . . hunting games he played with the other boys while the girls played house . . . being the youngest aboard the small boats that went out to catch whales four times longer than the boats . . . not strong enough to handle paddles as his companions did but really happy because he was often the first to spot the whales . . . moving to Bon Accord, to Pangnirtung, to Padloping . . . transporting patients by dogteam from all over Baffin Island to the hospital in Pang and not losing any on the way . . .

"There's so much more, you'll never finish it," he said in Inuktitut. "You should stay longer. You come too late, you leave too soon."

In 1996, Etoangat went to Ottawa to receive the Order of Canada for his life's achievements. A few weeks later, he died. I did come too late. I did leave too soon. It doesn't matter how fast you run, how much you pack into a day, there is never enough time.

And yet I have been winging it for longer than people expect. Recently, a reader wrote from Inuvik to compliment me on some stories I had written for a northern newspaper. "Back in the 1960s I used to enjoy your mother's stories on living with wild animals in British Columbia. I especially remember *There's a Seal in my Sleeping Bag.* How nice that you became a writer too, and that you even use her name." The reader was very surprised when I wrote to tell her that the person she was reading in the 1990s was the same Lyn Hancock she remembered from the 1960s, a Lyn Hancock who never did have any children.

I have grown older but I probably have not grown wiser. The knack I have for attracting trouble is a direct result of winging it—taking chances, talking to strangers, following whims. So far I've survived, perhaps because of a guardian angel, perhaps because of all the understanding people I've met in the North, perhaps because I have not forgotten how to laugh, especially at myself.

And I've never felt the yen to go back to London, Paris, Athens, and Rome.

Swimming to a Trapline

MY MOTHER USED TO WARN ME against taking rides with strangers. But Whit's invitation seemed too good to miss. I had met him in Fort Nelson, Mile 300 of the Alaska Highway, while I was waiting for a bus. I was on my way south to Vancouver, British Columbia, after a four-month trip around North America searching for wild places. Soon, I sighed, I would be out of wild places and into civilization. Then I met Whit. He said he was a trapper but he didn't sound like one. And that was intriguing.

"I have to check out one of the cabins on my trapline tomorrow. Do you want to come?" he said simply.

"How do you get there?" I asked just as matter-of-factly.

"Drive the Liard Highway to the Nelson River, take a barge, drive a private forestry road, hike five miles or so, then swim."

Suddenly, it didn't seem so simple.

"You sound as if you're an Aussie, you should be able to swim a river," Whit continued in response to my startled expression. "And it's only forty yards across."

I didn't want to destroy his image of Aussie girls as tough and adventurous. But sunbaking beside the surf or swimming a few lengths of an indoor pool scarcely qualified me as a strong swimmer.

The Liard and Fort Nelson rivers have long been highways for fur traders and prospectors, hunters and trappers. They were still highways in summer for river scows and barges, and in winter for dogteams, snowmobiles, and seismic machines. But now an all-weather gravel highway had been punched through the Liard River Valley between the old fur trading posts of Fort Nelson and Fort Simpson. Streams and rivers were being bridged; log cabins, once accessible only by river in summer, could now be reached all year by road. The pioneering way of life was rapidly becoming civilized. Swimming a wild river would be a challenge. I wanted to see if I could do it. Perhaps that was my main motivation.

"Of course, we could go by boat but it'd take longer to organize and you say you have to get back to Fort Nelson for the two o'clock bus," Whit said, interrupting my thoughts.

"Right, let's swim," I decided.

Whitton Anderson was no ordinary trapper, or at least he didn't fit into my image of one. His gait gave him away as a cowboy; his drawl, a Texan. His home cabins in the bush (so he said) had saunas, stereos, and stained-glass windows. He ate game and the animals he trapped, but he chose escargot and filet mignon for dinner in town and cooked Eggs Benedict for breakfast on the trapline. Books by Conrad, Vonnegut, and Schroeder were scattered beside the latest boxing magazines at his town base. He kept informed on Canadian and American literature; in fact, we shared the same literary friends.

Next morning, as we clattered out of Fort Nelson in an old car bound for the Liard, Whit related his story. His dog, Nikki, half malemute, half German shepherd, snarled at me from the back seat. Nikki, Whit's only companion on the trapline, didn't want to share.

Born on a ranch in Texas, Whit had been a cowboy, rodeo rider, and boxing coach. But he'd always "run the bush." So had his family. His son, Bry, was studying for a doctorate in history at an Oregon university but would probably take up trapping when he graduated. "He'll be the most educated trapper in the whole north country," said Whit proudly. His daughter, Donna, was a dancer and a flautist for a symphony orchestra in Seattle.

His wife, Vi, was a business executive in Mission, but according to Whit, she was one of the best bush women anywhere. "My family can all ride a horse, pack a gun, throw a knife. When the kids were young, Vi and I took them into the wilderness and they had to learn how to survive, else they'd go hungry or freeze."

We turned off the Alaska Highway onto the new Liard Highway at Mile 317. Nelson River Ferry Open 7 A.M. to 7 P.M., said the sign at the junction. Our time was limited.

The Liard Highway runs 240 miles to Fort Liard and Fort Simpson and is the first direct link between British Columbia and the Northwest Territories. Although interesting historically, important politically, and convenient for tourists venturing into Nahanni National Park and the Mackenzie Mountains, it has been described by some as rather a dreary drive. It isn't if you stop to meet the people and explore opportunities waiting for you by the roadside. For years, I had "done" the Liard: I had driven, hiked, flown, skidooed, and dogsledded this historic route. Now I was going to swim.

We reached the Nelson River in less than an hour, stopping only to birdwatch at streams and listen to beavers sounding at sloughs. At the Nelson, Mile 27.6, machines were taking giant bites of mud from the · banks in readiness for building a bridge. We waited for the barge. The ferryman recognized me from the previous week when my truck got stuck in the mud for fifteen hours on an ungravelled section. He was surprised to see me here again. He was even more surprised when he heard that I planned to swim his river.

"It's in full flood," he said disbelievingly. "We measured the current last night, nine kilometres an hour, the fastest it gets." I tried to look calm.

"The company that's been barging this river for years says it's impossible too," added Whit casually.

I was beginning to wonder if I would see that ferryman for a third time. "Still, you can take a look and see what you think when you get there." Whit tried to sound reassuring.

I tried not to think of the current swirling tempestuously against the barge as the tug pushed us over to the other side of the river. One of the construction crew had told me that the bridge planned for the Nelson had to be unusually long (about four hundred yards) and unusually strong to match the current at high water. I didn't remind Whit that he said the river was a mere forty yards across. Somewhere, he'd missed a zero.

The ferryman shovelled a dirt ramp for our car on the other side of the river and waved us good-bye. I was uncharacteristically quiet.

We turned west on the Liard Forest Service Road (recently opened all year to allow summer logging) and headed in the direction of the abandoned Hudson's Bay Company trading post of Nelson Forks. About half an hour later, Whit stopped the car and said, "Here's where we walk." Nikki, who'd been snarling at me throughout the journey despite Whit's remonstrations, bounded across my shoulders and jumped outside. "He knows he's going to be home soon," Whit said. I didn't feel as sure.

"Nikki's probably the best bush dog in the whole north country," Whit commented as we hitched on our packs. "He's always with me, even when I drove heavy equipment one year for Cadillac mine at Nahanni. Nikki rode the cab on my front-end loader. He's saved my life twice, once when he pulled me from a fire in my cabin and again when he broke the charge of an attacking black bear."

"Talking of bears," I interrupted, pointing to the muddy track ahead, "those tracks are pretty fresh and those bears have been eating fresh berries."

"Sure, plenty of bears around," Whit shrugged. "We should see one or two but don't worry, Nikki will protect us if it's necessary."

As we trudged along the colourful, weed-fringed trail which once had been a logging road, ravens belled overhead, nighthawks fluttered, and hawks screamed, but we didn't see the owners of the plentiful tracks. This was Whit's trapping area. Inevitably, the conversation turned to his job. Unlike many trappers, he lives along his trapline all year. Occasionally, his family visits. He and his son, Bry, had just been doing some wrangling near Muncho Lake.

"Part of me doesn't like trapping," he confessed, guessing what I was thinking, "but people, especially those from cities, criticize when they don't really know anything about it. Most animals don't die of any great pain, they freeze. And we're not killing all the animals off as people say. This country is loaded with wildlife. We farm the land, we have to. I want my kids to have just as many animals around when they trap as there are now for me. I bet more wildlife is lost when habitat is destroyed by bad logging practices than by hunting and trapping."

He answered my unspoken questions. "My cabins are less than twenty miles apart and I check my traps often. I use Conibear traps when I can but they're not always the best even for the animals. You know, Lyn, boxers and trappers have a lot in common: they can't be dumb, they have to out-think the opposition. I enjoy the challenge of trying to out-think the animals. That's why I use a lot of snares. It's fast becoming a lost art."

Whit was sympathetic to the animals he trapped, but he shared the trapper's traditional dislike of wolves. "I kill any I see," he said emphatically. "They kill my dogs, they take my fur, they kill moose. It's them against me in this country and I'm determined to out-think them. And don't think they won't attack you. Wolves chased my neighbour Jimmy Stubby for fifteen miles. For the last one hundred yards, wolves were taking his dogs right out of their harnesses. Jimmy finally holed up in a cabin and kept them away by beating on a stovepipe. He thinks the wolves down south that he hears city people talk of must be different kinds of wolves than up here because he knows from his experience that these wolves can and do attack."

I had no intention of getting into an argument on wolves and trapping when, at any given moment, my thoughts were on cabins and swimming. Moreover, Whit changed the subject and the contrast intrigued me.

"You know I really love this country. I've travelled the world, but I prefer it here. I'll never go back south. The land around the Liard has the most spectacular sunsets and sunrises anywhere. They would blow the mind of Van Gogh. I look at the colours and they bring tears to my eyes. I've almost had accidents when I've concentrated more on looking at the scenery than on my skidoo.

"This is a very poetic land. You have to get emotionally attached to it or else you'll be burned. It has a lot to offer but it is no place for unintelligent people. It demands a lot from you, physically and mentally. It challenges you constantly in every way."

My own challenge was coming closer when, after trying several dead-end game trails, we finally found the one through the poplars that led to the river opposite Whit's cabin. For fifteen minutes, we followed faint blaze marks through the trees. Increasing numbers of willows and horsetails told me that my moment of truth was at hand. We emerged from the willows and crossed the bog of thick, black silt that edged the roaring river. The mud was like a magnet. We had to exert considerable effort at each step in order to extricate our boots. Nikki, on the other hand, seemed to have forgotten his annoyance at my intrusion and scampered down to the river, obviously overjoyed to be back in the bush. At last, the mud gave way to pebbles and we stood at the edge of the Fort Nelson River.

"Well, there it is," said Whit, pointing to a log cabin half hidden in trees above steep mud banks on the other side. "What do you think?"

I was trying not to think at all. I was trying to forget that the ferry-man said we'd be swept several miles downstream by the time we got to the other side. Or that we could float all the way to the Liard and perhaps the Mackenzie. Or that, yes, we could even drown. Well, I was headed for the Arctic Ocean later in the year: why not take a shortcut now? Don't be facetious, I scolded myself. Why do I try to be funny when life is most serious?

Whit was still waiting for an answer. "Are you coming?"

"Sure," I replied offhandedly. "You could have put on better weather, though. Pretty cold and gloomy compared to yesterday when you extended this invitation. Hope the drizzle stops!"

Would it matter in the water? Teetering on one foot, I tugged off my boots and wool socks, removed my jeans, and shivered into a swimsuit. Whit stayed clothed but wrapped food, his gun, and spare dry clothing in plastic bags to be left at the river's edge for our return. I got him to take a picture of me before I added my cameras to the bag.

"I usually build a raft," my companion explained, "but somebody's taken the axe I leave on a tree back in the willows. And anyway, we don't have much time if you still intend getting the last ferry back tonight to catch that bus."

As an alternative mode of getting some gear across the river, he put a change of clothes and a blanket in two large plastic bags, blew them full of air and tied them together. He looked like a huge green butterfly. Now I wished I had taken his picture. But then, poised on the pebbles in rain, ankle-high in mud, I had thoughts only for the river.

"May as well get it over with," I said in mock confidence as my bare feet met the murky water and felt the current. I wanted to experience the wild. This was it.

"Head for the cabin," Whit instructed. "Be careful of sweepers sticking out from the bank. You'll be swept downstream but it doesn't matter, you'll eventually hit the bank on the other side and we can walk back upstream to the cabin. Remember, I'll be right behind you if you get into trouble."

I couldn't test that promise because as soon as I plunged into the chilly, grey, rain-swollen waters of the Nelson River, the current seized hold of me immediately. Like all Australians, I had passed through swimming school, but somehow my strokes had suffered from some Down Under syndrome and I used a unique method not shared by other Australians: a combined crawl and frog kick. When I got tired of taking in river water, I changed to breaststroke, though front and back leg strokes never seemed to match.

Whit, control of his movements hampered by his awkward, inflated, garbage-bag wings, was swept downstream more quickly. I soon lost sight of him, but Nikki, satisfied that her master was fine, swept over to check on me with a fast dogpaddle. "Oh, no, Nikki, don't start trying to get rid of me now: I'm in danger of doing that for myself," I thought. Nikki now seemed only to be trying to help. I felt reassured.

The cabin had fast disappeared in my downstream dash, lengthening the hike we'd have along the beach. I tried to keep my eyes on the other side, but it was too discouraging to see my destination receding in the distance despite each stroke. Better to swim sideways and look where I'd been. Although I might be on my way to the Arctic Ocean by water, at least I could see some progress. Actually, after fifteen minutes or so, I was surprised and elated to find myself halfway across the river, thanks more to the currents than my inimitable swimming strokes.

Ahead, sprouting weirdly from the eroded banks, were sweepers—tree trunks reaching over the river. Sweepers could be friend or foe. Whit had warned me against being flung into their midst. Still, I was hoping to use them to stop my pell-mell rush downstream. I would have to be accurate and lucky. My plan worked. As the branches swept toward me in a blur, I reached out, grabbed, and held on grimly with all the strength I could muster. Like some lumbering hippopotamus, I stepped out of an eddy and hauled myself to shore through thick, black, cloying mud. I had reached the other side. Only then did I realize I was cold.

Five minutes later Whit and Nikki arrived. Having decided not to hamper my movements by floating over a change of clothes, intending instead to rely on a fire quickly made in the cabin, I wanted to set off immediately along the beach despite the mud; however, Whit recommended we climb the banks and hike the trail along the top. The trail would have been a good idea *if* we had found it.

I bushwhacked ahead to avoid getting colder while Whit, stopping long enough to put on dry clothing and spare footgear, followed. The floor of the forest was thickly clogged with shrubs, vines, and fallen debris, better under my bare feet than I expected. Not so the wild roses and blackberry bushes that did full thorny battle with my naked skin as I thrust arms up to shield my eyes and bulldozed into the brambles bound for Whit's luxury cabin.

"Stop for some bug dope," called Whit from behind. "The mosquitoes are eating you alive."

Stopping me for a spray of repellent was a kind gesture on Whit's part, but it made the bombardment all the more concentrated. The mosquitoes were the worst in thirty-seven years, so the barge people said. The night before, mosquitoes in this area had even made the national news. It seemed now that they were amassing their entire forces to do battle on me. They probably had no-one else. I doubted there were any other exposed bodies along the entire Nelson River.

Whit gave me his dry shirt and forged ahead to look for the trail. "Creek ahead," he called. "Bit muddy and steep. Are you still okay?"

"Sure," I called back, slapping mosquitoes and squelching to my calves in the creek. Groping for spine-free branches, I hauled myself to the top, and to my relief we hit the trail. A hundred yards ahead was the cabin.

Nikki got there first and grabbed her dinner, a fat woodchuck. We had to wait for ours.

This is my home. Treat it as you would your own but replace the wood when you leave, said the sign above the door.

"It's not finished," Whit explained apologetically as we bent to go through a low door into the cabin's dark interior." The windows haven't been cut from the logs yet and the floor's still dirt."

Something must have been lost in the communication. I had been expecting a cabin with stained-glass windows and a library. That cabin, Whit explained, was another nineteen-mile trudge through summer muskeg. "I'll take you there in the winter when the country is ice-hard and we can go by skidoo," he recommended. I was disappointed but I said no more.

"This is the cabin that came with the trapline. It's not one of the ones I built myself. I have to finish it, though, as a home this winter." He went on to explain that two of his other cabins on lakes to the north had recently been destroyed, one by fire and the other by vandalism.

"I don't know what happens to some people when they come north," he complained. "They leave their manners and the rules of civilized conduct at home. They barge in where they're not wanted. If you're there, they expect you to feed them; if you're not, they take what they want anyway. I've gone back to my cabin and found everything taken, even skillets and coffee cups off the walls."

Fortunately, this time the tourists had left us enough wood, although the cups, teabags, and mosquito coils were gone. Whit soon had the dim interior of the cabin illuminated with a can of lit grease and warmed with a fire in the forty-five-gallon drum stove. While we dried, he talked of the new home cabin he would build, not on the riverbank where it was too easy to vandalize but high on the ridge in the Poplar Hills that he hoped most tourists would find inaccessible.

Vandals and fire were not his only problems. He had just learned the beautiful glade of trees around the cabin we were sitting in would soon be clearcut. This would be the last time he would see it pristine.

"Good trappers manage their traplines like farms and try to leave the same number of animals for their kids," he said, "but after the forestry guys finish logging here, they will have killed more fur in three months than I will have killed in twenty years."

I glanced at my watch. Ugh! Now that we were dry and comparatively warm, it was time to get back in that river. We allowed ourselves an hour for things unforeseen, called Nikki from the bush, and set off for the riverbank. We were to need that extra hour. Swimming back was to be infinitely more difficult.

"Let's walk upstream half a mile or so," suggested Whit, "so we'll land on the other side closer to our gear." His strategy was to dive in where the current slammed into a steep bank so that we'd be doing the hardest swimming while we were feeling strongest. "Push hard for the sandbar on the other shore," was his last instruction before he disappeared from my view. I would not see him again for almost forty-five minutes.

I stepped into the water to find it far colder than on the way over. I was tired and I was hungry. I knew I was going to have trouble.

Putting mind over matter, I charged into the current and tried to slice the straightest path through the maelstrom. This time it was different. Harder. Faster. I was getting nowhere and I was tiring quickly. I seemed to be flung back to the bank I was trying so desperately to leave.

Nikki didn't want to go in either. Her howls and whines and barks echoed down the river in loud, vibrating crescendoes as she ran up and down the bank. Buried in waves, I couldn't see Whit. Had he drowned? Was that why Nikki was so frantic? For a moment, I looked back, treading water and losing ground. What had happened to Whit? Not that I could have done anything constructive. I could scarcely help myself. I forced myself to keep moving. Nikki kept barking, running back and forth from the cabin to where we'd gone into the water.

I almost panicked. Then I saw a tree lodged in the middle of the river, its stubby branches protruding from the water as if it too were calling for help. If I could just get to it in time, it would provide a resting spot for stiffening arms and legs and a vantage point to look for Whit. *If* I could reach it! I seemed not to have the extra reserves of strength for the necessary effort to beat the current that relentlessly continued to push me downstream. Stupid me! I should have taken a chance on keeping dry and floated some chocolate bars over with me, something to give me energy to reach that tree.

My imagination kept me sane. I felt I was a character in a suspense movie. I reached the tree at its topmost limb, lunged, missed, was swept past to the next branch, lunged and missed again. So it continued with every branch I tried to grab, all the way down the tree. One to go. Would I get it? Just as the imagined music swept to a climax, I made one final thrust forward in the water, made contact with the last branch, and clung desperately with both arms and legs.

Slowly, as I gained breath and more energy, I pulled myself up to straddle the trunk. Above the water, I could see Nikki, a white ghost still running madly along the sombre bank; and then to my relief I saw Whit, his giant butterfly bags ballooning to each side of his head, many yards downstream.

I could hear him encouraging Nikki to get in the water. But the distance between the two was fast widening. Damn it, dog! We had no time to waste. The last ferry left in less than two hours, and we had more than five miles to hike followed by half an hour's drive to reach it. I didn't want to spend a night in the car on the deserted Liard Highway. I knew Whit would never leave Nikki in the bush. Nikki, start swimming! I added my cries to those of Whit, at least mentally. Did the dog know something sinister about this river that we didn't? Probably she couldn't understand why her master had stayed such a short time at their cabin. Why, he hadn't even killed a moose!

Perhaps if one of us reached shore the dog would come. Still straddling the log, I carefully edged up the tree again until I got to the top. The effort seemed silly but I wanted to have at least a tree-length start on the current which to me was now a living thing, an enemy to be beaten, a challenge to be mastered. I hated leaving my life-saving island but to get the agony over with, I plunged into the current again. I hoped to be swept into a bay to halt my imposed dash downstream. Stay afloat. Keep moving. Push yourself. Drive across the current. Aim for that bay. Push again. And again. Nikki kept crying. Whit kept calling from somewhere downstream.

Then—amazingly—still some distance from the shore and almost outside the saving arms of the bay, my feet hit something solid. A submerged tree? Sand. I was in a back eddy of the river and had hit the sandbar. I could *walk* to shore.

When I pulled myself from the river, I almost welcomed the quicksand. Fearing hypothermia, I kept moving, stumbling through the mud, hobbling over the pebbles to where we'd left our gear a mile or so upstream. It was more difficult than pushing through the bush but infinitely better because it was on the right side of the river. The mosquitoes joined the blackflies and all made a beeline for my bare wet skin. Whit had the repellent in his floating "suitcase."

I was dressed and scraping off the black ooze when he appeared. He had thought I was lost to the river at the same time I thought he was. Not seeing me at all until I'd climbed onto my "island," he had let himself float downstream at the river's pace in hope of getting into a position to help me.

Seeing both of us safe on the other side of the stream, Nikki finally capitulated and plunged in. "Good girl, that's my girl," Whit encouraged while munching mouthfuls of cheese, sausage, and chocolate bars. A check with our watches revealed that we'd been in the river an hour.

The ferryman stared in disbelief when Whit told him we'd both swum the river. "No big deal," said the trapper.

As for me, I was glad this Aussie with the funny swim pattern had faced the challenge. I was glad I'd "done" the Liard again before the new bridge and the new road tames this wild country.

Now I could catch that bus.

The Road to Nowhere

"HEY, YOU'RE GOING THE WRONG WAY! Going south is a heck of a way to get to the Arctic Circle."

The deckhand grinned as he waved us into the last place on the Victoria-Port Angeles ferry and winched up the gangplank. He was laughing at the sign on the side of our camper—To the Arctic Circle with Lyn Hancock in a Datsun.

"We're going north eventually but right now we're headed to Death Valley in California," I retorted.

We would be the butt of many more jokes over the next month, and I would have to explain many more times that, despite my mobile billboard, my parents and I were breaking-in a new truck and camper the easy way by a civilized trip south through the United States. After that, we would be testing the toughness and dependability of a standard-equipped Datsun sports truck and a small economy-model Buccaneer camper by driving them along the Dempster Highway as far north as it was possible to go on any public road in North America, or for that matter, the world. Our aim was to be the first private vehicle across the Arctic Circle.

The travel departments of the respective territories assured me that the new road being built between Dawson City in Yukon and Inuvik in Northwest Territories was open and would reach the Arctic Circle by the end of that summer—1973. It was not to be. The respective highways departments guessed better than the tourism departments. Poor weather, remote logistics, uncertain financing, and criticism by politicians and environmentalists were to delay completion of the road to the Arctic Circle until 1976 and to Inuvik until 1979.[1]

The Dempster, in the making since 1959, was called Dief's Dream. It was part of Prime Minister John Diefenbaker's vision of the North, one of his Roads to Resources, which he hoped would stimulate mining, logging, oil and gas exploration. Building roads "from igloo to igloo" through the vast empty spaces of Canada's Top End was expensive, and cynics called the Dempster a Road to Nowhere.

It followed a route taken in the early 1900s by the Royal North-West Mounted Police, who did gruelling month-long dog team runs between Dawson City, Fort McPherson, and Herschel Island. It was named after Corporal Dempster who directed the search for a missing RNWMP 1910-11 patrol which has been immortalized in literature as *The Lost Patrol.*

Characteristically, I planned my expedition along the Dempster at the last minute. Not that I wanted it that way. My long-suffering parents, Ted and Doris Taylor, had just arrived in Canada from Western Australia by freighter in the company of ten other passengers and 2,500 sheep after a long voyage that had taken them to Singapore, Malaysia, Hong Kong, and Japan. They were looking forward to a year-long family visit with me and my husband in our home near Victoria at Island View Beach. Instead, they were welcomed in Vancouver with the sudden and devastating news of our divorce. A 15,000-mile trip through the backwoods of western North America seemed a good way for me to "get away from it all." Many go north for similar reasons.

Our truck was the economy model without extra springs, radial tires, or mountain rear-end ratios, a baby beside the four-wheel drive vehicles with their large motors, automatic gears, oversized tires, and gigantic winches that we were to find along the muddy tracks that pass for roads in the back country of British Columbia, Yukon, and Alaska. To make matters worse, we were overloaded with three people, their personal luggage, food, camping equipment, typewriter, tape recorder, cameras, research material, boat, motor, extra tires, and gas cans. Many times the contents of our cupboards would be bumped open by the backroads and fill the camper floor.

"I hope you're not going to take us up too many mountains with this load aboard," Dad complained. Being the cautious type, Dad was to tangle with his daughter on more than one occasion as I led him from the burning sands, dust storms, and searing 118-degree heat of sub-sea-level Death Valley to the rain, snow, and clouds of the mountainous Dempster. Somehow our Datsun survived, and we did too.

Our north began on the widely advertised but not-yet-officially-opened Cassiar Highway which links the Yellowhead Highway in British Columbia with the Alaska Highway in Yukon. Every gas station within hundreds of miles of the Cassiar warned us of the new road's dangers with grimaces and "best of luck" good wishes. With conditions worsened by relentless rains that made gumbo of the track, and enforced waits for sections to be built, we slushed northwards on an unfinished road which later in the season would be closed completely because of adverse and unseasonal weather conditions.

Except for bulldozers and other construction machines, we were about the only vehicle on the road. On one occasion near Meziadin Lake when we ran out of road completely and ran into half a dozen heavy earth-moving vehicles and soft sinking mud, another truck pulled up behind us. It was a well-equipped Cheyenne with four-wheel drive, a 350 cubic-inch motor, automatic gears, huge oversized tires, aluminum bug screen, and a gigantic winch mounted up front.

"Beautifully equipped for this road," Dad commented enviously. "Where have you come from?"

The Californian replied, "From the Yellowhead on a stinking road. Where have you come from?"

"Same place," Dad grimaced.

There was an incredulous look on the man's face. "Really? In that Datsun?" he finally stammered. He turned back but we crawled on.

Limping along from one unmarked pothole to another, manoeuvring across innumerable streams and temporary Bailey bridges, and worrying constantly about flat tires and broken springs, Dad, a former speedcar driver, was given to grumbling. "You have to be nuts to drive on roads like these, splashing black clouds of slush to the windows every time the wheels turn."

Mum shuddered at the gumbo our boots hauled back to the Datsun after every picture-taking foray. Nevertheless, for the rest of the summer, she insisted on sluicing down and sprucing up our truck and camper on a daily basis so that it looked as if we were being slung around the north by helicopter. It was only at the end of our six-month journey as we rolled back into Victoria that she left on the crud as a mark of pride. WE TRAVELLED THE ALASKA HIGHWAY BOTH WAYS said the stickers on big Winnebagos, but the Alcan was a carpet compared to the tracks we tried that summer in our little Datsun.

We travelled every backroad in the Yukon and a few more in Alaska. We did every dead-end side road off the Alaska Highway, the Top of the World Highway in Alaska, and the Nahanni Range Road and North Canol Roads in the Yukon until they petered out in the mountains of the Northwest Territories.

Friends warned my parents that their daughter would turn them into nervous wrecks in a week, but when I left Mum and Dad for a couple of days on comparatively civilized roads in Alaska to enjoy normal recreational travel on their own, they attracted trouble without any help from me at aptly named Troublesome Creek.

In post-divorce, cashless economy mode, I planned to pay for our adventure travel by taking photos of the truck and camper in interesting positions. This often meant driving on the wrong side of the road or against a glacier or nudging the edge of a cliff to achieve the best angle. Photo opportunities always came unexpectedly, which meant a sudden stop in some appropriate location, a rapid gathering of props such as binoculars and lawn chairs, and a set-up scene with my parents in place, perhaps reading a map or guide book or sipping a drink. And then we were back in the truck looking for the next location.

To add order to such a "winging it" approach, I tried to plan our nightly camp spots. Unfortunately, we rarely reached a sufficiently picturesque destination at a time which coincided with my parents' notions of normalcy. "Look, there's some normal people," my mother would point out as we passed campers in the late afternoon. "Sitting in lawn chairs in a proper camp spot, reading a book and having a drink before dinner." Invariably, the planned photo opportunities eluded us and we wound up camping in some unphotogenic gravel pit because it was midnight.

So at Troublesome Creek on their first night alone, Mum and Dad parked the truck on the right side of the road (for a change), set up their chairs, poured the wine, and prepared to enjoy a relaxing evening without having to smile for my cameras. Perhaps in an hour or two, they would prepare a leisurely meal.

Suddenly, a squeal of brakes and loud shouts interrupted their reverie as another camper pulled up in front of them. "Hey! There's a grizzly and two cubs coming along the road. You'd better get out of here." Without waiting for a reaction, the man roared off down the highway.

As Dad explained afterwards, "We packed up as fast as we could and shoved stuff in the back of the camper. We intended to get in the cab and drive off but the grizzlies were galloping towards us so we dashed into the camper instead. Unfortunately, we left the door of the truck open and the bears got inside—two cubs and as much of their mother as could squeeze through the door."

I could imagine the mess and my mother's reactions as the grizzlies rooted around the glove compartment for chocolates and lollies (candy) and tore up the upholstery. I tried not to imagine what the owner would say when we returned his truck to him at the end of our travels. Meanwhile, Mum and Dad knocked wildly on the glass that separated the cab from the camper and rattled saucepans to distract the animals' attention. When this failed, they appealed to the bears' sense of taste and smell by throwing out biscuits (cookies) from the back of the camper.

Dad continued the story. "I kept throwing biscuits one at a time and then the whole package to entice them out of the cab. Eventually, they tumbled out of the truck and chased the biscuits. I grabbed my opportunity, dashed from the camper to the cab and raced off down the track." He grinned sheepishly. "I must have gone a mile when I suddenly remembered Mum. I'd left so fast I couldn't remember if she was still safe inside the camper or—if she'd followed me out of the camper and was left behind with the bears."

Fortunately, Mum was still pressing her face against the glass window at the back of the camper trying in vain to attract her husband's attention. But Dad didn't notice and he couldn't stop because the bears were barrelling down the road at top speed after him. "I drove all of five miles before they gave up and I lost my fear of being followed."

After that, I think my parents were glad to have me back. I met them in Whitehorse. Our intention was to drive to Dawson City to begin our drive on the Dempster, if not to the Arctic Circle then as far as the road went. However, plans changed dramatically after a chance meeting with canoeists on the Yukon River.

To mark the seventy-fifth anniversary of the 1898 declaration of the Yukon Territory as part of Canada during the peak of the Klondike Gold Rush, Yukoners were celebrating a year-long series of events.

Meeting my parents in Whitehorse coincided with the arrival of the 75th Anniversary Canoe Pageant which was re-enacting the entire route of the stampeders from Skagway to Dawson City over the Chilkoot Trail, across Lake Bennett and down the Yukon River. The party of sixty-two people included forty paddlers from Alaska, Yukon, Northwest Territories, British Columbia, and Washington in five twenty-five-foot fibreglass canoes, two officials in a speedboat, and a support team from the Canadian Armed Forces who travelled in seven river boats, two freighter canoes, and a helicopter.

The group had just clambered over the Golden Staircase, the near-vertical 1500 feet of shattered boulders that leads to the summit of the Chilkoot Pass, a trail still strewn with debris left by the thousands of men and women who sought their fortune in the Klondike.

It was now preparing for a five-hundred-mile paddle down the Yukon River and an arrival in Dawson City on August 17th for the town's annual Discovery Day celebrations. The entire trip lasted twelve days with stops at Tagish, Carcross, Whitehorse, Carmacks, Minto, Fort Selkirk, and Dawson for local celebrations. These included hootchinannies, special Yukon parties that featured the imbibing of a unique liquor known as Yukon Hootch.

When the flotilla arrived in a community, the army's five-man gun crew, dressed in period costume, fired a smoky, noisy salute from a one-hundred-year-old cannon, which caused everybody to clap their hands to their ears but which added authenticity to the celebrations. Also on hand was a slimy, green and black, fifteen-foot-long monster that first appeared with the paddlers' arrival in Lake Bennett and was to re-appear at each community en route. Upon close inspection, the monster bore an uncanny resemblance to one of the army's scuba divers.

"We're having a lot of fun," said Glenn, the army lieutenant in charge of the pageant. "You should come along."

I couldn't resist the invitation. The tourism department suggested I write a few stories and take some pictures. The teams suggested I paddle part of the river with them. The army suggested I ride in their helicopter to vary the view. And so, one day after the invitation, my parents took the land highway to Dawson City as planned while I took the unplanned marine highway. We arranged to meet in Carmacks, Minto, and Dawson, the only places where the river and road came together.

Although sprint races were held in each community and points earned by the teams contributed to the overall competition, the event was more a re-enactment than a race. I didn't really know this when the team from British Columbia invited me to paddle their canoe. Baldy Jackson, captain for the day, assigned me to the bow. I had no paddling experience but I was determined not to let my team down. I tried to follow Baldy's advice. "It's not the power you put behind the paddle that counts, it's the rhythm . . . Don't thrash or swing, just skim the water or you'll never last the day." The day? I thought. For the sake of the team, I'd expected to do only an hour. "Don't rub," Baldy continued. Rub? Rub what? "If we'd rubbed like that, we wouldn't have had any boat left by now." I caught on. I'd been rubbing my paddle against the side of the canoe.

I cleared everything from my mind—blisters, back, knees, background—and focussed on my paddling. Dig, dig, dig, no skim, skim, skim . . . Switch after ten strokes, that was Baldy's way. Skim, skim, skim . . . Don't stop. Just keep on going. Anxious to keep up with the paddler behind, I just paddled as fast as possible. The banks rolled by, the miles rolled on. Morning passed into afternoon. When we eventually stopped, my mates informed me we had paddled eighty-nine miles.

Baldy steered us ashore to make camp for the night. I tried to get out but my muscles were stiffened to the day's position. The crew carried me from the canoe.

It wasn't till the following day, after the first aid person's medicines and ministrations, that I found I could walk. And then my paddling crew told me I hadn't been in a race. "We wanted a more relaxing day—that's why we put you in the bow—but you paddled so fast setting the pace we had no choice but to try to keep up."

After that, I thought it safer to fly. The helicopter crew decided that their photographer had to improve her image. She couldn't go on wearing boot laces that didn't match. "We'll fly you into Dawson to buy some more then get you back in time to film the canoes paddling through the Five Finger Rapids," said the lieutenant.

I jumped at the opportunity of taking my first helicopter ride till I climbed aboard and found the chopper open on two sides. Sitting on the floor and dangling my legs over the edge of nothing did not appeal to my fear of heights, nor did it assuage my tendency for suicide. Willy clipped a seat belt around my thighs. Glenn plonked a helmet on my head. Chris handed me a harness attached to the floor of the helicopter. I struggled into the harness, hopelessly entangling myself. The crew waited till their laughter subsided before helping to free me from the jumble of ropes.

As we rose effortlessly into the air, flattening the bushes and banking over the canoes, I hung on grimly to a circle of steel wire on the floor of the chopper and edged closer to the opening to take pictures. I tried to dangle my legs nonchalantly like everybody else instead of nervously sticking them out in front of me, ramrod-style. I wished my parents could have seen their daughter dangling midair on her first helicopter flight.

In fact, they did. Dad told me later, "We couldn't find you on the ground or on the water so we looked in the only place left—the air— and that's where we saw you. We waved. Didn't you see us?"

Despite my fears, looking down from a helicopter was a wonderful way to see and appreciate the wide, twisting coils of the Yukon River and the sandbanks and islands midstream. It also allowed us complete freedom to drop down to fish in remote creeks and visit pioneers such as the Bradley brothers at the Pelly River Ranch. Finally, we made it to Dawson City to accomplish our mission, the purchase of new bootlaces. The trip cost me thirty-nine cents; I hate to think what it cost the taxpayer.

It was in Dawson City that I became the Yukon's first female sourtoe. At that time, I couldn't qualify as a female sourdough because I hadn't seen the Yukon River through freeze-up and break-up, so being a sourtoe had to do. I earned the distinction when a well-known Dawson resident persuaded me to drink, not a mock Iceworm Cocktail of spaghetti strands that normally is given to tourists, but an authentic Sourtoe Cocktail of prospector appendage dipped in champagne.

Only in the Yukon where tales are told of frozen corpses cremated in ship's boilers or of longtime partners affected by cabin fever ensuring an exact division of their possessions by sawing in half their boat, cabin, tent, and stove—only in the storied Yukon could a Sourtoe Cocktail evolve.

When I popped into the Sluicebox Lounge of the Eldorado Hotel in Dawson City, one of the local characters challenged me to drink a glass of champagne in which had been dropped one very large, very old, and very ugly big toe.

"Back in the twenties," explained Captain Dick Stevenson, "over by Glacier Creek in the Sixty Mile country, a couple of oldtimers by the name of Otto and Louie Lichens used to trap, prospect, and run rum into Alaska. They travelled under the very worst of weather conditions so the Mounties weren't able to catch them. On one such trip, Louie's moccasins got wet in an overflow, his big toe froze, and gangrene set in. Otto got Louie well plastered with a bottle of Overproof Rum and with a pair of horse snippers chopped off the toe, using a red hot iron to cauterize the wound. These two brothers kept every thing, every picture, every newspaper, every letter, and even Louie's big toe pickled in brine. Four years ago, my wife, Lou, bought their cabin, and when we were cleaning it out, there was this big toe in a pickle jar—and I've been saving it ever since to initiate the first Yukon Sourtoe contest.

"I had to ask five people before I could get somebody to bring it into Dawson for me. They'd take one look and shove it back in the cabin and leave it there. In fact, you're the first female who could even look at it without fainting."

I'd gone along just to take pictures of the first male to accept the challenge, a young outspoken Californian tourist, Daniel Ness, who was travelling in a battered 1949 half-ton pickup truck that had done "331,000 miles with an expectation of doing a million more." Daniel was on his way back home from Alaska where he'd been winched across a river to shoot a grizzly bear with a pistol at twenty-five yards— or so he was saying when I walked into the bar.

While waiting for the arrival of Bartender Pete to immerse the sour toe in the champagne with his silver tongs, Daniel and Captain Dick were competing with each other in the telling of gory stories. Captain Dick would describe how a grizzly lacerated the scalp of an eighty-year-old prospector, who lay for weeks in his cabin before being rescued, and Daniel would counter with the grisly exploits of such early American war heroes as Liver-Eating Johnson. It was a relief when everything was assembled for the challenge.

As it says in the "Ballad of the Yukon Sourtoe," Bartender Pete pulled "the fearsome monster" out of the jar with his silver tongs, and plunged the Toe to the bottom of the glass. The cork popped from the bottle of champagne—a liquid especially selected for its transparency—and three glasses were filled.

"A jagged nail and wrinkled skin, a ghastly yellow streaked with green/The vile thing seemed to glisten with a sickening sheen/Captain Dick was seen to shudder and turn a ghostly pale/When the loathsome thing splashed in the drink and he saw the jagged nail."

"He reached and grasped the frosted glass with quaking hand/And a hush fell among the gathered band/The glass he raised to quaking lips/ And with a shudder took a mighty sip."

Dick quaffed his with the flourish of one who had done it before, Daniel lingered to savour the attention he was getting from the crowd in the bar, and asked for another.

"Lyn, you're next," said Captain Dick.

"No way," I protested, "I'm here just to take pictures. I've got people waiting for me."

There was no way of making a graceful exit from the clamorous crowd. Trying to get the experience over with as soon as possible, I grabbed the glass, closed my eyes, and downed the drink quickly through furrowed lips. A handy slice of banana cream pie helped to erase the memory.

I'm glad I became a sourtoe when I did because if there had been a next time, I doubt an entire banana cream pie would have sufficed. Although the Toe had been cleaned with a toothbrush dipped in wood alcohol and placed in vodka between contests, I heard Captain Dick remark casually, "Guess we'll have to dehydrate it and try a rock salt preservative. The Toe has been in vodka too long. It is beginning to disintegrate."

At that point, I left.

By the end of August, I was back in the Datsun with my parents and heading up the unfinished Dempster Highway for the climax to our northern odyssey. Only graders and government pickup trucks ventured the route with us.

"It's a road good for nothing," complained the prospector over coffee in the Klondike River Lodge at the entrance to the Dempster. "No good for logging or farming, and mining's no better than anywhere else. It's no good for people and not much better for animals. It looks like the moon, barren and empty."

For me, that was the Dempster's attraction, but my parents may not have felt the same way. Dad was an old goldminer and a longtime Jack London fan, but I am sure Mum would have preferred shops and rose gardens.

The rain and fog that had plagued our way since spring continued into fall. Despite the bad weather and the desolate loneliness of the land, my parents were fascinated by the grandeur of the scenery and the vibrant colours of the autumn tundra. The North was beginning to cast its spell, even on my mother.

It rained continuously, but Dad thought that the sun must be shining to gild the poplars so vividly and flame the tundra in such fiery orange and blazing red. From afar, the ground was one vast, riotous watercolour. Underfoot, in a more intimate view, our boots pressed down crinkly white, lettuce-like lichens, crimson ground willow, bronze buckbrush, and multi-coloured moss into little pools of melted permafrost.

From the beginnings of the Dempster at Mile 0 to where it sank into a puddle at Mile 178, and then all the way back again, we were constantly fascinated by the landscape. (Despite the recent trend to kilometres, Americans and residents of the north country still talk of northern roads in miles, especially the Alaska Highway and Dempster, and especially in 1973.)

The Dempster began in trees, but by Mile 42 it left the wooded valley of the North Klondike River and climbed through the Ogilvie Mountains, above canyons, to the alpine tundra at the summit of North Fork Pass. Nearby, the famous landmark of Tombstone Mountain was still mantled in last year's snow.

Two legendary couples lived in cabins along this part of the Dempster and were the road's only permanent residents: Bob and Julie Frisch at Mile 6 and Joe and Annie Henry at Mile 33. Bob is best known for his long treks of hundreds of miles through mountains and across tundra. Once he walked clear across the Yukon through a grizzly reserve to Old Crow. The people who live in this remote community had not seen a boat arrive nor heard a plane. They were stunned to learn that Bob had walked.

Joe Henry tramped this country on snowshoes along his trapline long before white bureaucrats in Ottawa dreamed of scissoring the wilderness with a road. And when the strangers came to put their paper plans in action, Joe was the one who guided them. He led the first cat train north to the Peel Plateau for oil and gas exploration crews; he led the engineers to survey the best route for the highway; he led the dogsledders to locate Jack London's Gold Rush cabin. Bob and Julie, Joe and Annie were away on the land during my first trip up the Dempster; I would meet them in person on later trips.

By Mile 51, the road dropped to the Blackstone River, which it continued to nudge for the next forty-two miles. This is an area rich in wildlife, and outfitters with horse trails into the nearby mountains make it handy for hiking.

A cloud of white-winged ptarmigan erupted from the willows at Mile 58 as we stopped at a sign which read Pete Jensen Outfitter. Smoke gusted from a cabin chimney. Two horses were hitched to a railing. Two wranglers met us at the door. I felt I was in the Wild West as much as the Far North.

We stopped long enough to revel in a few hours of extemporaneous northern hospitality with guides, Bill and Joe. I discovered later that Joe was Joe Loutchin, the famous Yukon fiddler. We had a rollicking time. We vigorously argued the pros and cons of wolf conservation, we herded porcupines for pictures, we chased a pet weasel in and out of the Datsun, and we danced some lively jigs to Joe's fiddle on the frost-heaved floor of the cabin. The fiddle got faster, our movements livelier despite big wet clodhopper boots, our spirits happier and the stove warmer till we finally fell down in exhaustion to fan ourselves at the open door.

The Blackstone is a good grayling river, especially where its west arm joins its east arm a short distance downstream from the bridge. It was here that embarrassment nearly cured me of poking my nose into other people's business. Dad wanted to go fishing so we camped at a respectable hour near a dusty station wagon that was so packed to the roof, leaving no space for passengers, that I thought it entirely abandoned. At noon the next day the car was still there, but there was no sign of life.

Curious, I crept over to investigate and peeked surreptitiously through the window. Amid the gear was a book, *The Yukon Story*, notebook paper with the words "gold" and "prospecting" scrawled several times in a bold round hand, a can of Aussie peaches roughly sawed at the edges, an old hat but no body. Should I open the door? Nervous, Dad beckoned me away.

I was having one last stare through the window when a face came suddenly into focus from under a pile of blankets. It belonged to Tom, a young biology student from the University of British Columbia. He was living in his car and spending the season line-fishing the Blackstone for an elusive and previously unrecorded fish that had been reported to his university by some construction workers. When we met him later in Skagway, he said that he had found his fish— though he had to resort to getting it in a net.

For the next fifty miles, the Dempster's panoramic landscape was broken only by a survival cabin, a bush airstrip, two primitive campgrounds, and a few battered fuel tanks.

At Mile 123, we reached a road maintenance camp and chatted to Sid and Hilda Carr, who ran a lodge nearby, the only one on the highway. Lodge is rather an inflated description for hotel-type accommodation on northern roads. The Ogilvie River Lodge consisted of one gas pump, two house trailers, and some storage sheds, but it did provide the only gas, food, and accommodation on the Dempster. The lodge has since closed but at the time of our visit, its menu offered "Baby Blue Whale Stuffed with New Cadillac—$6800," "Virgin Mermaid on the Half Shell—$585—limit one per customer," "Little Seal Sandwich garnished with Polar Bearies" and "Saddle of Mule (with or without stirrups)." Northerners are known for their sense of humour.

Amenities may be poor on frontier roads, but people add richness to the northern experience, something you cannot buy. Hilda Carr was born in the village of Moosehide close to Dawson at a time when the native people still had half a dozen traditional fish wheels in the Klondike River. Hilda's father trapped in winter and worked as a recorder on the gold dredges in summer. She mourned the changes as people moved from a subsistence economy on the land to a wage economy in modern towns. She regretted the loss of dignity that government handouts had brought.

53

"Moosehide was such a close community then. Teenagers would get together and go out in sleds to cut firewood for the old people. Kids protected their elders. Now it seems that nobody cares."

Hilda sat down with us at the table as we ordered another round of coffee. "When I first came here to the Dempster, I wondered what I could possibly do to fill my time especially in winter. Now I find that with this business, my trapline, and five kids in school on correspondence, the days go by so fast I don't miss living in a community at all."

She did admit to feeling depressed in winter when for two months the sun doesn't shine. "I had aches I never heard of before. Still, last winter was very warm—50 below. Three years ago, it was 75 below."

Sid came in from fixing a flat and joined us. "Lots of wildlife around here. This year we had a lot of wolves. We'd sit on the porch and look at them in the yard. We thought it was fun till one got our puppy. We heard a ruckus and chased the wolf till it dropped the pup. And last fall, thousands of caribou came through the valley almost up to our front door. They were like a big, rolling brown carpet."

We chose not to argue the pros and cons of the Dempster as a detriment to caribou migration and took advantage of a break in the rain to continue our journey. The next ten miles of road gouged a narrow way through the grey talus slopes of the Ogilvies, whose gravel sides seemed to hang in suspension as if some sudden noise could easily send down an avalanche of slate and pebbles.

We inched gingerly up a long winding hill above timberline to reach the summit at Mile 160. Beyond the bare rolling hills to the northwest was Old Crow on the Porcupine River; to the east were the Richardson Mountains; and at Mile 235, the Eagle River, where a major bridge would be built. We had climbed a thin black ladder into the clouds. The land around was hidden in fog. We could use only maps and our imagination.

"Only writers, biologists, and construction workers are crazy enough to come up here," Mum said caustically as I clambered back in the Datsun after photographing the absolute nothingness that surrounded us.

An hour later at Mile 178, we followed lights and the hum of generators into a village of interlocking trailers and sheds that formed the Dempster's northernmost construction camp. Project engineer John Hudson, a polite, precise Englishman, welcomed us with the words,

"So you're 'Lyn Hancock in a Datsun,' I presume, on your way to the Arctic Circle? Well, you're not going to make it this year. The Circle's another forty-seven miles, and that's as the raven flies."

Due to the wide publicity given the Dempster in 1973, a few private vehicles had reached camp before us. However, all but one had been turned back by weather, road conditions, or the construction crew. John told us that a Winnebago had crept by them one day, but it was too large to turn on the narrow elevated roadbed (berm) so the driver had to inch back along the muddy track in reverse, quite a difficult feat.

"Tell you what, go as far as you can and if you get stuck, we'll get a grader to get you out." I smiled thankfully. I knew I'd find some advantage to carrying that sign.

It was pelting rain and we had only half an inch clearance over deep, wet, boggy ruts but Dad and the Datsun got us through. We stopped at a gigantic mudhole that signalled the end of the available road and hoisted the flags of British Columbia, Yukon, Canada, Australia, and Japan. Thanks to the truck's short wheel base, we were able to turn around without asking for help.

Ahead was hand-cleared muskeg. A line of red plastic ribbons marked the rest of the route. They pointed the way to the Arctic Circle at Mile 251, to the Northwest Territories border at Mile 289, to Fort McPherson at Mile 342, and to Arctic Red River, where at Mile 378 the Dempster would eventually join the already constructed end of the Mackenzie Highway and run north as one to Inuvik at Mile 456.

John watched me dream. "Do you want to go farther? The surveyor can probably take you another three miles." I accepted immediately.

Leaving Mum and Dad back at camp to deal with the aftermath of our truck in another bog, I trudged with Jim Copp along the cutline. Trees cut down by axe and saw and machete had been left in line on top of the muskeg to act as insulation and protect the permafrost. The permanent imprint of old seismic lines that crossed the cutline attested to a less sensitive way of doing things.

We reached the end of the cutline. Ahead were only flags. Soon this highway would reach beyond the Arctic Circle to the Arctic Ocean. Only a dribble of people had been this far north on a public road. Would the Dempster's empty loveliness be marred by the essential accoutrements of expanding civilization? Would its fish be depleted and its wildlife be scared off by roadside potshots?

As if reading my thoughts, Jim said quietly, "Don't worry. We're trying to affect the fragile northern ecology as little as possible. We clear by hand and build on a berm two to five feet above the surrounding ground. We follow stringent rules to protect the land and the wildlife—it's the first highway to have a land management plan. John Hudson, I know, wouldn't want to be associated with anything he didn't feel was right or for a good purpose."

I wondered about my own motivation in wanting to be where few had been before.

Back at camp, where John had invited us for supper, Erva and Florence, the cooks, had no such misgivings. A cheery couple, they had come north, they said, "to get the frontier feeling of being at the beginning of things." They bubbled over with enthusiasm in telling us of their experiences.

Florence started. "You should have been here when we first came. We didn't have anywhere to stay. The guys had to shovel a bunk for us out of the snow. A kitchen and rec room had been plopped down in the mud and that was all. There were no walkways between the two rooms. I told the guys, 'Do you think we're kangaroos?' You'd better put something down to get us out of the slush."

Erva cut in. "The stove was an old diesel one and you could never tell what temperature it got to. It smoked so bad one day that fifteen guys came running because they thought the kitchen was on fire."

Florence added. "I got into the habit that every time the stove smoked, I'd yell 'Fire, fire!' But it got to be like crying wolf. One day it did make a big blaze and no-one came. I kept yelling and eventually someone thought I was desperate enough so they came with a fire extinguisher and put it out."

"And then there was the time the hot water system blew up," Erva grinned. "Honestly, I never thought we could make a livable spot out of this place. But here we are. I wouldn't want to be anywhere else."

By the end of the evening, Mum was tempted to apply for a job as a northern cook. The money was good, but the mosquitoes were a deterrent. Jim said he held the record for the Mosquito Index. "You swat somebody's back and then count the corpses, in my case eighty-two." John added, "You make your recreation where you can. Slapping mossies is one of our games. We have an Insane Index too but we'd better not talk about that."

It was early summer 1979 when I made my next trek up the Dempster. By now, the road had reached Inuvik, but it wasn't yet officially opened; most travellers ended their trip at the Arctic Circle because there was still no bridge or ferry to get them across the Peel River farther north.

This time, I was driving a compact four-wheel drive Subaru Brat pickup truck with a light, easily removable, fibreglass canopy and a specially designed luggage rack of light steel tubing to hold extra gas tanks, an eleven-foot inflatable rubber raft that weighed only forty-one pounds and a 4.5-horsepower Mercury outboard motor. This time, my trip was planned but I wanted to be ready at a moment's notice to take advantage of an opportunity—to inflate my boat for an hour's fishing, to pack it on my rucksack for a hike to an off-road lake, or to throw it on a bush plane. Brat backpacking meant that as much as possible had to be dual purpose: my storage box doubled as a kitchen table and office desk; my waterproof nylon ponchos doubled as a tent.

In the few short years since it was possible to drive to the Arctic Circle, travellers from around the world—South Africa, Switzerland, France, Holland, and the ubiquitous Germany and Japan—had come to "do" the Dempster. They had written messages in bottles or scratched their names and addresses on a huge orange-painted tractor tire that hung from a large log frame set up by road construction workers.

Here at Eagle Plains, the Ogilvies are left behind and the road climbs treeless into the sky to face the ramparts of the Richardsons, the next great mountain chain. On this vast intermontane plateau, you feel literally on top of the world.

The Eagle Plains Hotel, built on bedrock at Mile 231, midway along the Dempster, is considered an oasis in the wilderness. Old photographs on the walls of each room depict the Dempster's history: in the restaurant, the story of Inspector Fitzgerald's Lost Patrol of 1910-11 and the search by Corporal Dempster for their bodies; in the lounge, the story of Albert Johnson, the Mad Trapper who was hunted down and killed by the RCMP at Eagle River in 1932; in the lobby, the history of cat trains, oil exploration, and road construction; in the bedrooms and corridors, vignettes of local personalities.

Eagle Plains is an instant hotel sitting smack in the middle of five hundred miles of what most people would call "nothingness." It was built in a rush to accommodate an expected fifty vehicles a day. Due to the Road Closed and Dangerous signs to the north and south, they never came. I sat with the staff in the bar and we entertained ourselves. My room at the hotel was dedicated to Constable Sam Carter, the guide for the Lost Patrol. His failure to locate the right route was one of the reasons for the demise of Fitzgerald's expedition. I hoped this didn't augur ill for my own trip.

As the scenery along the Dempster is ever changing so was the colour of the road surface—white, black, pink, yellow, grey, or brown to match the material with which it was surfaced. As I neared the Richardsons the elevated ribbon of road ahead was pure white; as I meandered among the mountains it became stark black.

This was my favourite part of the Dempster. Not even several hours of bombardment by a battalion of mosquitoes while I walked to the sheep lick at Rock River could dampen my delight in the Richardsons, in every way a sharp contrast to the Ogilvies.

From each side of the pavement-black road, a treeless green land swept like a golf course to mountaintops that were round and brown. This is the traditional spring migration route of the barren-ground caribou Porcupine herd, the animals most likely threatened by the opening of a pipeline through their calving grounds or a road route to the Arctic.

I had missed the caribou, but there were encounters with other animals to cherish. Like the arctic ground squirrel who kept batting my dangling lens cap with his curious front paws, too close for me to take his picture . . . the varying hares who scampered from their roadside flowers at my approach . . . the willow ptarmigan who stayed by my feet and, thinking itself camouflaged, refused to fly away . . . bald eagles fishing the Ogilvie River . . . short-eared owls hovering above the buckbrush . . . jaegers screaming into the muskeg.

And the grizzlies. I was dozing when I saw them, a blur of brown and then two more. In haste, I pulled my camera from a scramble of maps on the floor beside me and snapped off a shot—quickly—in case they disappeared. Darn. They were too small an image to reflect the drama of the moment. I scrabbled feverishly through the scatter on my lap to find longer lenses. My fingers fumbled. I sneaked a glance to cement them in my mind. Oblivious to my presence, the three came closer, the mother grizzly munching in the willows, her two cubs gambolling behind. At last. The biggest lens snapped into position to frame the family for posterity—or so I thought.

I didn't have to look behind to know what happened. The shouts. The running feet. My bear reached to full height, sniffed, stared, then lumbered into the bushes out of sight. "Sorry about that," said a voice apologetically from the enormous home on wheels that loomed above me. So much for my priceless picture. The memory remains.

For more than thirty-six miles I wound through the Richardsons to reach their summit near where the Yukon hands over the Dempster to the Northwest Territories. Here at the Continental Divide, water flows west to the Pacific Ocean and east to the Arctic Ocean.

Except for two confusing mileposts sticking up on each side of the road, one saying *458* and the other *468*, I would have never known that I had reached the border. A large yellow billboard had been erected the day before. As I read it, I thought pessimistically of the Lost Patrol.

There is NO public ferry service at the river. NO gas, NO accommodation and NO communication. Do NOT travel when the road is in a wet condition or whenever it is raining. If you proseed [sic] beyond this point you are travelling at your OWN risk. GET it?

For the next forty-six miles, the road oozed downward through thick mud to the Peel River. Except for short periods at freeze-up and break-up and in winter when an ice road is constructed, travellers can now call on a free government ferry to take them over the Peel. But when I drove the Dempster before its official opening, the long-promised ferry had broken down; indeed it hadn't yet arrived. At the Peel crossing, a sign on the northern side of the river told travellers that the Dempster was closed and dangerous—not much help for those on the southern side. Tourists who had read about the Dempster in national magazines had headed north unaware of ferry problems and delayed construction schedules, and almost all turned back at the Peel in disappointment or disgust.

I didn't know if I would have to abandon my Brat on the banks, swim the four-hundred-yard river, then backpack, wait for a helicopter, or expect a barge, but I was determined to get to Inuvik. Many and varied were the tales passed along the road, over the airwaves, and on the printed page about the difficulties and dangers in fording the Peel: illegal substitute barges, trucks and campers chancing a private scow and going overboard, alternative travel by plane and river boat.

According to the latest reports, Willy Simon of Arctic Red River was operating a little barge measuring ten feet by twenty and powered by a forty-horse outboard for prices ranging from thirty to fifty dollars a crossing. But when I got to the Peel, a sign on Willy's barge read Use At Your Own Risk. Gone Fishing.

I sat at midnight beside half a dozen abandoned vehicles on the wrong bank of the river and pessimistically wondered how I was going to get to the other side. After all my cockiness in coming north against all advice, was this really going to be the end of the road?

Two kids were playing in a scow a short distance down the beach. Above them beside an open fire, a woman, her face obscured by a floral scarf, was bending over a blackened kettle.

Mary Vittrekwa smiled a welcome and invited me over the willow stick threshold into her tent. Her husband, Willem Vittrekwa, eighty-six years old but bright-eyed and alert, was reclining on a pile of sleeping bags and contentedly smoking his pipe.

Like all the Gwich'in families I was to meet on the banks of the Peel, Mary and Willem were gentle and gracious. Making excuses for her "poor house," Mary stoked the fire anew to make tea and poured a stream of Ritz crackers onto a plate. They were rapidly snatched up by a bevy of grandchildren who crowded into the tent with us.

The Vittrekwas (whose name means "don't cry") had shunned the easy life of nearby Fort McPherson to live almost year round on the land: fishing here till August at Eight-Mile Joe's (called that because it is eight miles from town) then "trouting" on the Rat River and hunting caribou till almost Christmas. "We sometimes go into town when it gets really cold," Mary said. "But the young people in town do too much drinking, look at too much TV. Our chief was shot, his son kill him with a knife and his wife start to drink then she die too."

The talk continued. I glanced at my watch. 12:30 A.M. Outside it was as light as the middle of a day down south. Whole trees were sweeping by in the fast spring current. Kids were throwing mud blocks in the water. Across the river, dogs were yelping, a diesel generator was puttering.

"You stay with us here tonight, camp next to us," Willem said, and then to my surprise, "We sure like you."

Maybe it didn't matter if I never got to Inuvik. Then, in embarrassment, I saw that by the clock atop the radio, it was really 2:30 A.M. I'd forgotten the time change of two hours at the border. Still, living on Northern Time, what did it matter?

Next morning I tore myself from my sleeping bag to watch Willem pulling in his fish—white fish, herring, and inconnu. He dumped them on a bed of moss and willow then went upstream several miles to get fresh water. Mary and I set to work to prepare the fish for the smokehouse. Expressing a solicitude my ineptitude did not deserve, she upturned a cooking pot for my seat, covered my lap with a tarp, and wore her best parky in my honour.

"I do this side, you watch, then you do that side," she instructed me as we sat down with *ulus* (crescent-shaped knives) to fillet the fish between us. And when I, inadvertently, sliced through the tail leaving nothing to support the fillets to be draped over the drying racks, I confessed apologetically, "I'd never make the Good Woman contest at Northern Games." She laughed and didn't seem to mind.

Mary Vittrekwa, like her sister Annie Henry, works hard. That spring, she had tanned eight moosehides, three for herself and five for other people. "They don't do it in town much any more," she explained. Much of what she does is given away. "I like helping the old people and the poor people on the river."

Later Willem added, "Lots of people come here and eat my dry fish and take pictures. I like meeting these people." So far, the road, which had only just reached the Vittrekwas' tent flap, had brought few outsiders. I wondered if this hospitable couple's attitude would change in subsequent years when tourists travelled the Dempster in greater numbers. Most likely, and perhaps luckily for the Vittrekwas, travellers with their thoughts on ferries and Inuvik would race on by and never know that Willem and Mary were there.

The people of the Peel did not need a ferry to cross the river. Peter James Vittrekwa was only ten but he had his own scow. Seventeen-year-old Dennis Blake not only had a dogteam for his trapline but he had a truck and ran his own taxi service—on the Fort McPherson side of the river. He also operated a backhoe, a loader, and a grader.

For all their mechanical sophistication, the kids were fascinated by the simple Sevylor. They blew up the boat with the plastic pump plugged into the Brat's cigarette lighter and then used the foot pump to cool the tea I poured. Dennis of the white teeth, curly hair, and cheerful grin had no need to struggle with the instruction manual to attach the

Merc to the motor mount. He knew instinctively what to do. Yet despite their madcap antics when the boat was assembled—gyrating in quick circles, vaulting floating debris, zipping in and out of the slower, flat-bottomed scows—Peter James was adamant that I go visiting downriver with them in his own craft. He didn't trust a blow-up boat for that.

Four miles upstream lived the Vaneltsi family. Their camp of neat white tents edged the riverbank like motel units. Spruce-legged tables were set with jars of bannock, dishes of moose, plates of dry fish, cups for tea. The smokehouse, shingled with sheets of bark and underlain with canvas to produce the right amount of heat and moisture, was full with fish. A caribou skin was drying above the smoke from a willow rib tepee.

As I followed the children up the steps cut from the river mud, my apprehension at our presumptuousness melted away as Percy and Emma came forward to shake hands. Annie looked up from her moosehide to smile shyly. Winnie and Kimmie grinned. Marty enthusiastically pushed me towards the table. Rosalie made tea. I felt like royalty.

Suddenly, a shout went up as Marty pointed downriver. "Daddy, Daddy." Excitedly, all tumbled down the bank as the head of the Vaneltsi family pulled into shore with his load of fish. He registered no surprise to see a stranger in his camp and invited me to stay for a boiled whitefish dinner.

By this time, Peter James, Dennis, and the rest of the Blake-Vittrekwa crew had climbed Shiltee Rock, an impressive limestone pillar overlooking the Vaneltsi camp, and were making shadow pictures against the skyline. "Come and see Shiltee," said Wanda of the beautiful smile.

We climbed the trail together. From the crumbling top were far-sweeping views of a river that now had life and a delta not yet reached that now had shape.

Wanda told me a story about Shiltee Rock. Once there was an old man who lived with his wife and children, three sons and a daughter. His daughter had magic powers. The man spoke to his boys, "My children, I want food. Let us go to the mountains." So they travelled to the mountains west of Fort McPherson. Only the girl remained behind with her mother, who said, "My daughter, when your brothers return you must not look at them." But the girl loved her brothers, she was lonesome for them and anxious for them to get back. She looked down the river on the sly and saw her brothers walking back. She said, "Mother, Mother, my brothers are walking back." All at once, her three brothers turned into stone, three rock pillars in a row, as well as their dog which was walking behind, and also the bannock her mother was making. [2]

Two of the pillars have succumbed to erosion by the elements and many climbing feet, but the main pillar still stood like a guard over the Vaneltsi camp.

True to Northern Time and my winging-it lifestyle, the Brat and I got over the Peel the following day. Thanks, I think, to Moccasin Telegraph, Joe Vittrekwa came in from Fort McPherson and offered to take me across in Willy's barge. He gave me no time to break camp. It didn't matter as I could easily come back for my belongings in the rubber raft. Fortunately, the Brat was small enough to be reversed up a couple of rough planks, and although I had a few frightening moments before it dropped with a thud onto the floor of the barge, the crossing was easy. Joe and a friend drove the two river scows which pushed Willy's barge to the other side. And then Joe left.

Ironically, despite my weeks of worrying about how to get myself across the Peel, I spent the next few days ferrying my new-found Dene friends across the river in the rubber raft. The Sevylor was an intriguing novelty in a land so recently linked to the Outside.

Once past the Peel, the drama of the Dempster was over—in the pioneering sense. The road now ran effortlessly east across the Peel-Mackenzie River delta to the Gwichin Dene villages of Fort McPherson and Arctic Red River (now called Tsiigehtchic) and then north to Inuvik. Most travellers rushed on by. "That's a shame," said John Scaife, a private investigator who came to Fort McPherson as manager for the Hudson Bay Company but who quit to spend his winters in the bush and his summers helping at the local motel. "All people seem to want to do is to hit Inuvik and then head south. But the people here are friendly, that's why I stay, and there's lots to do and learn."

Much later in Inuvik, I was to meet strangers who thanked me for stopping by in Fort McPherson. "You shared our culture and took it with you. You will always be our friend." One of these was Mary Jane Vittrekwa, Mary's daughter, whom I met for a few moments at the motel. When I returned south, a beautiful moosehide watchband beaded by Mary Jane was waiting in my mail. It was inscribed with the words, "A token of our friendship." My new friend married a year or so later and went to live in Old Crow. On the day that TV came to Old Crow, she switched on the set to CBC Vancouver and saw me showing her watchband to the interviewer as a memorable moment in my northern travels.

It's easy to miss the picturesque community of Arctic Red River (Tsiigehtchic) at the confluence of Arctic Red River with the Mackenzie River, and that summer everybody did. To reach Tsiigehtchic you have to ask the ferry captain to drop you off and come back later, otherwise he'll take you straight across the Mackenzie River to join the Dempster.

Unlike Fort McPherson, Arctic Red River had no public accommodation, and the Bay man told me he was leaving for lack of business and TV. But the village, for many years a traditional fish camp, has an interesting old Roman Catholic mission set on a photogenic bluff and several Hudson's Bay Company buildings that demonstrate the architecture of different eras. It deserves a visit.

Fortunately, I detoured to Arctic Red River on Treaty Day, an annual event when, accompanied by Mounties in full red regalia, federal government officials pay treaty—a symbolic five-dollar bill—to every villager on the treaty list.

I knew in advance of the problems with the ferry over the Peel. I didn't expect any problems in crossing the Mackenzie. In fact, I loitered on a hill above it while taking photographs of Arctic Red River. Suddenly, a truck pulled up beside me and a voice said, "You'd better hurry, you'll miss the ferry and there isn't another one for a week. It's going in for refit." Northern Time means adapting to the moment.

From Arctic Red River, the road (now called the Mackenzie Highway) headed north along the eastern edge of the vast Mackenzie Delta, cleaving a straight path between miniature stands of spruce and tamarack, sidling past sloughs abundant with waterfowl, and punctuated with more places to camp than I had seen since Dawson.

Civilization seemed to come all at once. Buses even ran on this section. And there were pullouts to gravel pits, tables, toilets and picnic sites, an airport, float plane docks, and finally, Inuvik. According to the words on its official monument, Inuvik is "the first community north of the Arctic Circle built to provide the normal facilities of a Canadian town."

Nevertheless, there was still a frontier feeling about the place and the people. Three cyclists cooking their evening meal by a roadside culvert were leaving for a two-year trip to Tierra Del Fuego, and they talked of others who would be arriving to do the trip between the Antarctic and the Arctic in reverse.

The Brat with its BC licence plates was a novelty and quickly attracted attention. A group of Dene men signalled me peremptorily to stop. "How did you get across the Peel?" one asked. Hesitantly, I replied, "In Willy's barge."

They laughed. "I'm Willy," he said.

Back home in British Columbia after my trusty Bratmobile survived seven thousand miles of mostly gravel, I drove over a nail in my driveway and got my first flat tire.

Five years later, I did the Dempster again, this time in April, a month considered spring in the north but which looks and feels much like winter to those from the south.

"Come and see spring in the Arctic," suggested Frank Pielak, a long-time northerner from Inuvik. "Long days, clear blue sunny skies, good fishing, no bogs and no bugs." Then, knowing I had the habit of teetering on the edge of things, he added, "Be one of the few southerners who've driven the Arctic Ocean."

So I left the drizzle and daffodils of the Pacific Ocean and drove the Alaska Highway to Whitehorse to meet him. It was minus 22 degrees Celsius, but he wore only sneakers, jeans, and a short-sleeved cotton shirt. Casual but experienced, he smiled at my longjohns, parka, and snowboots; at my amazement that not yet were seatbelts mandatory in the North; and at my surprise that the locals often travelled this frontier country without four-wheel drive.

"How was the trip down the Dempster?" I asked.

"Wonderful," Frank exclaimed enthusiastically. He said that caribou were crossing the bare road in the spruce forest, chickadees and snowbirds were fluttering round the pussy willows, dippers were riding the waves on ice-scalloped lakes, Dall sheep were licking salt on the sidehills, and an orange moon rose over the Ogilvies. He'd even strolled the Arctic Circle in shirt sleeves.

Then why, I asked myself ruefully one day later, was I riveted to my seat in his Bronco looking out at a white, white world—the sky, the land, the road—and me. I was white with fright. I sat silently, rigidly, nervously fingering my seatbelt as the Bronco ploughed through a blizzard. Lying in the snow were the wings of a Cessna that had flown too low and the roof of a house trailer that had blown off the road.

What road?

"A bit hard on the eyes, hard to see the road edge, sure a different day than yesterday," Frank commented laconically at the wheel, "but it wouldn't be spring without a snowstorm."

Once past the plateau and through the mountains, we could make faster time on a flat, wide road through the delta. Frank was anxious to get to Inuvik for its spring carnival. He was to be crowned King of Muskrat Jamboree.

"Think we could make a short detour to Fort McPherson?" I asked. "I'd like to say hello to Willem and Mary Vittrekwa if they're not out trapping. Mary Jane who gave me this watchband is in Old Crow but I'd like to see her parents."

"Waste of time, Lyn," Frank shrugged. "Anyway, it'll be difficult to find them, the houses all look the same and anyway, they may not remember you, it was a long time ago."

I persisted. All the houses did look pretty much the same, but everybody knows everybody in these small communities so we soon found where the Vittrekwas lived. I stepped inside the porch and the first thing I saw on the wall was a gallery of photos I had sent years before and the first person I saw at the door was Mary Jane. She smiled in immediate recognition.

I bent over to take off my boots. As I straightened up, she said, "I hope you don't mind. I've worn them once." And into my hands she placed a pair of new lavishly beaded and furred moccasins.

"But I have nothing to give you in return," I protested.

"It's enough that you remembered. Thank you for coming."

Willem and Mary on the sofa behind nodded in agreement. It may have been blizzard-like outside but there was a world of warmth inside.

Despite the detour, we reached Inuvik in time for Muskrat Jamboree and the Top of the World Ski Meet, two ways in which northerners celebrate the end of cabin fever. Kids, looking adorable in their bulky but colourfully embroidered fur-trimmed par-kas, mitts, and moccasins, waddled around Twin Lakes and went for rides in toboggans or plastic milk carriers. Their parents played tug-of-war or raced their skidoos, then warmed themselves over coffee and caribou stew in tents with a willow brush floor.

We had driven to Inuvik on an all-season land road, albeit covered with ice. Now we were to embark on a 108-mile water route to Tuktoyaktuk via the ice-covered Mackenzie River and Beaufort Sea. I had never driven on ice roads before and I was apprehensive, espe-cially as four people had died the day before when their car careered around a bend, their wheels spun in the snow, and they slammed into an oncoming truck. People told me of graders falling through the ice even when it was four feet thick. "Drive slow," warned a friend, "and watch the overflow."

Despite the warnings, I didn't really know what an ice road was. Frank explained that sometime in December or January when the ice is considered thick enough, a grader snowploughs a route along cer-tain channels of the Mackenzie River and Kugmallit Bay in the Beau-fort Sea. It is important to scrape through the snow cover first so that the cold winter air thickens the ice. Sometimes, water is sprayed onto the road to freeze and thicken the ice further. It didn't seem possible to drive normally over slabs of ice even if they were six or seven feet thick. "Surely we need four-wheel drive?" I asked incredulously. "Nope," Frank replied nonchalantly, "people up here drive ordinary cars on ice roads all the time."

Ice roads were built to facilitate travel to drilling sites and supply camps in the oil patch of the Mackenzie Delta and the Beaufort Sea. Flying in fuel and heavy equipment to remote camps and settlements costs a lot more than building ice roads. For at least four months a year, ice roads were, and still are, busy highways for people from Inuvik, Aklavik, Tuktoyaktuk, and the bush camps in between. They are also important elsewhere in the North.

Frank and I left the geological survey ships waiting for breakup on the banks of the Mackenzie and drove onto the East Channel. I re-membered how, fourteen years before, I had launched my rubber boat at this same spot. Frank talked of the times he'd nearly capsized in gales on the Mackenzie, how waves came crashing over his bow, how, soaked and shivering, he battled ashore to make a fire.

It seemed odd that we'd both boated down this wide white road between the drifting snow packs that defined it. The Mackenzie Delta is an impossible maze of channels and islands and ponds in summer; it seems infinitely more confusing in the uniform white of winter.

At least I didn't have to worry about falling into a ditch as I had a few days before while winding through a whiteout on the elevated Dempster. Our road now from snowbank to snowbank was about four lanes wide. Running down the middle was a one-lane-wide track of slippery glare ice. Frank avoided it and drove on the snow-brushed section to one side. "The channels are narrower closer to Tuk," he said. Was that preferable or did I detect an ominous note in his voice?

The sun was only an amber glow in a leaden sky. "It'll soon be blue, you wait," Frank promised.

Impatient for colour, I asked him to stop. He did so, carefully. "Gotta get some colour pictures somehow," I called blithely as I knelt down in the middle of the glare ice and swept away the snow with my hands.

"How much road are you going to clear like that?" Frank asked amusedly from the window of the Bronco.

"Just enough to show that we're driving on an ice road," I retorted, continuing my manual snowplough.

I was amazed by a closeup look at the slabs of ice we'd been driving on. So many colours. Not white but all kinds of green—jade and olive and emerald; all kinds of blue—royal and sapphire and ultramarine; and shades like turquoise in between. So many shapes. The slabs were over six feet thick, Frank said, but broken into streaks and blobs and spatters by fault lines, overflow cracks, and air bubbles. The tiniest of splotches twinkled like jewels.

The ice was so shattered that I returned rather gingerly to the Bronco. I marvelled we didn't break through the ice and freeze in the water. Or that we didn't slither off the road.

After my intimate view, I was content to see the rest of the road through the window. We barrelled down the East Channel, past the Caribou Hills, past abandoned Reindeer Station where eighty herders and their families lived in the 1930s and 1940s; past a de-activated Imperial Oil camp at Tununuk; past the turnoff to the abandoned whaling station and trading post of Herschel Island where a party of Finns, Swedes, and Austrians were using ice roads to get to places even more remote; and finally, onto the sea-ice of Kugmallit Bay past the graves and driftwood remains of Kittigazuit where in the 1800s over a thousand Inuvialuit lived and hunted the beluga whale.

Signposts sticking out of this vast white expanse of land were intriguing. They pointed out detours around glare ice, bumps, and private ice roads leading to who knows where. One, obviously placed by a humorist, read Third Avenue.

Ptarmigan were remarkably tame. Frank slowed down obligingly while I tried to take pictures. Their spring plumage was just emerging—black wing tips and black feet and a clear red crest over the eye. As we got closer, they arose from the road like clouds of fluttering tissues, only to land again close by on the bare brown branches of the willows.

By the time we reached the sea ice, the sun, although soon to set, was shining brightly and the sea was blue, intensely blue, cerulean blue, just as I wanted it to be and just as Frank had promised.

The ice road of the river had been wide and flat; the ice road of the ocean was a fantasyland of whipped cream and meringue, a naked Pavlova dessert. I felt confined in the truck. I wanted to walk over that expanse of sculptured seascape. I wanted to reach the horizon. I tried and fell on my rump amid the frozen waves. I took the rest of my pictures while sea-locked in the snow.

"Better than falling out of a boat?" Frank commented facetiously when I staggered back to the Bronco.

"Saves a tripod," I retorted as soon as I could manage flippancy.

It was amazing that we could barrel along at sixty miles per hour, our inside tires on the ice lane, outside tires on the snow shoulders, and not slip or swerve or spin. Something to do with momentum, Frank said. Probably more to do with experience, I thought.

As the setting sun turned the ice of the ocean a dramatic orange in the west, a rising moon delicately filtered the pale blue sky in the east. It was almost midnight but the white of the land and sea in between seemed to make the day last longer. Twilight seemed forever. I stood on a bank at the end of the Tuk peninsula and looked out over an ocean of ice that had no horizon. To the north the sea and sky were one.

We celebrated our safe arrival in Tuk with Randy and Katey Pokiak at the Beluga Jamboree. Randy makes visitors part of his family, whether he is trapping in January, hunting polar bears in March, ice fishing in May, catching whales in July, or hunting caribou in September.

He is equally adept at explaining permafrost, oil drilling, and land claims as he is at skinning pelts and driving dogteams. I had known him only five minutes when he picked up Katey from a tea boiling contest on the ice and asked her to fry me some slices of caribou from the hind quarter sitting on his kitchen floor.

After lunch, he rounded up a babysitter for one son, Enook, put the other one, Lucky, behind him on the skidoo and invited me to visit the pingoes three-and-a half miles away by *qamutik*. "You'll be more comfortable in the sled," he said solicitously. I zipped my parka close around my face but prepared to put up with frozen fingers in order to take pictures as we sped along.

Comfortable? We rolled through Tuk and past the Roman Catholic mission boat *The Lady of Lourdes*, permanently anchored on a concrete pad in the middle of town. We left behind the houses with their polar bear skins flying like laundry in the wind and hurtled across frozen land and sea to the pingoes, ice-cored hills, volcanoes of ice, that are Tuk's most prominent landmarks. The *qamutik* bounced over the bumpy ice. "Okay?" gestured Randy. "Perfect," I grimaced with a nod as I stashed my cameras and curled my hands in my groin for warmth.

Perfect I was not, but it was worth the discomfort to experience the life of northerners who were still tough despite their preference for skidoos not dogteams, for electric-powered houses, not seal-oil-lit *iglus*.

It had taken many years to build a road to the Arctic Ocean and many years for me to reach the end of it. Some day there may be many more roads built up here in the name of progress. Like Erva and Florence, I am glad that I had the privilege of being at the beginning of things.

NOTES

[1] I have simplified this. The Dempster doesn't actually go to Inuvik, it goes to meet the Mackenzie Highway which was already built, i.e., the road was being constructed at each end at the same time. It seems incredible that the "someone" in the travel department who gave me the wrong information re opening of the Dempster should be out by three years but it happened.

[2] With thanks to William Nerysoo Sr. for providing a detailed version of the Shiltee story.

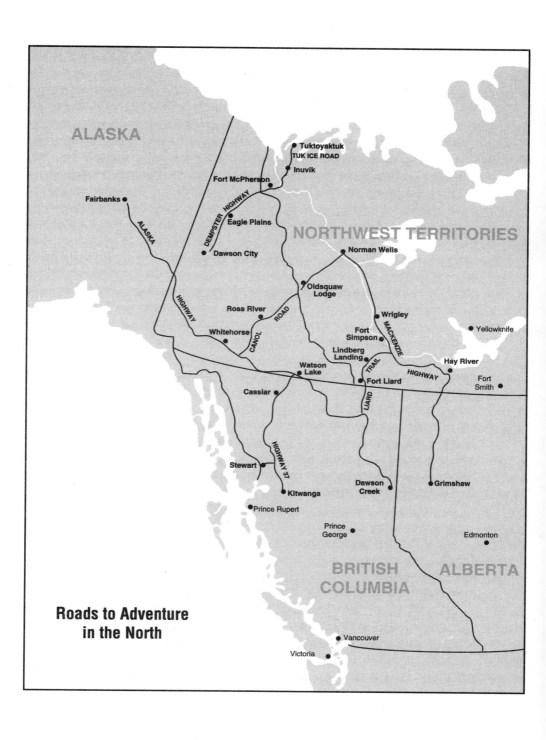

**Roads to Adventure
in the North**

A Garden of Eden
in the Barren Grounds

AS SOON AS I HEARD that Sam Miller, a wildlife biologist working for the Government of the Northwest Territories, was building a naturalists' lodge somewhere in the Mackenzie Mountains near the Yukon/Northwest Territories border, I knew that I had to be there.

"I haven't been to Sam's place myself," said his wife, Sandy, over the phone from Yellowknife. "A bunch of his wildlife buddies are helping him build the lodge during their summer vacation. Just ask people on the North Canol Road where Sam is. You should be able to drive as far as the Amax weather station in a vehicle but you'll have to backpack from there."

I found Sam's Place, later called Oldsquaw Lodge, in 1979, the Year of the Brat. Having already driven the South Canol section of the road in 1973 with my parents, I was certain that my trusty truck would get me safely 136 miles along the South Canol Road from the Alaska Highway to Ross River, but reaching my undetermined destination on the North Canol Road would depend on weather, the distance to Sam's Place, and the submarine ability of the Brat to ford streams, especially past the border into the Northwest Territories where the road was not maintained.

"Backpackers sometimes get as far as the Mackenzie River," said one adviser; then he added grimly, "but some of them die first."

"The road's crawling with pebble pounders," encouraged another brightly. "You'll get lots of help when you break down."

"You won't make it past the border in an ordinary car," determined a third. "You need a jigger to get you to Norman Wells."

Of rum or rye? No, he meant something in six-wheel drive. Well, the Brat was pretty ordinary-looking but it did have four-wheel drive for emergencies. And as far as my advisers were concerned, emergencies would be abundant along the North Canol.

Like many Yukon roads, the Canol (the name stands for Canadian Oil) was built to develop mineral resources: in this case, to service a pipeline from oil fields at Norman Wells on the Mackenzie River over 480 miles of largely unexplored wilderness to a refinery at Whitehorse on the newly-built Alaska Highway. Supporters of the project worried that a likely Japanese invasion during World War II would cut off supplies to Alaska.

The Canol project was one of the most staggering construction achievements in the world. It was more than a road, a pipeline, a telephone line, an oil field, and a refinery. It encompassed sixteen thousand miles of supplementary pipelines through Yukon and Alaska that radiated from Whitehorse to Skagway, to Fairbanks and Tanana, to Carcross and Watson Lake; well over a thousand miles of access roads that included a winter road from Grimshaw, Alberta to Norman Wells; as well as a dozen airfields, many pumping stations, tank farms and innumerable camps.

Some 4,000 engineers and 10,000 civilians took up the challenge. Working with the United States army was the contractor Bechtel-Price-Callahan who, on June 15th, 1942, posted the following now-famous sign in its employment offices across North America:

THIS IS NO PICNIC

Working and living conditions on this job are as difficult as those encountered on any construction job ever done in the United States or any foreign country. Men hired for this job will be required to work and live under the most extreme conditions imaginable. Temperatures will range from 90 degrees above zero to 70 degrees below zero. Men will have to fight swamps, rivers, ice and cold. Mosquitoes, flies and gnats will not only be annoying but will cause bodily harm. If you are not prepared to work under these conditions

DO NOT APPLY

What made the achievement even more staggering was the fact that it was completed in less than two years during one of the worst winters on record. The first surveys to seek a feasible route were made in June 1942 and the first oil reached Whitehorse in April 1944.

But oil flowed only eleven months. The Japanese tide was turned and the war ended. With shipping lanes free again around the world, it became far cheaper to supply oil to Alaska by tanker. Moreover, the diameter of the Canol pipeline was limited to six inches, too small to carry a commercial volume of crude oil.

In the years after the war, the Norman Wells oil field reverted to local production, the Whitehorse refinery was dismantled and shipped south, and the Canol road was abandoned. Hundreds of trucks, jeeps, bulldozers, innumerable pallets of parts, storage buildings and camps for as many as 4500 people were left mouldering in the bush.

On the Yukon side of the border, the Canol road was maintained in summer to get prospectors and miners to their camps as soon as the ice went out in May. With major discoveries of minerals such as lead and zinc, barite, and tungsten in the 1960s and 1970s, the Canol came to life again.

The South Canol is a lush land of rushing rivers, quiet lakes, high mountains, and deep canyons. The road crosses many streams, undulates beneath spectacular peaks, and runs along picturesque lakes.

Miners are not the only ones who use the Canol roads. At Quiet Lake, I met Tony Fritz, a greybearded Yukoner who netted trout commercially on the lake. I traded help in bolting his transom with a ride to check his nets.

"I'll never leave the Yukon," Tony chortled as we hauled aboard a thirty-seven-pound lake trout. "I eat when I feel hungry, sleep when I'm tired, and always feel healthy. I go Outside only at Christmas when I visit my wife and son in Victoria. Down there, everybody talks about dying but in the Yukon I feel young."

Tony gave the same reasons most people gave for liking Yukon life. "You feel free here. You can live quite cheaply—fish all year, kill a moose for winter, live in a tent all summer. If I want, I can earn more than a hundred dollars a day. But what good is money? Some work till they die but they can't spend it in heaven. Oh, I like to make money, don't get me wrong, but I don't want to work too hard at it."

He said he cooked for twenty-seven years and built a lodge at Little Salmon. "I run a trapline in winter now. Want to come along? I have nice cabins and I'm out all day on the skidoo." He paused for a moment then continued, "How old are you?"

After I gulped out the answer, he breezed on with disarming directness. "That's good. You could probably take it. Most young girls nowadays don't have the patience to stand a trapline for long."

Going with the flow is one of the joys of my life but I decided to head on down the road. I could always check out Tony's trapline on the way back.

From Quiet Lake, the Canol climbs along the Ross River to its summit at Lapie Pass, one of the most photogenic spots in the Yukon. Here the Lapie River is punctuated by a string of little lakes and splashed with slender islands. Just before the road reaches the junction near the community of Ross River, it squeezes through the canyons of the Lapie then oozes low over the floor of the valley.

The architectural style of Ross River (population 196 in 1979) was definitely Pioneer-Frontier: the native log cabins set in sergeant-major lines on one side of the road, the trailer-type government buildings in similar fashion on the other side, and scattered around, the usual jumble of workshops, oil drums, and broken-down vehicles. There was a store, a hotel, a gas station and a post office, although at first glance it was difficult to know which was which.

One house was distinctive: the Spanish-style white home of millionaire miner Al Kulan, who discovered the huge Cyprus Anvil mining deposit. I had had coffee with Al six years earlier and he had invited me to return to go prospecting with him in the mountains of the North Canol. Now it was too late. In 1977, he was shot point blank by his former partner in the bar of the Welcome Inn, a violent twist which seemed out of harmony with Ross River's otherwise quiet, deserted air.

Apart from this claim to fame, most of the action in Ross River takes place down at the Pelly River crossing where the Yukon Government runs a free cable-operated barge between May and October. Prospectors and miners use it to head for the creeks. Big game outfitters load horses on it for going to their summer grazing areas and fall hunting camps. Boat owners use it to launch their flat-bottomed scows.

With the North Canol even less travelled than the South Canol, I took the precaution of borrowing a comealong winch from Ed Russell, the friendly conservation officer. I lightened the Brat's load by storing my motor and raft in his workshop. Even I, the eternal Pollyanna, was beginning to be pessimistically affected by such signs as the one at the Pelly ferry, No Facilities For 235 km, and the notice at the suspension foot bridge, Use At Your Own Risk.

Good grayling pools made the first ninety miles of the North Canol worthwhile despite an otherwise unprepossessing appearance as it rollercoastered along drumlins, crossed innumerable creeks, and sidled past lakes and sloughs. Three Indian women were hunting hares by Marjorie Creek. Ed's wife, Heather, had told me the men in these women's families returned for the winter to the settlement, but the women, all in their eighties, lived in their tents on the Canol year round.

When I trucked up the Canol in 1973, the road was strewn with assorted junk left by the United States Army after they abandoned the Canol pipeline. Six years later, the old camps with their trucks, construction vehicles, pallets of spare parts, and wooden wannigans were lined up neatly along the road as if on parade. As I climbed into one of the cabooses, a porcupine, disturbed from munching on the walls, erupted his quills in a halo that intimated no angelic intentions and waddled past me to the door.

The first crossing of MacMillan Creek—with the spectacular peaks of the Itsi Range in the background and the river rushing by at my feet—was one of the most picturesque spots along the road. It was midnight when I stopped to make camp, light enough to read maps and make a meal but not the best light for photographs. Having decided to wait till morning, I took great pains to pose the camp for a calendar-type perspective: the blue tent here, the folding orange table-cum-storage cupboard there, the yellow chair to one side of the picture and the fall-tinted Brat to the other. Of course, at dawn, it rained.

But even leaden skies and cloud-hung mountains couldn't obliterate the beauty of the next thirty miles to the border, even if I had to carry it more in my mind than my camera.

This was where most of the exciting mining discoveries were being made. Short access roads led to white tent camps whose roofs were covered with brightly coloured tarps to act as handy identification points for helicopters.

Just at the point where in better weather I would have been glassing the Itsi Range for mountain goats, I turned off on one of the mining access roads to see how far the Brat could get to timberline.

Four miles farther on, I sneaked past a grader, rounded a bend, and pulled up beside Jim Dodge, a mining engineer from Yukon Barite. Jim was friendly, soft-spoken, and an easy conversationalist. Very quickly, I learned that barite is a mineral used in making drilling mud for lining oil and gas wells. With the next nearest source of high quality barite far away in Nevada, Yukon barite was much in demand at the time by drillers in Alaska and the Beaufort Sea. Today, Jim Dodge is still collecting a little barite, but other mining camps along the North Canol Road have been dismantled. Present-day miners now look for gold in these hills as did their predecessors one hundred years ago.

Jim was on his way to pick up a drill in Ross River and wanted to make the Pelly ferry before closing, but he didn't seem to mind talking.

"We put this road in three years ago but it's taken a long time to get everything checked. Seems to be choppers popping in all the time, checking to see if grades are low enough, that caribou and waterfowl nesting habitat aren't disturbed, that there's no erosion of stream crossings . . . they even check on cigarette butts. I remember one time we had a truck turned upside down off the road. We weren't allowed to take the cat off the road to get the truck out. We were just about to shovel the load from the truck when a chopper load of environmentalists jumped out with their clipboards. They gave us permission right there and then to move the cat twenty feet off the road to get the truck upright."

"I wonder if we're that tough in other places."

"Well, it's really a good thing," Jim replied, to my surprise.

"That's strange for a mining man," I couldn't help saying.

"Yeah, I was just about blacklisted down in the States," he laughed in return.

We got back in our vehicles. "Will I make it to the end of your road?" I asked.

"Sure you will. The government guy came up in an ordinary front-drive Subaru to do the final inspection. It was a miserable day, snowing, and the road was green. I groaned and thought, 'Oh, not today,' but he came and signed the inspection. He said if he could make it in his Subaru, the road was okay."

I drove off confidently, and around the next bend I almost ran into a bull caribou with a gigantic rack of antlers still in the velvet. Yukon Barite didn't seem to be disturbing this caribou.

Higher up, snow still edged the road, emphasizing how short a time the mountains let men in. I managed another seven miles before the Brat wound around its last pinnacle and refused to go farther. This was the point where barite would soon be removed. Only graders dared to go farther.

Back at the Canol, the road through the magnificent Macmillan Pass climbed steeply to six thousand feet. Each crossing of the Macmillan Creek was smaller than the one before, until at the border, Mile 147, the sixth crossing was just a gurgle. This is the Great Divide: on one side, the creek goes on to the Yukon River and thence to the Pacific; on the other side, the alpine ponds drain to the mighty Mackenzie and then to the Arctic.

I had made it to the Northwest Territories. But I'd been warned that this was as far as I could go.

Ahead downhill, horses were grazing, their bells tinkling as they hobbled on the tundra. It was still raining. Bob Badger, a wrangler from Alberta, was bending over his campfire as I drew up. "Come in for a coffee," he said cheerfully. "You're not gonna go much further anyway."

Inside the tent, I met Mike, the second guide. Bob and Mike were rounding up horses for the opening of hunting season which began July 15th. They would be taking them to Redstone River, another 170 miles into the Mackenzie Mountains.

"Want to come with us?" Bob suggested. "But you'll need a horse to get over the rivers. The bridges are all out between here and the Mackenzie. With all this rain lately, the waters are far too high for your clearance."

A mile or so past the border, the Brat breasted its first crossing of the Tsichu River without being flicked into four-wheel drive. Six miles farther was an old camp, a much-patched two-storey wooden hut, a junk pile of World War II army vehicles, a line of trailers, a field of gas barrels, and a row of modern trucks. Once an army maintenance facility, Canol Camp 222 was now Amax Northwest Mining Company's weather station.

"You're Lyn Hancock, aren't you?" said the fair-haired, bearded young man in greeting as I swung open the top half of his Dutch door. "Sam Miller said you might stop by. I doubt you'll get that Brat over the next crossing of the Tsichu, though. Why don't you stay overnight in the trailer and try crossing tomorrow. Would you like some hot chocolate?"

Moccasin Telegraph works faster than radios in these parts!

Greg Riggins and Anne Joslin were hired to prepare the old Canol camp for a winter of solitary confinement among the blizzards and glaciers of Macpass. Their job was to make weather observations five times a day for Amax of Canada, whose MacTung deposit, which straddles the border at Macpass is the largest known tungsten deposit in the world.

"The demand for tungsten is greater than the supply right now," Greg explained. "Amax is hesitant to develop this site because the price of tungsten goes up and down like crazy. So they're just doing preparation studies, like seeing if the weather's okay for flying tungsten out in a 747. The Fish and Wildlife guys don't want them to build a permanent townsite like Canada Tungsten has in the Nahanni country. Instead, they want Amax to fly workers in from Whitehorse for a month at a time."

Greg and Sue were a happy-go-lucky but practical couple who seemed well-suited for twelve months of isolation. "It's difficult to keep this place warm in winter but we're still going to enlarge the windows for watching wildlife. It's a great moose area. They say hunters mass here in the fall with just two questions: 'Got any gas?' and 'Seen any moose?' The moose congregate along the Tsichu to feed on a particular type of willow and use the river for easy travel. Of course, the resident band of wolves use it too. Dall sheep live above us and woodland caribou move through. You could hardly walk outside in early June when the ptarmigan were mating without knocking into them. Now they're on eggs so they're hiding."

The record rains that had plagued photography the previous day continued all night, and next morning the Brat met its match at the second crossing of the Tsichu.

Greg volunteered to try and ford the river in his Ford crewcab, which had higher clearance than my Brat. Leaving Sue behind to watch weather and monitor the radio, Greg and I ploughed into the rushing water beside the broken-down bridge. The river rose a yard on each side. It was like descending into a maelstrom, and for many moments I wished I'd not left the raft behind in Ross River. This was not driving; this was boating and swimming.

Greg changed gears continually. Slowly, we churned over the pebbled bed and hauled up through the mud on the other side. But this was only the first channel of a much braided river. After burrowing deeply through the muck of the next "portage," we inched forward into another arm of the stream. And then it was UNDER the only part of the bridge still standing. Chicken me! I should have been swimming the river outside the truck to take photographs of our crossing.

"This is the deepest part," Greg sang out cheerfully as we crunched through the swirling current and finally hauled up the bank on the other side of the Tsichu. There were five more streams to cross before Sam's Place.

We didn't make them. The next stream was fast, deep, and many-bouldered. Greg picked a channel through the rocks but his truck slid sideways on the greasy bank. The two left wheels bogged deeply into the muskeg and stayed there. Backpacking had begun.

"I'll go with you till we find Sam," said Greg. "He's sure to have a truck with a winch to get us out."

We hitched on our packs and set off across the Mackenzie Mountain Barrens, an undulating treeless plateau that is eighty square miles in area and surrounded by a thirty-five-mile crown of spectacular mountain peaks. The Mackenzie Mountains are the most extensive uninhabited mountains in North America, and, if you exclude the polar deserts, perhaps the world. We were mere specks in the middle of this vast wilderness.

It was hard to believe that thirty-five years earlier, the thin ribbon of road that now unfurled in front of us to the distant horizon rang with the songs of thousands of soldiers pitching pipe and cursing mosquitoes.

> "The night is light
> Mosquitoes sho-do bite
> Look up de river
> And see mo' damn pipe."

Despite the seeming emptiness and soundlessness of the tundra in the far distance, there was much to experience close at hand and underfoot. Wolves had walked our path no more than an hour earlier. Perky ground squirrels chattered at our intrusion or fought their own noisy battles. Ptarmigan, refusing to fly till we'd passed far from their nests, ran clucking from our feet. Then, with white wings flashing in graceful arcs, they flew back to the willows where we'd first encountered them.

Seldom reached by vehicles, this part of the road in the Northwest Territories had more to offer the historian or tundra scrounger than the more accessible section in the Yukon did. Trestles of old bridges still stood above the muskeg like some wooden Stonehenge; pieces of pipe, all sizes from two to six inches in diameter, still protruded from a thin layer of dirt; insulators still hung from slanted poles; bundles of copper-clad steel wire still trapped antlers of passing caribou.

About three miles farther on, we arrived at another abandoned Canol building. Smoke curled from an old garbage barrel. "Sam's moved," Greg sang out from inside a wooden wannigan. "He was here a few days ago. He must have decided to camp where he's building. Look over there to that knoll. That's where they are. Heave ho, it's just another few miles."

Sam had chosen well. The knoll was the only protruberance on the Barrens within a radius of twelve miles and an excellent vantage point for viewing and attracting wildlife. One hour later, we passed Marquis Lake, climbed the knoll, and found Sam and his buddies sitting on a pile of logs and taking a quick lunch break of pork and beans.

We had found Sam's Place. Now I was to meet Sam.

A soft-spoken man with long hair and a shy twinkling smile looked up at our approach. "Hi there. How far did you have to walk?"

"About twelve miles," answered Greg. "Wonder if you can give us a lift back to the truck? We're ditched back at the second crossing of the Tsichu."

"Sure. We've got a few logs to heft first."

While the men worked on the logs, Sam told me about some of his hopes and dreams. For the past five years he had been working in the Mackenzie Mountains studying grizzly bears. Now he wanted to share those experiences with others.

"My family lived with me during the grizzly project between May and October at our base camp by Godlin Lake. We always had lots of visitors, mostly biologists, hunters, mining people, and everybody used to tell us how lucky we were to live there. So I got to thinking of ways to help tourists experience this area. But it bothers me if people want to see only big things—large showy animals like grizzlies and caribou or the highest mountains or whole fields of flowers. I think you can get closer to nature by appreciating little things. A single flower is more attractive than the big splash a whole field of them makes. I can't always promise grizzlies, moose, and wolverine, but I can guarantee lichens, dewdrops, sunsets, reflections in a tundra pool, and weather—being hot and tired, cold and wet—these should be part of the experience too."

The name Sam chose for his lodge reflected the same understated way of doing things. "I like oldsquaw ducks. They're great talkers. You can hear them from a long way off, especially in spring. Oldsquaws usually nest further north on the Arctic coast and the High Arctic islands. This is the first time they have been recorded here on the Barrens. You also get long-tailed jaegers, Lapland longspurs, wheatears and snow buntings. Normally, they nest further north. Birders should have a field day."

The Barrens has been declared an International Biological Program (IBP) site for its unique ecology. Its name belies the abundance that greets those who can be parted from their vehicles. Of course, along this part of the Canol, that's one decision you don't have to make. The road does it for you.

Because the Barrens is such a large area and rises through varying habitats to a rim of high mountains, it is home to an overwhelmingly large number of plant and animal species, not only alpine tundra species but arctic and boreal ones as well. Sam said he'd counted over 120 species of birds, over 200 species of vascular plants and an incredible variety of lichens, as well as 31 species of mammals—a veritable Garden of Eden.

As we rumbled back to the Tsichu to rescue Greg's truck, Sam added more details. "The most obvious mammal you see here is the mountain or woodland caribou. It doesn't form huge herds like the barren-ground caribou, but it is gregarious and seldom travels alone. The Barrens is a critical post-calving feeding ground, and all summer you'll see small groups of two to six—sometimes up to sixty animals daily—in front of the lodge. They come here to feed on the lush plants of the flats and to use the ridge tops to get away from insects. I reckon the Mackenzie Mountain Barrens is the only place in the world where you can see caribou constantly day to day."

Sam's enthusiasm for his lodge was infectious. He was anxious to get most of the buildings closed to the weather before winter came. Opening was still two years away. The summer construction season is short in a land where snow doesn't melt till June and falls again in August. Yet already two cabins were walled and roofed, and the main building framed. Construction was laborious and expensive. All building materials had to be hauled for hundreds of miles along the Canol track, across creeks, through mud and over ice and snow.

"I'm scrounging as much as possible from the road and the camps," he laughed.

Building from Canol debris cut Sam's costs but it also added uniqueness. The past met the future in the building of Oldsquaw Lodge. Guest cabins and sauna came from bridge timbers; Sam's tiny cabin was a six-holer (toilet) for enlisted men; the dining room and gatepost were formed from telephone poles; all building supports were from pipe; door trims came from the lattice work on the side of army trucks, door knobs from camps, and beds were army cots. Sam was an artist and craftsman as well as a biologist and builder. That winter, he would painstakingly refinish and varnish all the old weathered wood and feature walls of the buildings so that in the light of summer's midnight sun they would glow gold with life again.

It was not Sam's knowledge of biology or his attributes as an artist that we needed that afternoon but his practical skill in extricating Greg's truck from the mud. With the help of a winch, a couple of trucks, and several sets of arms and legs, we succeeded just as the first of the season's backpackers came hiking up to the river.

We watched in fascination as the heavily laden hiker, still wearing boots, fought through the water at waist level. We winced when his sleeping bag dipped into the stream. How would he fare for the next two hundred miles of unpopulated wilderness? How would he cross a dozen more rain-swollen streams still ahead? Had he made arrangements to cross the biggest one of all, the mighty Mackenzie? And right now, how was he going to get his boots and sleeping bag dry?

"Wonder why he's carrying two rifles?" said Sam, shaking his head.

We introduced ourselves when the hiker, soaked but optimistic, staggered to our side of the stream. He spurned Sam's invitation to the Oldsquaw camp and felt sure he could make it to the Mackenzie River.

"What are you doing for food?" Sam asked.

"Plan to knock porcupines on the head," the hiker replied cheerfully as we left him on the bank to dry out—and to pursue his dream.

Eleven years later, the Canol road would be declared a National Historic Site and dozens of adventurers would tackle its heritage trail. Backpackers, horse riders, motorcyclists, and snowmobilers would pass by Sam's door—in all seasons. Some made it.

Experiencing Canol country is easier if you stay at Oldsquaw Lodge. It can be just as adventurous. Even getting there.

During the 1980s, I visited Sam's Place several times, characteristically on the spur of the moment when I found myself in the Yukon. I flew to Camp 222 from Whitehorse and Sam picked me up in Nellie, a distinctive aquamarine bus that some called "a crummy" and others called just plain "crummy." Nellie has also been called "a boulder bouncer" and "a spine-splitter." One visitor remarked that the twenty-five-mile ride was all that it was cracked up to be; another that every bump was worth it.

I found the best way to ride Nellie was to wedge myself tightly in the back seat with my companions, hang onto the seat in front, clamp my feet to the floor, and be mentally prepared to jerk and lurch over the ruts, crunch and scrape over boulder beds, splash over rivers, and slide along ravines. I just psyched myself into liking the journey.

To discourage others from driving the same route, Sam didn't repair the "road," although he cached the odd Canol plank to help in emergencies. (Some said the whole ride was an emergency.) Depending on your desire for excitement, you could stay aboard Nellie— or walk. It took the same time. Even if you stayed inside, you still had the opportunity to watch for wolves, moose, grizzlies, and the ubiquitous caribou from Nellie's wraparound windows

Sam's Place is now George and Brodie's and Norm and Barb's Place. Like Sam, they are respected biologists who share their love of the Barrens each summer with guests at Oldsquaw Lodge. Miners and weather watchers have abandoned the old North Canol Road, but naturalists and hikers still trek out from the upgraded airstrip at MacPass on foot or in crummy to savour the wilderness.

Most wildlife sightings are still made from the windows of the lodge. It's a simple, two-storey log building built like an observation blind with open beam ceiling, six skylights, and picture windows on three sides. It is flanked by five cabins also built like blinds.

I remember the wolves I saw the evening I was lounging in the library enjoying one of Oldsquaw's remarkable sunsets. After a nondescript day, suddenly the midnight sun gushed from the clouds above the Barrens and the iridescent glow of a triple rainbow struck the black hail- and rain-filmed crown of mountains that rimmed our horizon. The sun seemed to play a game of peekaboo as it slid across the sky, lighting each peak in turn. Soon it would be sunrise.

I watched as the sun glinted the tundra pools and lit the rain-filled rut of road that sliced the Barrens at the bottom of the knoll. With Sibelius's Second Symphony playing softly behind us in counterpoint to dozens of twittering cliff swallows flitting in and out of balcony nests in front of us, the stage was set.

To the left, a bull moose, silhouetted against a sunlit lake, strode ponderously, decisively, over the patterned ground towards a cow with young. They browsed together beneath the serrated edges of Keele Peak. To our right, below the rounded breasts of the Three Sisters, a group of mountain caribou grazed quietly.

Below our windows, a gyrfalcon sat motionless on a boulder staring intently at a scurry of arctic ground squirrels that scampered from mound to mound. Some, be-whiskered with grass, stood stiffly on furry plus-fours with their front paws held demurely on their chests like prayerbooks. But at the whirr of the gyr's wings, they would flick their tails, trill like chainsaws, and bolt down their burrows. Foisted, the gyrfalcon flew to the gatepost, a popular perch for raptors at Oldsquaw Lodge.

I eased myself from the cushions and crossed the carpeted floor for a closer look.

"A wolf! A wolf at the window," I yelled, then cursed my spontaneous outburst. A large brindled wolf with alert, chestnut-backed ears and black-tipped tail returned my stare through the sun-warmed glass. It was standing beside the cabin steps, scarcely two yards away.

My ecstatic yodels of surprise galvanized a dozen people to action. I hurtled downstairs for a camera with Susan close behind. Sam rushed out to waken the cook, who had been waiting all summer to see a wolf. Zoe dropped her plant book and grabbed her binoculars. Gene changed his glasses and Gus focussed his telescope. Everybody pressed their noses against the windows.

In thirty seconds I was back upstairs, but the wolf had gone. Not far. He seemed reluctant to leave. He sauntered across the hummocky tundra that sloped gently down to the road; then he stopped, turned around, and stared. He trotted on, then looked back again. We watched in awe for half an hour.

Ironically, two of the guests who had seen everything that week except a wolf were inside their cabin—sleeping. There is no room service or telephone at Oldsquaw Lodge. The guests never knew till next morning at breakfast that a wolf had been at their door.

"It pays to be persistent," advised Sam. "Keep glassing and scoping and scanning—the tundra, the sloughs, the lakes, the slopes of the hills, the crests of the mountains."

Dorothy Dickson was one guest who took his words to heart. It was rumoured that Dorothy stood scoping from the windows of the lodge so long that she named all the caribou individually. One evening her patience was rewarded by seeing two wolves stalk, chase, kill, and eat a caribou. She was engrossed in watching a group of sixty when a cow, calf, and yearling came grazing into view within 350 yards of her scope. Fifteen minutes later, another calf appeared, this one a loner.

Suddenly, Dorothy noticed two wolves, a thin, black bitch and a more robust brindled male, trotting along the Canol from the south. The pair stopped often to look up at the lodge, and once they followed each other in urinating against a bush. A larger group of caribou seemed oblivious to the predators, but a small group of three moved farther west. Dorothy lost sight of the lone calf. The wolves seemed peaceful too: they moved about 300 yards to the west and lay down among the hummocks. The bitch, more alert, sat up several times to stare back in the direction of the lodge. Fifteen minutes later, the wolves meandered farther west again.

All of a sudden, a caribou jumped up from behind a hillock and ran in wide zigzags over the rough, patchy ground with the male wolf in close pursuit. Dorothy reported later that the chase covered at least two miles, took six minutes, and the animals reached speeds of eighteen miles an hour. She was intrigued by the caribou's choppy upright gait in strong contrast with the low but powerful strides of the wolf.

Eventually, the wolf drew level with the caribou's left hip, leaped, and bowled his prey to the ground. Four times the caribou got to its feet but each time it was brought down. There was much excited tail wagging as the bitch arrived and the two wolves fed. They continued eating for three quarters of an hour, alternately pulling at the carcass, chewing, urinating, and defecating. Dorothy could see the bulging belly of the male, two miles away. Meanwhile, the larger group of caribou, seemingly oblivious to the killing, kept on grazing.

A couple of hours later, the guests hiked across the tundra to examine what was left of the kill. They found it was the lone calf.

At Oldsquaw Lodge you can see wildlife from the windows, but you can also see wildlife from your bed. I opened my eyes one morning to the sight of six gyrfalcons honing their flying skills across the skylight. Then, as I sat upright in my sleeping bag, through the window I counted fifty grazing caribou—some bulls but mostly mothers with young. Six gyrs and fifty caribou before breakfast was a good way to start my day.

I got even closer that afternoon—too close.

Sam always knew where the herds were, but I—stumbling over mounds of moss and grass, sloshing through sloughs and muskeg, elbowing awkwardly on my stomach, and hiding behind ice-cored palsa hummocks—I hardly knew where my feet were.

"Keep your head down but set up the tripod and wait for the herd to come into your picture," Sam whispered when eventually I caught up and fell down beside him in the dirt. Snow-capped glacier-hung peaks with serrated edges against an intense blue sky circled my horizon. What a backdrop for caribou!

I waited for the herd to come closer.

Suddenly, into my frame strolled a cow and calf. Click. The mother circled, trying to push her insistent offspring away but it did manage a quick slurp.

"It didn't get much," I complained.

"Only needs three seconds," Sam noted briefly. "Be quick! Not too many people get nursing shots."

Click, click.

"Lyn, move your camera to the left and up, quickly!"

Still pressing my eyes to the viewfinder, I swung the long lens to the side and gasped as a white tail and brown rump loomed into full frame. I clicked, but I was too close to be in focus and I had no opportunity to change lenses without disturbing the animals. The two caribou continued to graze, heads down, on the other side of the same palsa we were plastered against. They were just a couple of steps away but I dared not move to put myself in a better position to photograph them. I had to be content to snatch glimpses of them from around the rim of the boulder.

Then, into one side of my frame came a white tail and a rump, and two spindly legs. On the other side of the frame came a pair of antlers followed by a whole head in profile. Unaware. Click. I was reminded of the children's game "Pin the Tail on the Donkey."

"My God!" I breathed, more in prayer than blasphemy.

It had to happen. They heard and saw me. Two full-faced stares and they were gone, cantering back to the herd still back-dropped by those incredible mountains.

"Sit tight," Sam whispered. He whistled.

Curious, a trio of caribou from the herd bounced towards us, their red velvet antlers glinting in the sun. They looked like the front guard of an army. Without warning, they wheeled in tight circles, not away but around us. A perfect picture. Of course, I was out of film and the camera lens jammed.

"Oh well," I sighed. "Hunting season opens today anyway. That's the last time those caribou will be so relaxed for a while."

"You know, in a minor way, we are harassing them, too," Sam reminded me. "Every time they use up energy by running, they need more food to compensate. Caribou need every bit of fat they can get to help them survive the winter. Perhaps we should stay at the lodge and look at them only through spotting scopes."

❉

Often, you have an encounter with wildlife for which you are totally unprepared. This was the case with a grizzly Sam came to call "Lyn."

I had been hiking behind Sam along Grizzly Creek on the way to an eagle's nest, and as usual, I was burdened down with cameras, tripod, and packsack, not to mention years. I was a long way behind.

I crossed the creek and was heaving up the steep bank on the other side when Sam suddenly popped his head over my horizon to say tersely, "Hurry up, Lyn, there's a grizzly up here."

A hundred yards on the other side of the ridge, a golden-brown hump was browsing among waist-high willows. Sam studied it through binoculars while, heart beating fast, I tried to unjam my camera lens, a frequent problem that summer. "It's ambling down towards the creek," whispered Sam. "If it crosses to the other side, you should be able to get safe pictures from this side."

As soon as the grizzly lumbered from our view, we crept quickly along the bank through the buckbrush and waited where we had first seen it. Five minutes passed. Sam filled in the time talking of people who had been mauled. All of a sudden he stood up, a determined look on his face. "That grizzly hasn't come out in the open yet as I'd hoped. It must be quite close to us; we can't see it; and we don't have a gun. No picture is worth ending up a vegetable. Let's go back."

Reluctantly, I hitched on my pack, slung the tripod over my shoulder, and started to follow Sam back the way we'd come.

We both saw the grizzly at the same time. "There's the bear," Sam said unnecessarily. "And it's onto our scent. It hasn't seen us yet. RUN!"

A quick glimpse of a galloping, backtracking bear rushing towards me was all I needed to take off down the slope to the stream. Perhaps the bear would lose our scent in the water.

Don't believe all you read in print. Fear does NOT give you wings. The packsack got heavier, the tripod more awkward (I didn't have the sense to leave them behind), and I got slower and slower. I didn't really believe this was happening to me. Getting chased by a grizzly seemed something you read about in books or magazines. In fact, what amazed me afterwards were my thoughts at the time.

This adventure could make a good story for *Alaska* Magazine. I devised a title. "Thoughts Upon Being Chased by a Grizzly." I even planned the lead paragraph. On the other hand, I didn't see how I could live to tell the tale. Never once did I give a thought to doing something practical like distracting the bear with my camera case, hitting it over the head with my tripod, giving it my lunch, or playing dead (I had read in books that such strategies might work).

I just kept stumbling along down the hill. All the time, of course, the grizzly was gaining. I didn't risk turning around to see by how much. Meanwhile, my guide was way ahead on the opposite side of the stream. Aided by gravity, I fell into the water at the bottom of the hill, staggered against the current, panted up the bank on the other side, and landed in Sam's arms at the top.

While I used parts of my lungs I didn't know I had, Sam told me what happened.

"The bear followed you to the stream but it didn't try to go across. It stood up on its haunches at the edge of the water, pawed the air— testing, sniffing, deciding what you were, I guess—then for some reason it abruptly turned around and galloped away."

"Did you get a picture?" I wheezed. What a great photo for the cover of *Alaska* Magazine! Me in a red jacket and yellow cap wading the stream against a background of full-frame bear standing on two hind legs with tundra and mountain peaks behind.

Sam gave me a withering look.

We sat in the buckbrush and autopsied the bear's behaviour: a pattern of intentional backtracking and challenge that Sam hadn't encountered before. I could see he was bothered. On one hand he wanted to bring people and wildlife together. Oldsquaw Lodge was the fulfillment of a ten-year dream. On the other hand, he wanted to protect the 1200 or so grizzlies that existed precariously in marginal habitat in the Mackenzie Mountains. Obviously, more people would attract more trouble and increase the chances that "nuisance bears" would have to be shot. As a result, he often turned a blind eye to bears he saw regularly in his spotting scope, despite the thrill they would give to his guests.

The bear that day became known as "Lyn's Bear."

And then there was the "Forget-Me-Not Bear."

I was hiking with Dan and John in the valley between Little Brother and Grizzly Creek, hoping to see a grizzly but thinking it more likely to find a caribou or wolverine, when Dan pointed out two hoary marmots play-boxing beside their burrows not far from a lush grassy stream. This was unusual. We expected to find marmots on the rocky slopes above.

While John and I lingered behind to observe the marmots' nimble antics, Dan strode back down the slope to tell our companions where they were.

A little while later, John and I stopped marmot watching to wonder why Dan, halfway down the hill on his way back to us, was sprawled out on a rock, his arms outspread. Was he trying to attract our attention? Or was he just tired? Both, as it turned out. First, he'd lie prone, then up he'd jump, make great circles in the air and then point back towards the rest of the group now standing at their telescopes. People at naturalists' lodges are always standing at telescopes so that was hardly unusual.

We looked idly over their heads and there in a grassy flower-strewn meadow was the well-known golden hump of a barren-ground grizzly—a grizzly oblivious to all the attention he was getting.

"Darn! We must have passed it, and now it's half a mile away," I complained to John. "The others must be getting a tremendous view from behind those rocks." John looked relieved that I wasn't suggesting we go back for a better look.

So did Dan when he reached us. He explained that the group had been amazed he'd bother to run all the way back just to tell them about a marmot. "You'll have to do better than that," they all laughed.

"Then, what'd you know, I was scanning the terrain past their heads—habit I guess—when I saw the bear. They got a kick out of me asking if a grizzly would do. I sure didn't expect to see it."

We spent an hour watching that bear in the forget-me-nots—digging the roots of *Hedysarum* (Eskimo potato plant) and *Equisetum* (horsetail), sitting on its haunches like a giant teddy bear, kicking its hind legs like a playful baby, occasionally lifting its head as if on sentry duty, then rolling over into a furry ball to sleep.

I wished I could have been closer, but the boys, friendly but firm, said no. "Don't even think of it." They reminded me of the bear I'd met two years earlier at almost the same spot. Perhaps it was the same bear, Lyn's Bear, but that time, its behaviour was vastly different.

"Let's call this one the 'Forget-Me-Not Bear,'" Dan suggested.

Perhaps you can get too blasé. A few days later, I said good-bye to my friends standing at their telescopes on the lodge balcony and climbed into Sam's truck for the trip back to Camp 222.

Sam is often silent, and we were passing Marquis Lake before he started talking. "I thought you'd have stayed to look at the Forget-Me-Not Bear."

"Where was it?"

"In the guests' telescopes. They could see it from the balcony."

Unbelievable. My friends had looked up to say good-bye but hadn't told me my bear had come back.

We had named him well. I won't forget him.

Sleeps I Have Known

IN THE TIMELESS LAND OF THE ARCTIC, where a summer day and a winter night are several months long, Inuit measure the passing of time by "sleeps." There are seven sleeps in a week—or there should be. Travelling as I do with packsack, camera bags, bed roll, very little money, and no fixed itinerary, I rarely know where I will end up at night—or if I will sleep at all.

Northern travel requires flexibility. In the old days, very few communities had hotels, so you plunked your sleeping bag down on the floor of a transient centre or a vacated teacherage. Even now, hotel space is limited and weather often delays flights. You must be prepared to share a room with strangers or doss down anywhere.

I have bunked on the floor of a deserted airport terminal, under a boat on the beach, on a church pew, half in and half out of a snowhouse, and twice in a hotel bathtub, the first time to keep warm when the furnace quit and the second time to keep cool when the air conditioning stopped. I even spent a night in a pipeline. Not yet have I resorted to a cell in a northern cop shop, but I did spend a night in a dump—the Pangnirtung community garbage dump.

Pangnirtung on Baffin Island is one of the most picturesque communities in Nunavut. The dramatic, ice-capped mountains that line Pangnirtung Fiord leading to Auyuittuq National Park earns it the nickname "Switzerland of Canada."

Keith MacDonald, Pangnirtung's economic development officer, had arranged for me to go to Ross Peyton's camp in Clearwater Fiord to fish and photograph beluga whales. Keith had chartered Peter Kanuyuk's brand new cabin cruiser, a twenty-eight-foot-long, fibreglass Chris Craft with a 225-horsepower gas-guzzling engine. Such a boat was a rarity on Baffin Island, which is better known for its whaleboats and wooden freighter canoes. Indeed, Peter had wanted a wooden-hulled workboat, but it wouldn't have been built in time to get to Pangnirtung before winter ice blocked off the community. He settled for the new sleek cruiser because it was available. He hoped to use it to transport tourists, fishermen, and supplies the eighty-six miles to the Clearwater camp.

There'd been hazards enough just getting the boat north. The dealer had put it on the wrong ship in Montreal and it ended up in Iqaluit instead of Pangnirtung. Peter had to drive it to Pang through ice-clogged Davis Strait. At last, it arrived safely and was ready to test its first tourist—me.

Peter's plan was to leave Pangnirtung on the high tide and sleep at Clearwater sometime that night. The boat had been chartered by the government and I was supposed to be its one official passenger, but in typically informal fashion, Peter invited his family along—which in northern terms meant not only his wife and children but their brothers and sisters and cousins. It took three freighter canoe-loads to get all of us and our gear to the middle of the mile-wide fiord where his cruiser was anchored.

Everybody excitedly tumbled aboard the unusual new boat in a melange of parkas, *amautis* (parkas with hoods for babies) and bulging plastic bags. Kids scrambled down the steps to explore the galley and mothers giggled to each other as they tested the bunks. It was the end of summer now and almost dark by eight in the evening. Above us, the thousand-foot-high walls of the fiord rose steeply on each side, further diminishing the light. Quickly, the men on deck lifted aboard one of the rubber boats and hauled up the anchor. Peter pulled out the throttle and we roared down the fiord at full bore. The unexpected jolt pitched me backwards and I piled into Rebecca, Peter's wife. She laughed as we helped each other up from the deck.

We nearly fell again as the boat made another sudden spurt, then stopped. Peter pulled up beside a freighter canoe and started talking in Inuktitut to two men standing in the boat, one in the bow and the other in the stern. One of the men kept pointing to an orange tarp that covered a big mound amidships. Did they want us to take on some of their freight? When three heads suddenly popped out from under the sheltering tarp, I realized they wanted us to take on three more passengers. My heart gave a leap. Our boat was registered for a maximum load of eight and we already had twelve. Where would the hitchhikers fit?

"No, we have enough," Peter said after some consideration. I breathed a sigh of relief.

"What time do you think we'll get to Clearwater?" I asked the skipper as he roared off again.

"We may not get there," Peter shrugged, staring into the quickening darkness. "It may be too rough."

It was already windy when our heavily loaded ark ploughed into the choppy waters of Pangnirtung Fiord. An hour later, the infamous Pang wind had whipped up the sea to whitecaps and we were wobbling dangerously in the swells. The women were quiet now and some of the children began to cry. I couldn't help sneaking a look for life jackets when we turned into Cumberland Sound.

As we bashed our way through the waves, it soon became clear that we would not make Clearwater camp that night. Nothing was said, but the engines shuddered, the boat wallowed through another turn, and we headed back up the fiord. After waiting for days trying to find ways to visit Peyton's place, I couldn't help feeling disappointed.

"We'll try again on the morning tide," said Peter back at the beach. "The wind may die down by then. Be back at the boat in four hours."

Four hours. Not worth spending a hundred dollars in the local hotel even if somebody was awake at midnight and a bed could be found. Not long enough to bother getting my tent out of storage on the other side of town. And I wasn't brash enough to ask the skipper if I could christen his bunks, even if the boat had been chartered by the government partly for me.

Everybody crowded off the boat with their innumerable plastic bags of belongings. All the Inuit had a home to go to, but I didn't ask to go with them and they didn't offer. It's not the native way. You don't knock on a door, you just walk right in. You don't wait to be asked, you serve yourself. You don't ask to stay over at a house, you just stay. But for this *qallunaaq* (white person), old habits were hard to break.

So where was I to bed down for the next few hours? The skies were dark and stormy and the wind was high. If I wanted shelter, I had to make it myself. So I did, at the only place close by and in view of the boat—the garbage dump.

You could probably build a house from a northern dump, but I didn't have time. The skies promised rain, and that late in the season it may well have been snow. I rejected my initial idea of upending old chairs and chesterfields, which would get sodden in an impending downpour, and concocted instead a shelter between two boulders from plastic, plywood, and aluminum guttering. I gathered together wooden boxes left over from previous years' sealifts, arranged them around me, and even fashioned a night table. Old canvas from the bottom of a canoe provided my floor.

To fit into the congested space and provide more protection, I pulled my knees into my chest, packed my bags around me and leaned back against one of the boulders. Fortunately, I had borrowed a four-star down sleeping bag for this trip so I scrunched that over the top. Meanwhile, the wind intensified and it started to rain. I looked longingly at Peter's boat bobbing about in the waves and thought of those empty bunks. It was impossible to sleep.

Two hours later, the wind lifted the plywood and off blew my plastic roof. I creaked out of my cramped position curled inside the sleeping bag and, holding a garbage-bag poncho over my head, hopped around the dump to look for a substitute roof. House repairs this time consisted of another crate, a piece of tin, and a stove pipe—unfortunately without the stove. Lights were twinkling from the line of houses up the beach, but this time I didn't want to attract attention.

By 4:00 A.M. the wind had whipped itself into a gale and the rain had become a deluge. I had no roof and most of the sleeping bag was drenched. This would be a night to remember. But, I thought ruefully, dare I tell? I hunched into my parka, wrapped myself and my cameras in plastic, and grimly waited out the next two hours.

Nancy Mannik and her grandson, Travis, giggle as they teach me Inuktitut outside their caribou skin tent at a traditional camp near Baker Lake.

Why did it have to rain when I spent the night in a garbage dump on the beach at Pangnirtung?

Moe Keenainak welcomes me to his house in Pangnirtung with a slice of raw seal. In Inuit homes, there's usually a seal, a caribou, a fish, or a chunk of *muktuk* at the door for people to help themselves.

'Twas the night before Christmas and all through the semi-subterranean sodhouse in Pond Inlet, it felt frigid, despite Jack Taqtaq's attempts to show me how to keep the cottongrass burning evenly in the *qulliq* (Inuit soapstone oil lamp).

Icebergs as big as houses sail beside us along the coast of Baffin Island.

Once a busy whaling station in the latter half of the nineteenth century for American, Scottish, and Inuit whalers, Kekerten Island near Pangnirtung is now a lonely historic park. Visitors wander along the boardwalks to see artifacts such as largecast-iron pots used for rendering whale oil, remains of houses and storehouses,graves, and barrels.

Please close the door! Henry Kamoyoak built us a snowhouse for a spring night at a luxury lodge in Bathurst Inlet.

Winging it by helicopter. Here at Hole-in-the-Wall Lake, the distant peaks and icefields of the Ragged Range lead you along a string of little known lakes to some of the most secret and beautiful places on the planet.

Is there gold at the end of the road? Mum and Dad try some gold panning in Bonanza Creek, Yukon, during a gruelling exploration of unfinished northern roads.

Nellie bogs on through muddy streams and boulder beds to get travellers to Oldsquaw Lodge via the old Canol Road. It is often quicker to walk!

Negotiating the Bellanca Rapids on the first raft trip down the Burnside River.

It pays to be slightly crazy when you live for months at a time on a radar site on Baffin Island. Chef Pierre skates in with the drinks at an impromptu beach party in the clouds as summer temperatures at Club Baf reach a high of zero.

You should pack your bikini as well as your parka when you go north, especially in the canyons of the South Nahanni River.

I catch my first fish—a 16-pound arctic char—at Bathurst Inlet Lodge and everybody hears about it.

My slab of roasted buffalo meat is a little soggy when the ice melts on my stove.

I enjoyed watching caribou on Baffin Island more than hunting them.

Normally, I keep a comfortable distance from the animals I observe (both for their sake and for mine), but here on Victoria Island, I was able to sit beside these muskox for hours. There was nowhere to go, either for me or for them.

By 6:00 A.M. the wind had abated and the rain had lessened to a drizzle, but skies were still dismal. Choppy waves slapped against the side of Peter's boat. The tide was right but nobody came along. It was Sunday morning. People were probably sleeping in. Or perhaps they had decided not to go to the fish camp after all.

At 10:00 A.M. a man taking his dog for a morning stroll stopped by. He probably thought I was some homeless derelict who'd stumbled into the dump after partying too much on Saturday night. I scarcely looked like a respectable, hard-working photojournalist. People generally live and let live up north and had I not spoken to him, he would have hurried on. I rattled my stove pipe to attract his attention.

"I know this sounds crazy but could you take a picture?" I asked, handing him my camera when he reluctantly picked his way towards me. "I want to remember this night."

I never did get to the fish camp at Clearwater Fiord, but several years later I met Ross Peyton, the owner, in the terminal building of the Pang airport. When my new state-of-the-art packsack fell apart, he helped put it together on the terminal floor while I was waiting for the plane to Iqaluit.

That was the same night I found myself in another unexpected sleeping place and this time with unexpected sleeping companions— a party of American surgeons who had been weathered in at a fish camp in Tongait Fiord. Unable or unwilling to wait longer for better weather, they had helicoptered out to the Pang airport with their boxes of fish. But you can't guarantee plane schedules in the north (just as you can't guarantee weather), and we were all suddenly bumped from the plane in favour of a big party of British students who had come in from hiking Auyuittuq National Park.

"Another plane will come for you soon," promised the airport manager breezily before he left for home. The terminal building was deserted, except for me and a dozen uptight doctors determined to keep their Monday appointments in another country on the other side of the continent. Doctors who had no knowledge of northern time.

The steep tunnel-walls of Pang Fiord are hazardous enough for planes landing in Pangnirtung but nigh impossible in high winds. Afternoon wore on into evening and still no planes came. By evening, frustration had worn to resignation, and the doctors asked me where they could sleep.

97

"Well, there's one hotel in town, but it's probably booked up with scientists, government people, and other tourists. You don't book rooms up here, you book beds. But you could try," I said, trying to be upbeat. "As you're all doctors, some could probably bunk down at the nursing station and the rest could try the church. I can fit two in my tent at the campground."

That night, a near hurricane swept down the fiord and the skies burst open in a tempestuous symphony of sound and light. My two tent-mates spent their night valiantly hanging onto my tent. When their enthusiasm flagged, I told them that a one-piece nylon tent was better than a multi-piece concoction of plastic, tin, and plywood on the other side of town. We had no sleep that night, but the drama of dawn erupting behind the peaks of Pangnirtung Fiord made it seem worthwhile—to me at least. And we were right there on stage ready to appreciate it.

Late next day after the first plane dispatched to Pang "went mechanical," the northern expression for engine trouble, a second plane managed to land, and eventually we all got to Iqaluit. I never did discover if those doctors kept their appointments. But I bet when they got down south they talked more of their night in Pang than they did of the fish they caught.

One of my most memorable sleeps in the North was the night I spent in an *iglu*, or as it is more specifically called, a snowhouse. Although I had been visiting or living in the North for more than twenty years at the time, I had never seen a snowhouse till I joined a group of international tourists for a spring experience on the Arctic Coast at Bathurst Inlet. It was spring for the Inuit, but at temperatures of twenty below, the rest of us considered it winter.

For more than a quarter of a century, three generations of people—the Warner family and the Kingaunmuit or People of the Nose—have been sharing their home in Bathurst Inlet with visitors from around the world. Guests usually sleep in one of the rooms of what was a Hudson's Bay Company trading post now renovated as a world-renowned naturalists' lodge, or adjacent in the historic Roman Catholic church with its insulation of caribou skins. Some guests slept in plywood *iglus* built for the Kingaunmuit. I wanted to try a snow *iglu*.

Henry Kamoyoak hunted for the right kind of snow—fine and dry—and built a couple of practice *iglus* at some distance from the lodge. Everybody enjoyed watching him construct the snowhouse, block by block, but only Bess, a guest from Indiana on her first trip to Canada, accepted the challenge of joining me to sleep in one.

"No, we don't want sleeping bags and a Coleman stove. We'll do it in the traditional way with skins and a *qulliq*," I said spiritedly to Boyd Warner and Sam Kapolak when they came to get us. I don't think I spoke for Bess, a glamorous young flight attendant who was used to warm climates and luxury living.

Fortunately, the boys disregarded my bravado and added sleeping bags and blankets to the sled of stuff they took for us to the snowhouse. This was fortunate for Bess as well because she was a practising Jew. She confided to me later that touching animal skins was against her religion. The children presented us with little jewel boxes carved out of ice. Inside, when we lifted the lid, were last season's twigs and berries. We were to need them all.

Our first problem was how to get inside the *iglu*. Not daring in the unaccustomed cold to remove our bulky parkas and knee-high insulated boots, we wriggled through the door on our bellies and crammed ourselves and our gear between the entrance and the raised ice platform at the back.

Iglus come in various sizes and ours was the emergency model. There was not much room. There were two reasons why I didn't close the door: one, the block of ice was too heavy, and two, one of us had to protrude through the opening if both of us were to fit. An open door might be colder but it seemed better than being stuck in a tomb if by chance it iced up.

The next problem was to get the *qulliq* lit. "No sweat," I said, squeezing to one side of the cooking platform. A *qulliq* is a halfmoon-shaped soapstone dish full of fat (seal oil or lard) with a wick of cotton grass along its straight edge. It is the only source of heat and light in the traditional snowhouse.

Bess and I couldn't find the wick. Any cotton grass left over from summer was well hidden beneath the snow at this time of the year so we lit the kids' gift-wrapped twigs and alder cones instead. Slowly, the flames spread along the *qulliq*, and I encouraged them higher by raking the melted fat against our tundra tinder with the pointed end of a muskox horn that Boyd and Sam had left.

We learned later that the blunt end of the horn was used in the old days to pound the blubber and squeeze the oil from the fat. To push the wick up and down through the oil or to separate the wick into strands for quicker burning, we should have used the flat wooden stick that we found lying beside the muskox horn. It is called a "tender," the stick that tends the lamp. There wasn't much left of the tender after Bess and I got through our attempts to raise the temperature inside the snowhouse. Part of the tender became fuel for our fire.

"You're doing well," said Bess encouragingly as the flames leapt higher. Too well. Trying to keep our fur-rimmed bodies away from the flames despite our cramped positions beside the cooking platform, we huddled inside our sleeping bags and stared up at the dome.

It seemed that big holes were appearing in our roof. "Do you see sky?" I asked ominously. "I think we're melting the *iglu*."

Bess stretched out of her bag, poked her finger through a thin layer of ice and reached—sky! "You're right," she said, rolling her eyes as if she was asking herself why she'd left her cosy bed by the stove at the lodge to join me by a *qulliq* in a snowhouse. A rapidly melting snowhouse at that.

"Interesting problem. I wonder how *iglus* melt. Do blocks of ice just drop on our heads? Do they drip on us like the Chinese water torture? Or do we end up in a pool of water like fish in a fish bowl? Worse, does it evaporate and we finish up with just sky above us?" I tried to sound flippant. "Well, they say that open-air camping is healthy."

I prattled on about other *qallunaat* who paid for the experience of spending a night in an *iglu*. "I remember Simone, a rather large lady from Florida, who squeezed into an iglu. She said it was vital to put some protection like a sleeping bag cover between the last block of frozen snow cut for the door and the doorway. If you don't, the block can freeze to the entrance and you aren't able to get out even if you pound on the ice."

Bess's mind was on other eventualities. "We'd better put the fire out," she said, coughing. "The fumes from that black fat are pretty smelly." Obviously, she preferred death by freezing to death by asphyxiation.

In the old days, Inuit women left a little bit of wick burning through the night so they wouldn't have to relight the *qulliq* in the morning. The men often made a new *iglu* every month if the old one glazed over. Neither Bess nor I wanted to live in a snowhouse for a month. We wondered if we could last a night.

We snuffed out the light—and the remarkable trickle of warmth given out by the flickering line of flame. We laid the caribou skins on the snow floor and curled up inside our sleeping bags in the fetal position. Bess just fitted across the diameter of the *iglu* but I, much taller and burdened with all kinds of camera gear, had to shove my legs through the door. Soon the temperature inside would be much like the temperature outside, but we hoped at least we had stopped the leaks from our roof.

Some time later, I was awakened by a plaintive voice saying, "Lyn, are you awake? My feet are frozen."

"Well, mine are not exactly warm."

"No, I mean really frozen, frozen solid. I can't feel anything in them any more."

Oh, no. She must be kidding. "Well, I guess David Kamoayak's wooden legs would be an advantage right now," I quipped, reminding her of an Inuit guest at the lodge who had lost his natural legs from frostbite. "I suggest you take off your boots and let the air circulate rather than wear them inside your sleeping bag. And I'll try to rekindle the *qulliq* and rub your feet till they thaw out."

Bess gave me a look which said she'd prefer a suggestion that we pack up and trudge back to the lodge.

"It's only 3:00 A.M. We can't wimp out now," I said in my most persuasive tone. "Do you think you can last till say, 6:00 or 7:00? Look at it this way. This is the first time you've ever gone camping. And in a snowhouse! What a story you'll have to tell back in Indiana!"

I didn't have the same bravado after we got the *qulliq* going again and the holes kept getting bigger in our honeycombed roof. The *iglu* was beginning to look like a bowl of Swiss cheese. Bess removed her boots and three pairs of socks, and thrust her toes into the flames.

"Bess!" I groaned. "You'll burn your flesh."

"It's okay," she replied with a satisfied smile. "I can't feel anything."

I grabbed her feet and wiggled them, toe by toe, in the warmed air above the *qulliq*.

It seemed a long time before she told me to stop. "I think they'll be okay now," she said bravely. "I know you want to stay so I'll try to go to sleep." She put on my thermal underwear, exchanged her gloves for mitts, left her boots off, and tamped out the flames of the *qulliq*.

"I don't think our snowhouse'll last another night," I said in mock despair.

"Good!" replied Bess as her head disappeared inside her bag.

Some time later, I woke to a voice saying plaintively, "Lyn, it's 6:00 A.M."

I took the hint. There wasn't much left of the *iglu* anyway. Bess returned to the lodge to sleep till noon, but I couldn't resist staying to experience Bathurst Inlet at dawn. The sky was blue, the light magical. It was worth a cold night in a snowhouse to be on hand to see the colours—a delicate, mellow salmon pink over the frozen sea where the sun had gone down and was about to rise again, a cool moonlit blue over the mountain behind.

❖

I remember another night spent in a traditional Inuit dwelling with a reluctant sleeping partner whose enthusiasm for adventure was perhaps less than my own. "Let's spend Christmas in the sod house," I suggested brightly to Frank as we bulldozed our truck off the sea ice, up the frozen beach, and onto the snow-covered land. In the darkness of December in Pond Inlet, 390 miles inside the Arctic Circle, I couldn't tell if Frank groaned or grinned.

We'd just tried, unsuccessfully, to string festive lights on an iceberg. Frank could be forgiven if he vetoed further brainstorms of mine: it was minus 40 degrees C, and our snug hotel room beckoned. But I was determined we'd have a unique Yuletide.

I wanted to experience the way Inuit used to spend Christmas, in the 1940s, the 1950s, and 1960s. They left their camps in the hinterland and drove dogteams into the settlement to join festivities with the Pond Inlet RCMP detachment, the Hudson's Bay traders, the Anglican and Roman Catholic missionaries. In most years at Pond there wasn't enough of the right kind of snow to build huge snowhouses, as people in the central Arctic did. But people gathered anyway, to celebrate with games, dances, and feasting. We could experience some of that lost atmosphere by sleeping in a sod house.

The Inuit had built an old-style sod house at Pond two months before, so that Elders could teach their children how their parents lived a few decades earlier. In the old days, Pond Inlet people built semi-subterranean, *iglu*-shaped huts using blocks of sod topped with whalebone rafters. The remnants of traditional houses can still be seen on the landscape around Pond. Seal and caribou skin insulated with arctic heather formed the domes of these houses whose only heat and light came from their *qulliqs*.

Today, the people live in modern accommodation with comfortable conveniences, but there is still the urge, especially among older people, to return to their roots and find privacy in the old way. One woman in Pond had a modified sod hut beside her house with newspaper on the walls, sleeping platform, and a black tea kettle hanging over the *qulliq*.

As superintendent for Hearn-Stratton Construction, Frank had just finished building a dozen duplexes in this isolated Inuit community on north Baffin Island. The new buildings were a sharp contrast to the way Inuit lived even five years ago. They were ranch-wall duplexes with central heating and up-to-the-minute plumbing. Some had carpet and shower doors.

Our teen-aged Inuit friends, born in heated houses, were amazed that I would want to sleep in a sod house—especially at Christmas when temperatures were minus 45 degrees C. "Too smelly," said Loretta. "Seal oil makes you cough," she added, screwing up her nose.

"Too chilly," said Judy with a shiver.

"Too scratchy," added Letia.

Our *qallunaat* friends were similarly incredulous. But Frank was the one I had to convince. We had met in Pond Inlet the previous summer, and despite the many times since then he had said, "You're crazy," he had asked to marry me.

Considering that my plan to light up an iceberg on frozen Pond Inlet had just been aborted due to a blown piston on the portable generator, I presented my arguments with care. Staying in a sod house, I urged, would be just the thing. We could revive the spirit of earlier times, I added. We could test our survival skills, I pointed out. *And our engagement*, I thought.

Frank was ominously silent. So I rattled on. "And it'll be easier to decorate than the iceberg. We don't need a generator. We can string the lights to the nearest house."

Frank sighed in resignation. My next grand plan was under way. With permission from the Elders and the help of our friends Pakak and Olassie, Pat Lewis of the Northern Canada Power Commission, the Bay, and Hearn-Stratton Construction, we strung 260 yards of electrical cord to the nearest house (which belonged to the school principal, who was in the Bahamas, blissfully unaware). We draped strings of lights around the dome, and turned them on (well, most of them).

Pakak's wife, Ellen, looked up from her Christmas baking, raised the yellow blinds she attaches to her kitchen windows to brighten the dark season, and smiled. So did many other Pond Inlet residents who stopped their snowmobiles to visit. The sod house, looking like a big bejewelled beaver, brought colour to the Arctic night and helped to make the settlement pretty for the festive season.

After supper, we forsook the heat, television, and private bathrooms of the Sauniq Hotel, filled all our gas tanks, and drove the truck to a spot as near as possible to the sod house. We left the truck running (as you do up here if you're not plugged in) and prayed it would keep going through the night.

Dressed in longjohns, sweaters, parkas, mitts, toques, and *kamiks* (caribou- or seal-skin boots) for the coldest night of the season, and carrying a case of Christmas goodies, decorations, and other festive fare, we staggered through the snow, past noisy chained dogteams to the edge of the frozen ocean—and our snow-covered sod house.

To be as traditional as possible, we spurned sleeping bags in favour of caribou skins spread on the sleeping platform. While I hung tinsel on the rafters and set out the wine goblets, cheese, shrimp, and oysters (no frozen char and caribou this time), Frank lit the dried cotton-grass wick of the *qulliq*. The flame flickered along one side of the soapstone dish to melt the seal fat and give out our only heat and light. "You're doing that as well as you turn on ovens and thermostats," I said encouragingly as he tilted the melting fat in the tapered dish to let more oil slide against the wick and increase the flame.

Just then, the plywood door of the hut opened to admit Taqtaq, an Elder who'd come to show us how to keep the *qulliq* tended throughout the night. Dressed (under his parka) in a suit and tie for dancing in the community hall, Taqtaq was a dapper little man who had come to Pond to visit friends for Christmas. Then fifty-nine years old, he was born in a sod house between Arctic Bay and Igloolik, and still made his living as a hunter and trapper. Taqtaq spoke very little English, but as he refined our *qulliq* technique and posed for Frank's camera, he told us he'd been to Montreal, Edmonton, and Vancouver.

"You can get TB from the fumes and smoke of the seal oil lamp," he warned, between coughs.

Some time later, Pakak, dressed in a traditional caribou parka, came to see how we were doing. "It's a long time since I played around with these things," he said with amusement. "I lived in a sod house near Igloolik till I was nine years old. Being the youngest kid in a sod hut was sometimes boring, especially when the others went out hunting."

Although ice glistened around the edge of the sleeping platform, reminding us that it was minus 45 degrees C outside and not much warmer at floor level inside, I was amazed at how warm the air became near the ceiling (perhaps 15 degrees C or 60 Fahrenheit) for those who could stand up. Unfortunately, lanky Frank wasn't among them.

"We need bunk beds in here," I joked. "Whalebone ones might be difficult, but now that Inuit are using plywood, they could do it."

Pakak told us that earlier sod houses used to be warmer because they were smaller and had thicker sod as insulation. They also were built with an ice porch to trap cold air at the entrance, not a plywood door like the one we had. And the walls of this replica were canvas and cotton instead of seal and caribou skin, which was far more efficient at preserving heat.

"I don't remember ever feeling cold," Pakak said, tamping the wick in a straight line. "My mother carried me in her *amauti* most of the time, but we all slept together naked in the one caribou-skin bag with the fur on the inside. We used our outer garments for pillows."

Taqtaq added that white people wear longjohns to bed in a caribou-skin bag because they don't like scratchy fur against their skin.

Frank and I would not have that problem. We intended to sleep in our longjohns *and* all the rest of our garments, both inner and outer. We would even forsake a pillow.

Neither Pakak nor Taqtaq wanted to spend the night in a sod house, whether old or new, so with a final adjustment to our *qulliq*, they left, Pakak to his family home and Taqtaq to the games, dances, and feasting in the community hall.

"You know, Frank, Father Mary told me it can get so warm inside a sod house that grass grows next to the lamp," I said when they'd gone. "I think I'll put on my Aussie granny's negligee and find out how warm it really is. Just an experiment, of course, to compare nylon and caribou fur." The idea of wearing a Down Under nightie up here intrigued me. It had travelled the world, from somewhere near the South Pole to somewhere near the North Pole, after all.

Exactly seven minutes later, with ice still forming around the sleeping platform, I was out of the nightie and under the caribou blanket, with enough layers of clothing to ensure I would not feel scratchy. I did not intend to stay up all night tending the *qulliq*, as I'd heard some Inuit women once did. I slept till morning. Not that you'd know when night ends and day begins in the bowl of bluish blackness that is the Arctic Circle in December.

"You're awake," I said in surprise to Frank. Then the truth, if not the day, dawned. "You haven't slept, right?"

"Right!" he said through gritted teeth.

"Do you want to go?" I asked, unnecessarily.

Within minutes, we had taken down our Christmas decorations, gathered together our goodies, pulled on our *kamiks*, tamped out our *qulliq*, and followed the cloud of exhaust to the truck. Happiness, in these climes, is a truck that's still running.

"Fancy, a lifetime of this!" mused Frank back at the Sauniq Hotel. "And what have you got in mind for next Christmas?"

❉

I admit my enthusiasm for trying new things does attract trouble. But then, life can get complicated without me even trying. Take the night I spent in a church in a small village in the Northwest Territories. The priest had given me the key to his church and a letter of introduction to the village. I was not aware of the contents of the letter, but I guessed it was a simple request to welcome me to the community and to verify that I had permission to stay in the church.

The church was a simple one-room log cabin which also served as the priest's home. He had his bed, table and chairs in the back behind the pews. Intending to get some sleep before I visited with the villagers, I went straight to the church, put my packsack down on the cot, snacked on some crackers and freeze-dried food, and started to write my diary.

People up north are not slaves to routine. They visit (and sleep) any hour of the day or night, especially in summer. I had just got settled when in came a young girl called Mary, the first of my visitors. We chatted politely for a while, I made her tea and while we were drinking it, another visitor arrived.

Adam was a tall, well-built teenager about fourteen years old. He had not been among the men who had welcomed me at the beach, but I learned from Mary that he could not hear or speak. A smile is always a good way to establish rapport. I smile a lot. I smiled, Mary chatted in English, and Adam sat in silence.

"You'd better watch out that the Bush Man doesn't get you," Mary warned.

"Is that like the Boogie Man my mother told me about?"

"It's a man with long hair and a frosty beard who comes out of the bush and takes people away."

"I want to get lots of sleep tonight ready for meeting everybody tomorrow. I'm not going outside to meet any Bush Man or anybody else," I told Mary when she got ready to leave. "Will you take Adam with you?"

People don't mind other people's business up north. She gave me a look as if to say, "Get rid of your own guests," then departed.

But how to do that when your guest doesn't hear and he can't talk? Naturally hospitable but not really knowing what else to do, I prattled on, poured tea and offered crackers. An hour passed. It was still light outside; it would be light all night, but I really wanted to bury myself in the dark of my sleeping bag and go to sleep.

Although I must confess that I can prattle on without needing a listener, it was disconcerting to sit there with a stranger staring at me so intently. Why did he stay?

Suddenly, Adam got up and walked over to a couple of posters on the wall of the church. They showed staircases: one with steps leading up to Heaven and the other with steps leading down to Hell. Adam stopped staring at me and started staring at them.

That was it! He thought I was a priest—or rather a priestess. It made sense. I had come out of the skies in a plane, I had the key to the church, I looked as if I was going to live there. Surely, Adam had come to discuss his spiritual problems.

Now I felt sad. Here I was a free guest of the community and I couldn't give him any divine guidance. I felt inadequate. Meanwhile, Adam kept looking from one poster to another while I, not knowing what else to do, just kept drinking tea.

The light outside was now warm and golden, that magical time near midnight when I usually rush around with my camera and take pictures. But all I wanted to do was to go to bed.

Another half hour passed. I decided to tell Adam exactly what was on my mind. I hadn't learned sign language, but I had studied mime and movement at the Royal Academy in England. My message to him was "I want you to go now because I want to sleep."

So I pointed to him, I pointed to me, I put my palms together and laid them against my cheek in what I believed to be a universal symbol for sleep, then I pointed to the bed.

Adam was galvanized into action but not the action I expected. Perhaps I got my signals crossed. Suddenly he left the two posters, rushed over to me, and lunged for places that left no doubt as to the nature of his problems, even in my naive mind. Adam had definitely not come for spiritual guidance.

I sprinted away from the bed, through the pews and around the altar—twice—with Adam in close pursuit. Several images went racing through my mind. I thought of all the people who had warned me that this could happen. I remembered the Dene trapper who took me on a seventy-five-mile circuit of his trapline by skidoo. "How come your husband lets you leave home to go around the country alone?" he said, while we bounced along the track. I remembered the women who couldn't understand how I didn't have a husband or kids and were flabbergasted that I didn't seem to want them. I remembered the many who said they envied my Huck Finn existence. And I ruefully remembered my girl friend Hilary who said that I courted trouble.

Well, trouble had found me now. A third circuit around the pews, past the posters, and I reached the door with just enough time to get outside. But what to do? I could hardly run through the village crying, "Rape!" Not proper etiquette for a would-be writer or a could-be priestess. Besides, nobody was around. People were either inside their cabins or out at their fish nets—minding their business.

I circled the church with Adam close behind. Once. Twice. On the third circuit, I pushed open the door, scooted inside, and rammed the latch shut. To my relief, he tried the latch once and then departed. Feeling thankful, I dropped onto the cot. When I caught my breath, I shoved the pews against the door, curtained the windows with clothing, and stayed alert till morning.

Perhaps my guardian angel was watching over me. I have never had any similar problems since, and if I had learned my Royal Academy lessons better, I mightn't have had them then.

You Never Know Where
Your Next Meal is Coming From

IT PAYS TO BE ADAPTABLE and have a sense of humour in the North—especially at mealtimes.

Inuit like to eat their meat raw, which makes sense in a land without trees and where fuel is expensive. Walk into an Inuit house and you're likely to find an entire seal or caribou on the floor at the door. All you have to do is reach for an *ulu* and cut your own slice. Imagine the time a harassed housewife could save down south if she used the same methods. As soon as she saw guests in the driveway, she'd whip out a frozen roast from the freezer and hand everybody a knife. No muss, no fuss. And, unlike northerners, she wouldn't have to hunt and kill her meat first.

Preparing country food may be simple, but getting it can be complicated. In Hall Beach and neighbouring Igloolik where I lived for a few months, Inuit eat *igunaq* or fermented walrus meat. Adult Inuit say it tastes like cheese: the younger generation have other less complimentary words for it. (They, like teenagers everywhere, prefer "white man's grub"—junk food such as candy, pop, and hotdogs.)

To make *igunaq*, Inuit roll up walrus meat in sausage-shaped bags of walrus hide and then bury them in summer under mounds of gravel.

These triangular caches extend for many miles along the shore, and people dig them up during winter and spring when the *igunaq* is well-ripened. Although Inuit have amazing skills in navigation, I am fascinated by how they tell whose *igunaq* is whose when the mounds are unmarked, buried under snowdrifts, and spread over a flat and featureless landscape. Perhaps it doesn't matter in a village where the philosophy is "share and share alike."

Whenever a hunter comes in with slabs of walrus or whale, everyone troops down to the beach to help themselves. Women cook up big cauldrons of meat and blubber on the shore and while the stew simmers and the blubber rises to the top, people sit around on the gravel chewing ribs and drinking tea. They eat some of the stomach contents raw and hang some of the meat in strips to dry. Leftovers go to the dogs.

Northern Foxe Basin is one of the few areas in Canada where walruses are still common and walrus hunting for food and ivory is a common activity. An Inuk hunter is allowed to kill four walrus a year for his own use, and some communities have community quotas as well.

As soon as I arrived in Hall Beach overlooking Foxe Basin, I spread the word that I wanted to go walrus-hunting for *igunaq*. I knew from previous experience that there was little use in planning a trip on a certain date. It would happen when it happened.

Most of the hunting takes place in the summer months between July and September when the walrus are hauled out on floating pack ice at variable distances east of the communities. In the fall months when the floe edge is closer, the walrus are closer too. But in Hall Beach at the time of my residence, the main floe edge was about twenty to twenty-five miles southeast of the settlement, which necessitated taking a long trip by twenty-two-foot freighter canoe across variably open water.

My neighbour, Shelley, had once gone walrus hunting with Eric Itoriligak, an Inuk who lives with a large extended family at an outpost camp about forty-five miles south of Hall Beach. For a few weeks each summer, Eric comes to town and camps on the beach to replenish supplies, repair equipment, visit friends, and see the nurse. Shelley seized the opportunity to go walrus-hunting with Eric, and despite running out of gas and having to paddle home, she came back enthralled with the experience. "Go ask him to take you, too," she advised. "But make sure you buy a lot of gas."

I hurried down to the beach to find Eric prising metal bands off a construction crate and his wife kneeling on the pebbles beside piles of rotting char and walrus. She was sewing a canvas tent with an old Singer sewing machine.

"Going walrus hunting?" I asked casually, sitting down beside them. "There are two of us who'd love to go with you if you do." Eric didn't reply. He looked out to sea and shrugged. I didn't know if he could—or would—speak English.

"I'll buy the gas. Ten gallons?" I said, a figure which Shelley had suggested.

"Thirty-five," Eric replied without further comment. This time, I shrugged.

A few days later, Eric knocked on the door of the old nursing station where I lived as a volunteer cook for the construction crew of the new school. "Be at the boat at 8:55 A.M. We go hunting," Eric said with a big grin. It was now 8:30 A.M. I was surprised. Inuit are not known for keeping such precise schedules.

Within minutes, I had thrown a smorgasbord of sandwich makings on the table for the crew's lunch, dashed off a tongue-in-the-cheek note promising walrus for dinner, picked up Frank, and got to the boat at the appointed time.

Frank, a carpenter and construction superintendent, looked a bit dubious when he saw Eric's equipment. Inuit still living off the land are a hardy breed and are masters of the makeshift and the scrounge. Despite rusty guns, unreliable motors, improvised harpoons, and boards for paddles, Eric exuded enthusiasm and an optimistic attitude to life. He met a kindred spirit in me when my rubber boots sprang a leak and I was forced to wrap my socks in plastic garbage bags from our lunches.

Although seven of his family had said they would be joining us, only Eric's teenaged sons, Brian and Jama, had awakened in time. Eric courteously laid an orange tarp topped by several caribou furs on the floor of the canoe for Frank and me, stashed the guns and harpoons, and eventually started the fifty-horsepower motor. At 9:15 A.M. we cruised away from the community over a pearly grey sea. It was 5 degrees C and cloudy, not much of a day for photography, but it was to be a great day for an adventure.

Hall Beach's Inuktitut name is Sanirajak, which means "flat," and that's the obvious word to describe its surrounding terrain. A flat grey tundra plain of marshes, pools, and lakes meets an exposed flat grey gravel shoreline, and then a flat grey glassy sea stretches to a seamless horizon. At a time when many of the old DEW (Distant Early Warning) line stations were being dismantled in environmental clean-ups, local Inuit requested that the twin radar screens of the station in Hall Beach be retained as a navigational aid. The radar screens in Hall Beach truly do live up to their nickname of Giant Billboards (or Drive-in Screens) in the Sky.

Twenty minutes from the community, Eric suddenly veered off course and drove the prow of the boat onto an ice floe. "Water," Eric explained with another grin.

"For tea?" I questioned innocently.

No, we were leaking! I looked down to see a milky liquid filling the stern. First my rubber boots and now our boat! Swimming was impossible in this frigid water and the nearest "land" was moving ice. I felt relieved I'd taken the precaution of informing the RCMP that we'd gone to the floe edge for walrus hunting and to expect us back by nightfall.

Frank helped Eric and his sons lift the heavy canvas-covered wooden canoe onto the ice and then watched carefully while they tipped the boat over and planned how to mend the hole. "I'm glad I have my own carpenter along," I teased, nudging my companion. Frank rolled his eyes a bit at Eric's solution—sawing off a piece of the grub box and nailing it to the canvas with a couple of nails—but the improvisation got us on our way again.

At least for a while. We shoved off the ice floe, and with Brian and Jama standing in the bow to direct a circuitous course through a maze of ice sculptures that looked like snowy mountain peaks, we continued on to the main pack.

"Do you think it'll last?" Frank asked, a little facetiously.

"Maybe yes, maybe no," replied Eric with a shrug and his usual grin.

"Well, at least as far as the next floe, eh?" Frank joked. Eric the Unflappable grinned again.

He was still grinning when, a few moments later, the bilge filled with water again. This time he pulled the plug from the stern board, and as long as we kept going fast, the sea stayed where it should. However, whenever he slowed down or stopped to let his sons shoot at a seal, water gushed in again. I didn't even need any walrus to make this trip an adventure.

Inuit elders usually take out a couple of boys with them on hunting trips, although till their mid-teens boys don't often get to shoot seals or walrus. On this hunt Brian and Jama stood side by side at the bow and shot simultaneously whenever the round head of a ringed seal popped to the surface or a blimp of a bearded seal appeared on one of the ice pans. It was clear that Eric was teaching his sons by participation, and such is the forbearance of the Inuit, he just grinned when they missed.

Despite being peppered with bullets, one huge bearded seal refused to leave its resting place on an ice pan. Sure that the boys would get it, I centred it in my camera's viewfinder and intended to shoot at the same time as they did. I heard three shots, but to my amazement, the seal slithered off the floe and disappeared, leaving no blood on the water. Usually the sea turns red when a seal or walrus is shot.

Eric gave some instructions in Inuktitut to the boys, rammed the canoe into the ice pan, and grabbed a harpoon; then all three jumped off onto the ice. When Frank grabbed the dangling bow rope as it slipped into the sea and jumped off too, I was the only one left on board. I picked up a wooden board for a paddle and kept the canoe nosed into the ice pan.

Where was the seal? I knew they could stay submerged for twenty to thirty minutes, although Eric said later they could last an hour. "It could be sneaking a breath anywhere under the lip of the ice pan," said Frank. The three Inuit checked the ledges on the far side of the ice and once I saw Eric throw his harpoon. It didn't make contact.

And then I saw the seal's head quietly emerge from a ledge a yard or so down. Eric threw the harpoon again but missed. The seal subsided. Again there was no sign of blood in the water. We waited ten minutes before Eric called, *"Tema"* ("that's enough") and we left, not really sure if the seal got away or not.

We reached the main floe edge at 1:15 P.M. "Lots of walrus everywhere," said Eric enthusiastically with an expansive wave of his arms that circled the entire horizon. I didn't see any walrus myself, but I did note that each ice pan was a dirty brown, the colour of buckwheat pancakes, where I imagined walrus had hauled out. Later, I learned that the colour was more likely due to the sea ice grounding on the bottom of shallow Foxe Basin and disturbing the silt.

"Lots of walrus," Eric repeated gleefully as he sharpened his harpoon head with a file and pointed the canoe to a mixed group of adults and young he'd seen hauled out on a small ice pan. As we circled the ice at a distance of about nine yards, all the walrus but two old bulls dived into the sea. None seemed concerned. The ones on the ice lifted their amply upholstered shoulders, faced off like two opposing gladiators then sank down into a single lump. The ones in the water milled around but made no attempt to flee.

Inuit hunters circle several groups of animals before they select a walrus to kill. Usually, they take the largest tusked animals although these are not necessarily males or the ones with the most meat. They must also consider the ease of butchering the carcass and bringing it home. Obviously, they prefer to shoot an animal on a large ice pan and hope it stays there rather than shoot one in the water where it can sink before they harpoon it.

Eric moved on to a group on another ice pan. Walrus are unpredictable. Normally, big old bulls are the last to leave, but in this case, the two on the second floe dived into the sea as we approached. "They can attack the boat, eh?" said Frank, noticing Eric's swift veering away from the oncoming bulls.

The hunter raised his eyebrows. "Yep," he replied briefly as he took off quickly to another floe. It was the first time I'd seen Eric so serious.

As we approached five walrus lumped together on the ice, Brian stood up at the bow ready to shoot. As the shot from his .303 rifle rang out, three walrus fled into the water, the one with short knobby tusks stayed put, and the fifth ("a woman," according to Eric) rolled over inert.

"Can you believe that?" I whispered to Frank in amazement. "The ones in the water are trying to get back onto the ice."

"The dead one's starting to roll off the edge. The guys are going to have to get it before it sinks."

That was no easy matter. To do that, the Inuit had to dodge the walrus that were swimming around the boat and the walrus that refused to budge from its dead buddy. While Eric circled the floe again, Brian and Jama fired shots into the air, banged on the side of the canoe, threw ice balls, and clanged their harpoons, but nothing would clear a path to their booty.

Meanwhile, the dead walrus had slipped off the ice and was rolling slowly over the edge. A minute or two later, it lost its grip of the ice and began to sink. Fortunately, its body came to rest on a submarine ledge, and there it stayed in a widening pool of blood. Oblivious, the three swimming walrus bobbed in the water beside it and redoubled their efforts to get back to the ice.

"You'd think they'd gag on that blood or want to get away," I whispered again to Frank. "Are they trying to help their dead companion or are they just plain stupid?" I asked rhetorically. A biologist explained later that walrus are as intelligent as they have to be. They tend to be gregarious and likely do not connect blood and inertness with death. They may have interpreted the dead walrus as just resting.

Unable to get the live walrus out of the water and with the dead walrus starting to sink again, Eric and the boys decided to risk a retrieval. Dodging the still-swimming walrus and with a wary eye on the walrus still acting as the centrepiece of the ice pan, the Inuit carefully cruised towards their prey.

Brian's harpoon hit its mark. Quickly, Eric whipped out his knife, slit a few holes in the neck skin, and laced a rope through the holes to lash the walrus to the side of the canoe. The lone walrus left on the ice opened one bleary eye but seemed to pay no further attention. Nevertheless, Eric wasted no time in heading to another floe about seventy-five yards away.

Then the hard work began. They had to get the walrus—an adult female probably weighing six or eight hundred pounds—out of the water and onto the ice. Eric wedged the canoe into a handy little cove, then, leaving Frank to keep the boat roped in place, he and his boys jumped onto the floe. Careful not to stand on the edge of the bouncing platform and risk falling into the frigid sea, I took up a position to observe the butchering process and at the same time relieve Frank on anchor duty.

Eric cut holes in the walrus's hide, threaded a sealskin thong through the holes, and with everybody's help, pulled the walrus's forequarters up onto the ice floe. The rest of its body dangled into the water, and we had to watch carefully that it didn't drop and disappear.

Eric was back grinning again as he sharpened his long butcher knives. Brian had shot the walrus, but I noticed that it was Jama who did most of the cutting up. Occasionally, Eric intervened to suggest a better place to make a cut or separate the choicest meat.

The Inuit butchered the walrus in sections, pulling up as much of the body out of the water as they could manage at one time. They peeled the hide, blubber, and meat from the skeleton in large slabs, cut off the head and foreflippers, removed the viscera, and pulled off the ribs. Then they cut the teeth, tusks, and penis bone from the skeleton, probably to sell to the Co-op store.

Permanently hard, two-foot-long penis bones often arouse comments and giggles from newcomers to the North. Later in the week, I bought a penis bone from the Co-op, and Sonny MacDonald, a famous Metis carver from Fort Smith, turned it into a work of art with a few deft chisel strokes. He mounted it on two brass legs and stood it on a moose antler. Few admirers of the great blue heron now in my living room realize its origins.

I was surprised at how much space the viscera take up in a walrus's body. The liver, heart, and kidneys are huge, which is just as well as these are prime cuts for the Inuit. Eric carefully set them aside before he hauled out the long snakes of intestines.

"He's looping them just like I loop my electric coils," Frank commented.

"Are you going to eat those?" I asked Eric.

He nodded dramatically. "Inuit eat everything," he replied, continuing to loop and then braid yards of intestines like a crocheted mat.

"What about those?" I asked as he threw away the last section.

Although Eric only sometimes spoke English, and I was never sure how many of my words he understood, there was no mistaking his reply this time. "No. Full of shit," he said very precisely. Then he almost doubled over with laughter at his own words.

The boys packed the slabs of walrus meat and ribs on the tarp at the bottom of the boat, stuffed the liver, heart, and intestines and some of the other meat into a sausage-shaped bundle of hide and blubber, and put the bundles on top of the slabs. Surprisingly, they scooped up what was left of the carcass and piled it neatly on the ice—for scavenging polar bears, I presumed. Finally, we had a quick cup of tea and pilot biscuits served on the hacked-up grub box.

Shelley had told me that Eric whipped up a walrus stew the day she went hunting with him. Despite the monochromatic sky and a sudden onslaught of rain, and despite our leaking boat, I was hoping for something similar. But suddenly, Eric looked at my watch and asked, "What's the time?"

"3:30 P.M.," I shrugged, wondering why time should be so important to an Inuk in the Land of the Long Day.

"My wife's coming home from hospital in Iqaluit on the four o'clock plane today," he explained in an uncommonly long English sentence.

Within the hour, the twin radar screens of the old DEW line station loomed out of the silvery sea-sky, and at the end of the next hour, we landed at Hall Beach to be greeted by Eric's wife.

We may not have had time for a walrus picnic on the ice, but thanks to Eric's gift of some of the most prized walrus parts, I celebrated their successful hunt, our adventure, and our safe return with my own feast of marinated walrus liver and a "hearty" walrus stew cooked in my own kitchen. Like Inuit teenagers, Frank and the rest of the construction crew preferred hotdogs. My companions were not gourmet adventurers at all, and even I declined Eric's offer of walrus intestines—especially the lower end.

Inuit are often surprised when non-Inuit eat the traditional Inuit way. Long ago, before I first went to the Arctic, I tried to prepare myself to eat raw meat by gnawing on a thawed beef roast. As I learned in the North, frozen raw meat is infinitely preferable to thawed raw meat. And frozen fish, seal, and caribou taste a lot better than frozen pork, beef, and chicken. Perhaps it depends on the situation. There is truth in the old cliché, "When in Rome, do as the Romans do."

❈

One December I made one of my typically spontaneous decisions and flew to Pond Inlet, about four hundred miles north of the Arctic Circle, to see what it was like to spend a winter in total darkness. Although I hadn't wanted to stay during the festive season, I did. I was one of the few non-Inuit in town for Christmas.

Meals were memorable. Christmas up north goes on for weeks. Celebrations in the form of feasts, games, and dances start in mid-December and continue nightly till the New Year. I had not one but many Christmas dinners in Pond Inlet.

Judy, the sweet teenaged waitress at the Sauniq Hotel, tore a page from her school exercise book and proudly handed me one of my Christmas menus. Scrawled across the lines were the words:

BEEF STEW
RICE
FRIED RICE

and for desert [sic]
CHOCOLATE CAKE WITH PUDDING

I still treasure that piece of paper—and the memory.

Rarely are there regular sit-down meals in Inuit homes. If visitors are hungry, they are expected to help themselves. Usually, there is a chunk of raw caribou at the door, a long-thawed, skin-crinkled raw fish on the counter, or my own preference, a pot of duck soup on the stove.

One night I walked into the community hall expecting to find tables laden with turkey, cranberries, and pie. For days, the local radio station had been soliciting volunteers to cook turkeys donated by one of the oil companies. The announcer even gave detailed instructions on how to thaw and cook them. However, the turkey feast had to be postponed when the women didn't realize how long turkey took to cook. Many of the women had boiled their birds. Somehow, turkey raw, boiled, or dried is just not the same as turkey roasted and basted in an oven.

Instead, we had a seal feast, which is the most popular feast of all. Even my Inuit friend, Iga, who prepares gourmet dinners that would be the envy of any restaurant in the south, craves seal meat. "Other meat is too dry," she says. Some women say it is the best meat to eat when they're pregnant.

Elijah, Kadloo, and Luti were dragging in three freshly killed ringed seals when I arrived at the hall. To my surprise, I learned that the women had harpooned them that afternoon during the seal-hunting contest. This must have been an arduous feat in the darkness. Traditionally, men do the hunting and women do the meal preparation, but on this night the roles were reversed.

Everyone waited patiently while the three men slit the seals neatly down the middle, stripped off the fur to be made later into mitts and *kamiks*, set aside the fat and the guts and the blood in separate buckets, cut up the ribs and muscle into chunks, and reserved the choice pieces of liver and heart.

Everything was laid out on long orange tarps, which rolled like a carpet along the floor from the door of the hall to the stage. Suddenly, everyone stood up and faced the stage. I couldn't understand the Inuktitut words, but when people started singing, I recognized the tune, "Praise God From Whom All Blessings Flow."

"We're thanking God for the seals, asking Him to keep them coming, and promising to make them useful," whispered Sarahme beside me.

As soon as the last note was sung, the Inuit swarmed to the floor with their *ulus* and butcher knives to grab what meat they could. Some knelt to eat lined up at the tarp table. Others filled plastic bags with seal, spread cardboard tablecloths on the floor around the sides of the hall, and gathered in groups for cosy family picnics. A few of the more opportunistic packed chunks of seal for people back home, although almost all the community must have been at the feast already.

I came without an *ulu*, but as soon as the surprised Inuit realized that I wanted to participate, I was offered liver, which, like walrus liver, is a delicacy. I knelt down beside the quickly disappearing carcasses in my blue satin party dress and wondered what my family in Australia would think of this Arctic Christmas dinner.

On other nights, I went to the community hall to find frozen chunks of fish, caribou, or whale spread out on the floor. Frozen tails of arctic char standing upright on the tarps reminded me of candle decorations. Often there were side bowls of fat and white stuff that looked like sultana-studded rice, but which, so I was told, were the semi-digested stomach contents of caribou.

In deference to my non-Inuit upbringing, my Inuit friends sometimes offered me Cheerios, macaroni dinners, or plates of traditional Christmas fare they'd picked up at the many Christmas parties, but I preferred eating as they did. Country food is far more nutritious than expensive store-bought southern food brought in by plane or barge. But there are some Inuit delicacies that I can't bring myself to eat.

Take *okshuk* for instance. Agnes and Fred Carpenter of Sachs Harbour introduced me to *okshuk*, which is bearded seal oil gone rancid. It is a popular condiment in Inuvialuit communities. I was strolling past the Carpenters' house with Miluse, one of my southern friends on her first visit to the North, when Agnes called out through the window, "Lyn, I've just got some fresh apples in on the plane. Come and have some apple crisp."

As soon as she heard that Miluse hadn't tasted country food before, Agnes discarded her offer of apple crisp and whipped up several sumptuous dishes of swan, goose, and caribou. And when Fred heard that I hadn't tried *okshuk*, he encouraged me to try it. "If you eat it long enough, you'll get to have an Eskimo stomach. You'll be able to do anything, even grab snow in winter without gloves. Every hunter eats some *okshuk* with his dry meat or fish."

Agnes added that her kids never had colds when they ate *okshuk* because it was chock full of vitamin C. She explained its preparation. "We cut the blubber of the bearded seal into strips, put it in a large can, let it melt and marinate for a couple of weeks. Then we keep it in the deep freeze but it doesn't freeze. It's an amazing oil. Try some."

I will almost always try something new in the North, but this was one time I wished I hadn't. With Miluse, Agnes, Fred, and a roomful of Carpenter kids watching, I dipped a chunk of dry caribou into the pot of *okshuk* and in an agony of shudders and grimaces, managed to force some down despite my shrieking tastebuds. My audience shrieked, too—but with hilarity. Grab snow in winter without gloves? I didn't think I'd ever be doing anything again.

To my consternation, Miluse tried some *okshuk* without being asked and even went back for more. Surely she was just being polite. Surely she didn't enjoy it. I begged for apple crisp.

I don't think I'll ever eat *okshuk* again, not even if I am starving. I have never been in that predicament but on one trip to the Northwest Territories, I came close—or thought I was.

I was invited to spend a week on Ray and Doris Beck's trapline at the Talston River, north of Fort Smith, learning how to drive a dog team. My companion Lee Smith was from New York and had never been to Canada before, let alone the Northwest Territories. Lee was a vegetarian. She guessed correctly that a native family in the bush would be eating mostly meat, so, while still in New York, she systematically habituated her stomach to accept smaller and smaller meals.

"I think I can probably go a week without eating anything," she confided when we landed on the frozen Talston River in our ski-equipped bush plane. "I booked this trip because I love dogs. I can't bear to see an animal killed."

I could see such expectations would be met with great difficulty on a trapline. We were welcomed with appetizers of dry caribou meat followed by a dinner of buffalo stew bubbling in a big black pot on the woodstove. Murmuring something about air sickness, Lee just had bannock and tea. After supper, Ray and his teasing teenaged son, Eric, stretched their lynx and marten skins and Doris dyed moose hair for her tufted moose hair pictures. And on the way to the outhouse we flushed a covey of ptarmigan. "Don't tell the Becks," Lee entreated. "Ray will probably shoot them for breakfast."

The Beck family provide what is dubbed subarctic serenity vacations in the boreal wilderness. Guests share their life on the land— hunting moose and buffalo, setting snares and traps, helping to dry meat, fish through the ice, chop wood, or join in other camp chores. If guests don't want to get involved in the trapping life, they can take a dogteam ride, snowshoe or cross-country ski, gaze at the northern lights, or just talk to Doris while she tufts moose hair, or Ray while he is training his dogs. Our hosts were part of a large family of Becks known throughout North America as champion dog mushers.

And that's what Lee and I had come to Talston River to do—learn how to drive dogs. As we approached them on our first morning, thirty yelping, howling Talston River Huskies ran around the dung that encircled their dog houses and lunged at us from the end of their chains. Nervously following Ray and Eric, we threaded a narrow, twisting corridor through them, thankful that the end of one chain didn't quite reach the next. These were no house-breed mix but working dogs with wolf in them.

"We'll give you the quietest dogs," said Eric, reassuringly. "And put Lyn in the lead, she's had experience."

Some experience! All I had done before was sit on a sled while a friend's dog team pulled me along the Muskwa River in northern British Columbia. When I fell out, the dogs dragged me like a human snowplough till they decided of their own accord to stop. I had provided no direction at all.

Ray and Eric set out each team's harness on the snow while Lee and I led "our" dogs to their places along the line. "They're your dogs for the time you're here. You feed them, water them, harness them, and drive them," said Ray nonchalantly.

My first lesson was how to recognize which dogs were mine: Boots, the stoic black and white leader; Happy, small, lively and living up to his name, following solo; big Relic and all-black Blackie in tandem behind.

My second lesson was how to slip the right part of the dog through the right part of the harness. I thought the dogs might have helped by proffering the correct paws, but perhaps they were testing me too. Ray and Eric murmured something about voice commands and how to stop but their words passed by me in a blur.

"By the way, where are we going?" I asked Ray who was kneeling beside me in the snow checking the harness.

"Our first night's camp is a tent about ten miles downriver," he said laconically. "Don't worry. Boots will stop when you get there."

At that moment, either because we had mentioned his name or because we had released our pressure on the harness, Boots stood up and took off. "Jump on the sled," Ray yelled as the line of dogs trotted past me.

Instinctively, I grabbed a handle and swung onto the back runners. To my amazement, I stayed there. I certainly hadn't needed the word "Hike" to get the dogs started. Ray had assured me they knew where they were going so I wouldn't need "Whoah" to get them to stop.

Although Lee's team was faster and her lead dog Oz (pronounced "Aussie") kept nipping my heels, I hoped she wouldn't use the word "Trail," a courtesy to request passing. In my first five minutes of dog driving, I wasn't about to chance a messy mix-up in the snow as two teams vied for the same narrow track. That would come soon enough.

So this was the subarctic in spring—silent, sun-sparkled world polarized an intense blue by my goggles; a frozen river snaking between naked poplar and willow in a land of little sticks. Here and there, the ice was broken by foaming water at several sets of rapids. I gritted my teeth a bit when the toboggan swung toward them, but the dogs kept trotting on. Lee was somewhere behind but I wasn't yet brave enough to risk an imbalance by turning around to look.

I felt as if I had the whole North to myself.

Actually, it was easy. All I had to do was to stand on the runners, hang onto the wooden bar in front of me, and with knees flexed, balance with the bumps. Easy—as long as the dogs kept to the river bank. Suddenly, Boots veered at right angles into the bush along a portage trail, and the dogs pelted through a slice of spruce trees. The sled swung crazily like a living thing, swerving, sideswiping, flying, almost flipping. I ducked to my knees at every branch. One of us—the sled or I—was going to get hurt.

I opened my eyes long enough to catch a glimpse between bouncing pompon tails to see Boots swing his team again at another right angle bend. The dogs disappeared from my line of sight, and my toboggan, careering around the corner, became a plane.

"Yes, you were certainly flying," Lee recalled later. I remembered the thud and the stars as my head hit the ice, packed hard, so Ray said, by all the heads that had landed at the same place in the past. "Yep, everybody falls there," he said offhandedly when he came to dig me out of the tunnel made by the dogs dragging me through powder snow. At least, my experience had taught me to hang on so I wouldn't lose my only transportation in the northern wilderness.

There's no worry, really. Ray or Eric always follow with teams a discreet distance behind, close enough to get guests out of trouble yet far enough away to give them the feeling of being alone with the river, the bush, the sky.

The dogs continued trotting along the river. "Talk to them," Eric had advised. Of course, as one who raced dogs, he wanted me to go faster, but I preferred a more relaxing meander through this vast silent land, especially in the comparative warmth of zero Celsius sunshine. I did manage a half-hearted "Hike. Put on your hiking boots, Boots," every time OZ nudged my heels. "Hike," didn't increase Boots's pace one bit. I wondered if "Whoah" would make him stop.

Around the next bend I had my chance to find out. Perhaps Relic was bored. Overcome suddenly by some romantic urge, he bounced on top of Blackie. Tangled legs and snarled harnesses didn't faze two mating dogs one whit, but as the team slowed to a jumble, I feared broken legs or a dog fight. I had to get them to stop.

"Whoah, Boots, whoah," I shouted. It didn't work. My lead dog kept pulling stalwartly despite the extra weight of the amorous couple. I had to try the hook, a fierce-looking iron anchor roped to the sled and used as a brake. Trying to avoid its teeth, I reached down gingerly to pick it up by the handle, jumped off the sled, and plunged the hook into the ice behind. That, my weight, and the increasingly entangled dogs brought us all to a stop.

Now, how to keep them stopped while I tried to unravel the team? I looked behind. Lee was laughing and taking pictures. Ray and Eric, in laid-back native fashion, were keeping a close watch but waiting to see how I'd go about solving the problem myself before they intervened.

Continuing to say "Whoah, whoah, whoah," to Boots, who was sitting on his haunches in the middle of the trail and seemed oblivious to the tied-together trio behind him, I sidled along the sled, ready at an instant to jump aboard if Boots suddenly took off. Kneeling beside Relic, Happy, and Blackie, I tried tracing the traces back from Boots, but none of my efforts resembled the way Ray had set out the harness that morning. Knots were the problem. It wasn't thread or string I was trying to unravel but real live sled dogs.

Fortunately, the Becks really had given me their quietest team, and eventually the dogs let me thread them in and around their harnesses. But not out. To do that I had to unsnap the lines and just hope they wouldn't run away and leave me up the river without a dog team. My scheme worked. With the dogs unleashed, it was easy to unravel the knots. As quickly as possible, I snapped the dogs back on the line and despite the hook still grabbing snow, they careered off down the trail again.

I caught the sled as it whizzed by, leaned down to pick up the dragging hook, and feeling quite proud of myself barrelled on to the next hazard. Eric had warned us that the hill ahead would make us parka-clad angels in the snow, but unravelling the dog line gave me confidence and I was determined not to fall. By now I realized that despite the lack of reins, I did have a part to play in driving the dogs. I could control the sled and the team by leaning to one side or the other. I even felt brave enough to take one foot off the runners and scoot to lighten the sled and make the dogs go faster. With every successful bend and portage, my cockiness increased to the point that I even took two feet off the sled and ran behind just like you see in the movies. I looked around and waved gaily to Lee. Ray and Eric seemed nowhere in sight.

And then came the hill. I was merrily ducking branches like a lively trampoline jumper and throwing my weight from one side of the madly swinging sled to the other when the dogs skewed unexpectedly around another right angle corner. I leaned out, lifted one foot off the runner, balanced the sled and began to congratulate myself on my newfound prowess as a dog driver. Yes, Eric, I'd made it. I looked around to smirk at my companions—then crashed.

Ray and Eric picked up an embarrassed, appropriately coloured, red parka-clad angel in the snow. This time, it was doubly embarrassing. I forgot to grab either the hook or the sled. Unperturbed and obviously not needing me, the dogs barrelled off into the bush. The professionals followed and brought them back. I clearly had a lot more to learn.

And not just about driving dogs.

Our camp that night was an aging canvas tent strung on spruce poles. We laid fresh spruce boughs on the snow, spread our sleeping bags on the boughs, and hurried outside to the toboggan to get frozen slabs of buffalo meat for the dogs.

"I wonder what we're going to eat," I whispered to Lee. "I'd like to try some buffalo myself."

"I've got some granola in my pack," she whispered back.

With the sun now fast disappearing behind the hills on the other side of the river, we were tired, cold, and hungry after our day of exercising. I looked forward to whatever the men prepared. I was not expecting to hear Ray say, "There's tea and salt in the grub box. Beyond that, you'll have to catch your own grub."

Lee and I looked at each other in disbelief. Was he serious? This was a do-it-yourself vacation, we were paying for the privilege of an authentic experience, and the Becks were supposed to assist us only in trouble. But did that include rescuing us from starvation in the wilderness?

Ray continued. "I admit it'll be hard this time of the year, no ducks, no fish, no berries, no trapline animals, few ptarmigan, and moose and buffalo tracks have been pretty sparse lately. Still, after you get your dogs fed and tied up for the night, you can try snaring rabbits."

Ray was the serious, silent type, but Eric was plainly enjoying our discomfiture. "Here's the buffalo meat," he grinned, "but remember it's only for the dogs."

The meat still had bits of curly brown hair attached, but in my current situation it looked quite appetizing. Perhaps I could steal some from the dogs when Eric wasn't looking, even if that meant wolfing it down raw as the dogs did.

We were in a chastened mood when Eric took us along a trail behind the tent to show us how to set rabbit snares with little circles of copper wire. If it wasn't for wondering where our next meal was coming from, I might have hoped he wouldn't catch anything. I admit I am the kind of person who likes to see the meat on the plate but doesn't want to think about how it got there. "Anyway, with our lack of trapping skill," I encouraged Lee, "these Easter bunnies will be safe."

Back at the tent, Eric suggested we start a fire. Ray had returned to spend the night with his wife, and Eric wanted to take a quick skidoo trip to his next line-cabin. "Sure, we can handle that," I said breezily.

While he roared off along the river, Lee and I set about making a safe, textbook-type, environmentally-friendly fire. We chose a location on a flat expanse of snow well away from the canvas tent; we collected deadwood at long distance rather than desecrate nearby trees and shrubs; we started the fire with little pyramids of sticks, a single match, and much bent-over blowing.

"Let's try barbecuing a few slabs of buffalo," I suggested to Lee after the flames shot upwards and the fire seemed to hold. "It's insurance in case we don't get any rabbits. And perhaps Eric will take pity on us and let us eat dog food after all. Me, anyway." I still couldn't believe that Lee was going to stick to her meagre diet by choice.

What we lacked in fire-making skills we made up for in enthusiasm. Ten minutes later, the frozen slabs of buffalo meat I had sneaked from the toboggan were laid out on a crosspiece of thin saplings set over a roaring fire on the snow. Leaving them to sizzle, we tied on our snowshoes and stumbled off to check our rabbit snares.

Our traps were empty. "Good thing we cooked that buffalo meat," I chuckled.

Was it? We returned to camp to find our buffalo patties floating in a shallow lake like charred waterlilies. Inadvertently, we'd made our blazing fire not on the snow-covered beach, but on the frozen river. The snow and then the ice underneath it had melted, leaving a shallow lake—and a soggy supper.

"You're weird," laughed Eric when he got back. "We Indians do it this way." He took his axe, chopped down a tree, cut up some sticks, poured gasoline onto the pile, lit a match, and within minutes he was cooking moose steaks. "We've got plenty of grub," he grinned. "Dad was just kidding."

We spent the rest of the week driving the dogs, touring the trapline, snowmobiling to the abandoned village of Rat River where the Becks had grown up, and enjoying the camaraderie of the trail. Lee was enthralled. As she came to know the Becks in person and realized how they interacted with the land, she came to accept their need to hunt and trap animals for food and clothing. On-the-spot participation is the best way to change attitudes. She even volunteered to spend the following summer with the family to look after the dogs.

On the last morning when that covey of ptarmigan fluttered up from the outhouse, she called, "Go and tell Eric—he can shoot some for breakfast." And when we sat beside each other on the plane going south, I ate her salad and she ate my filet mignon.

❀

In the North you learn quickly to go with the flow. Take the time I joined a group for a boat ride up the South Nahanni River. I went aboard thinking I was a guest but learned suddenly that I was the cook.

The South Nahanni River has the honour of being a World Heritage Site as well as a Canadian Heritage River. This means that its scenery is world class, on a par with the Galapagos Islands in Ecuador and the Pyramids in Egypt. It is often called the Yosemite of Canada for the beauty and variety of its outstanding landforms, a fast-moving mural of twisted mountains, deep winding canyons, unique karst features, spectacular waterfalls, and unusual rock formations.

Long before tourists came from around the world to canoe this river Mecca on organized expeditions, I hitched a ride into Fort Simpson in a float plane to follow my own dream of running the river. I had made no preparations, but according to the word on the street, Ted Trindell, a highly respected Metis trapper, boat builder, and river guide, was selling his outfitting business to Rod Norwegian, a Slavey trapper, and a Nahanni trip could be in the offing.

"So you want to see the Nahanni," Ted echoed when I found him repairing a scow on the banks of the Mackenzie River outside his house. "Rod's doing his first trip tomorrow. I'll see if you can go along." And that was that.

I was to do two extemporaneous trips up the Nahanni that summer, but it was Rod's trip that was the more memorable—and mainly because of the meals. Rod was a handsome, youthful-looking, forty-eight-year-old father of twelve, a man raised to a nomadic life on a trapline in the bush. When I met him in Fort Simpson he was driving a taxi and operating heavy machinery at the airport. My expedition to Virginia Falls on the South Nahanni River would be his first undertaking as a guide and outfitter.

His friend and navigator, Alfred Thomas, still spent his life as a hunter and trapper. Once, when stranded on the Flat River, a tributary of the South Nahanni, Alfred built himself a boat out of spruce bark and drifted down to Fort Simpson, a distance of almost three hundred miles. It was Alfred who provided our meat. Fortunately, although I didn't appreciate the significance of this at the time, Alfred bagged a moose on the eve of the expedition.

Our group consisted of Mickey and Derrick, a middle-aged couple from High Prairie, and Bill, Donna and Gloria, youth workers from Yellowknife. All were on their first wilderness holiday in the north. I was looking forward to a leisurely cruise upstream and the opportunity to snap a photo or two. Until my guides told me otherwise.

"It's lunchtime and you're the cook," Rod told me casually as he nosed our long wooden scow into a mudbank on the Liard River, a morning's motoring upstream from Fort Simpson. To my astonishment, he handed me an enamel basin of raw moose meat and a copy of the *Northern Cook Book* open to the chapter headed "Jellied Moose Nose."

Up till then, my camp cooking was limited to adding water to the freeze-dried foods I carried in my backpack. I had no experience catering to groups, especially customers paying hundreds of dollars for their dream trip on the Nahanni. Oblivious to what was awaiting them at my hands, the passengers jumped ashore to explore. Alfred tended the scow and Rod carried a cardboard box of groceries and cooking gear up the bank.

Nervously, I scanned the recipes in Rod's cookbook, recipes that required such exotic ingredients as charcoal seasoning and juniper berries and such methods as simmering in wine for two hours and marinating for two days. Then I took a quick peek into a couple of cardboard cartons of miscellaneous groceries that Rod had swept randomly from the shelves of the Hudson's Bay store the day before; a furtive glance at the number of people in our party (eight); counted up the number of meals we would be eating (fifteen); and came to the rather uncomfortable conclusion that much ingenuity would be needed to make this basin of moosemeat last the five days of our expedition.

I was glad Alfred was a hunter. Otherwise *we* might be among those who never returned from the Valley of Vanishing Men, one of the Nahanni's claims to fame.

That first night we splurged on Moose Steaks. The second night I plunked celery and a can of tomatoes on top and called it Swiss Moose. The third and fourth nights I cut up the meat into strips, added onions and peas and we had Moose Suey. The fifth day I rounded up what was left and hey presto, Moose Shish Kebabs! To my surprise, Alfred's wash basin of moose outlasted the journey in quantity—if not in quality.

Taking a cue from our taciturn, nonchalant hosts, we managed to adapt to the informality of the trip. Bill, Donna, and Gloria had the carefree abandon of youth on their side. Derrick, still jangling a crammed key chain from his office, coped with his sojourn away from civilization without comment. But his wife, who had never been camping before, confided pluckily one day while I was doing a knee-bend over the Coleman, "I'm really a very fussy person and some of these things are a bit hard on me."

She grimaced as I picked out a mosquito that had just flown in to fry itself to death in a pan of onions and gritted her teeth when I tried unsuccessfully to brush sand out of the blueberries. I didn't let her—or anyone else—watch when I gave the moose its daily dip in the river to wash the maggots off! The Subarctic can be surprisingly warm in midsummer, and we had no refrigeration.

Fortunately, my companions were all good sports. Everybody pitched in to load and unload the scow, build fires, set up tents, and blow up air mattresses. Rod and Alfred handled the scow but they left camp chores to their customers. Such was their casual laid-back attitude that sometimes it seemed as if the guests were taking the Slavey guides on this trip and not the other way around. Yet, in a way, this gave the journey its special appeal.

❊

Twenty-two years later, I travelled the Nahanni again, this time the North Nahanni River, which flows into the Mackenzie River seventy-five miles downstream from Fort Simpson. I was standing in the line-up at the Northern Store when Loyal Letcher, a fledgling Dene entrepreneur, invited me and two of my friends to spend a day on the North

Nahanni in his jet boat. Like Rod before him, Loyal was taking guests on his first commercial trip.

I had tried to get up the North Nahanni once before in a sixteen-foot rubber raft with a fifty-horsepower motor, but I had managed little more than a mile. The river that June was on a rampage. Its delta was strewn with debris, its banks were stripped five yards above the normal high water mark, and trees dangled down the eroded banks at all angles. Naked roots formed a bamboo-like curtain down to the water, which was the consistency and colour of Cream of Wheat.

After a couple of miles of battling the strong currents, dodging stumps of black spruce lodged in mud banks and logs hurtling downstream, I finally found where the deepest channel lay. But not for long. With the river in flood, my navigation maps were useless and within minutes I was grounded.

Pushing free with my paddles, I swung the motor out of the water and cautiously pikepoled up the swirling stream. Four feet, three feet, two feet, one foot. STOP. I hit bottom again. Pushing off once more, I snaked a precarious path through the snarl of roots and trees, barely holding my own against the fourteen-knot current. I dared not lose power lest I swirl helplessly among the sharp snags. Crawling along at a mere half mile per hour despite my fifty-horsepower motor, I eventually found a place to camp in midstream on the fine silt of a sparsely treed island. I jumped ashore, only to squelch ankle deep into mud. Struggling painfully, I made it the hundred yards up the beach and fixed the anchor line around a bush. And when finally my tent was pitched against the majestic backdrop of the Mackenzie Mountains, I felt the long haul was worth it. But that was as far as I went up the North Nahanni.

Doing the North Nahanni twenty-two years later in a nineteen-foot jet boat with Loyal and his chief guide, Foster Norwegian, was certainly a different experience. The two young men were in their first year of running one-day jet boat trips on the North Nahanni as an alternative to week-long paddling trips on the South Nahanni. They were also building a log cabin naturalists' lodge at nearby Cli Lake.

With two of my Ottawa friends, Len and Cairine, we left Ndulee ferry crossing on the Mackenzie River at 9:00 in the morning and didn't get back till 11:00 that night. "I didn't know a day could have so many WOWS!" exulted Cairine on her first trip to the North.

Unfortunately, forest fires had been burning all summer and were still burning as we cruised down the Mackenzie and up the North Nahanni. A grey shroud veiled the landscape merging sky, water, and land like a Toni Onley painting. Foster drove the boat. He made it look easy. With visibility less than a mile because of the fires and a river whose swift and powerful current showed itself in an obstacle course of eroded banks, dangling sweepers, naked roots, and bobbing deadheads, he had to make split navigating decisions.

"Sit down, we'll have to give her to get through these channels," Foster warned, his brows furrowed in intense concentration. With an unerring instinct for the right path and picking up speed to get over the shallows, he leaned into the turns. He rode the river like a cowboy, but we always felt comfortable and confident in his ability. This river was the boys' childhood playground and they obviously enjoyed sharing it with visitors.

We explored all their favourite places—relatives' hunting camps, traditional lookouts, historic cabins. "Do you see that log cabin up there, perched on the edge of the cut bank?" Loyal asked as we followed his gaze. "There used to be two cabins, but one has already fallen into the river. It was owned by a fur trader. People said he kept his money in tin cans around his cabin. But he fell through the ice on the North Nahanni delta and it wasn't till spring that they found his skull. The money was never found." Like the South Nahanni, the North Nahanni has its legends.

We slowed down to look at a moose with calf, a sauntering black bear, skeining geese, soaring bald eagles. Foster defied the currents and debris to get us as close as possible to the animals. Meanwhile, Loyal, a Renewable Resources officer and Assistant Forest Fire Management officer for the Government of the Northwest Territories, kept up a lively and informative commentary on the animals' lifestyles.

"Look, there's another moose, quick get your camera," he called suddenly. As Foster swung the boat in the direction of a moose trotting along the beach, and I dived for a telephoto lens, I couldn't help think how different this younger generation was from its predecessors.

My mind went back to the day Rod and Alfred took us on a hike to see sheep at a salt lick in Deadman Valley on the South Nahanni River. As we strolled across the sandy delta, I took pictures of flowers among the pebbles of the braided stream bed, Bill took pictures of me, and

132

the rest just enjoyed their relaxing walk in the warm sunshine. We scarcely noticed when Rod pointed up the delta. "Wolves," he said almost casually in his quiet voice.

Oblivious to our presence and with the wind in our favour, not theirs, a family of five wolves came loping down the delta in a straight path towards us. Thrilled, we scrummaged for our cameras and with fingers nervously feeling for dials, waited tensely till the wolves—parents and three young pups—reached close range. We watched in amazement as the animals got bigger and bigger in our lenses. Wide angle, normal, portrait . . .

Just as I was about to click the shutter, a shot rang out, followed quickly by another. The two adults crumpled immediately. I clicked a picture of three young pups leaning over the dead bodies of their parents and learning fear for the first time. Aghast, I looked behind. Alfred had just shot the wolves we were trying to photograph! We were shocked and disappointed, but it was as natural for our guides, who were hunters and trappers, to shoot wolves as it was for us, visitors to their land, to shoot pictures.

Attitudes are changing—in the North as elsewhere. On our trip up the North Nahanni, Loyal and Foster lost no opportunity to point out the wildlife and to position us for the best photos. As we passed the entrance to the Tetcela River that wriggled rapidly to join the North Nahanni, Loyal said, "That's the way to Cli Lake, first a jet boat ride, then a three-mile hike through a gap in the mountains. Fishing's great but only catch and release and shooting only with a camera."

There were other differences. Several times that day, we stopped to eat. Some stops were for snacks such as tea and bannock or juice and cookies. Others were full-fledged meals. Each time, our guides were eager to tell us what they knew of the local surroundings.

"Time for marshmallows and a wiener roast," Loyal announced at the base of Lone Mountain. The smell of smoke was still thick in the air. We could feel the mountains rising up around us, occasionally we caught glimpses of them in sporadic sunlight, but we had only the map's contours to prove they were there.

Lone Mountain is the summer home of Garth Hildeman, a geologist who, two decades earlier, had fallen in love with these landscapes and built himself a log house on nearby Cli Lake. He lived a solitary existence there till summer when he was dropped off by helicopter on top of Lone Mountain to watch for fires. Unlike other fire wardens, he needed no midseason break. If he left at all, he hiked down the mountain and bushwhacked home across the muskeg to check his garden. Tales about Garth's bush travels are legendary. People tell of him walking sixty miles regularly into Fort Simpson to check his mail.

"Garth is to be the naturalist for our lodge on Cli Lake," Loyal said enthusiastically as he handed me a freshly sharpened willow stick for our wieners. "He's walked all over this country."

"The trail to his lookout goes up that hill," Foster pointed. "Take a walk while we prepare lunch."

Our trip up the twisting North Nahanni ended beneath surrealistic smoke-hazed mountains at Battlement Creek, thirty or so miles from the river's confluence with the Mackenzie. Beyond the towering palisade of the Nahanni Range, the tributaries of the Ram and Tetcela beckoned us to the high country. Upstream, the wiggling canyons of the North Nahanni called us farther into the mountains. But we had only the day.

I accompanied Len and Cairine on a walk up Battlement Creek while our guides prepared a final meal. We offered to help, but the boys were adamant. "No, just relax. There's a good fishing spot across the creek," Foster said. "I got some Dolly Varden there last week."

We were treated like royalty. Foster set up plastic chairs for us to relax in comfort. I don't ever remember sitting in chairs on a wilderness expedition. Loyal handed us soap, water, and towels to wash our hands before eating, which made me ashamed of my usual camping habits.

And the supper was sumptuous—Cli Lake whitefish, pork spareribs, beans and pan-fried potatoes, bush tea, bannock, and homemade berry jam. "Wow!" I grinned as I sat back comfortably in my easy chair and accepted a dish of whitefish AND spareribs loaded with vegetables. "This is a bit different from my first trip on the Nahanni."

For the next fifteen minutes, I regaled the group with my memorable trip by scow with Rod Norwegian twenty-two years earlier when the guests did the chores, we relied for food on what was hunted, and I was appointed rookie cook. I left nothing out, not even the maggots in the moose. When I finished my tale, Foster handed me dessert. He smiled quietly. "Yes, I know. Rod was my Dad."

❊

After my impromptu apprenticeship cooking on the Talston and Nahanni Rivers, I have learned to prefer making pictures to making meals. Given the choice, I leave wilderness cooking to the professionals.

The most spontaneous meal I have had prepared for me in the wilderness was high in the clouds at Baf 3, a state-of-the-art radar site on Brevoort Island, one of a chain along the Arctic Coast that is part of the North Warning System, a modernization of the DEW line. To keep their employees happy living for three months at a time in a metal cocoon on a blizzard-ridden mountain in the clouds in an area which averages 150 days a year of fog and 322 days of frost, Frontec Logistics tries to ensure that meals are sumptuous and superb.

"We even have beach parties beside our outdoor swimming pool," said site-supervisor Ken with a grin, pointing out the window to a rectangular concrete pond filled part way with murky ice water and flecked with falling snowflakes. It looked like the foundation of an old building.

I arrived in summer but in the yard the fuel drums were hung with icicles and trucks had turned into ice sculptures. Weather can change in seconds on Brevoort Island, and there were ominous warnings on the walls of Baf 3:

BEWARE FALLING ICE FROM THE ROOF WHEN YOU WALK OUTSIDE. TIE A ROPE TO HAUL YOURSELF BACK IN A WHITEOUT. ALWAYS PARK INTO THE WIND.

"Would you have a beach party today?" I dared.

"Sure, why not? You can't wait around for weather here," Ken beamed. Congeniality is a tool for survival when you live on top of a gravel pile looking down over a 1200-foot precipice.

Dinner that night was a brief but mad beach party around the pool. Dave drove the barbecue into position with the front end loader. Derek rounded up a diving board and ghetto blaster. Jack set up patio furniture. Kevin erected an impromptu sign that said *CLUB BAF*. Ken flipped the steaks and Pierre donned his chef's hat to skate in with the drinks (which because Frontec's sites are dry were coloured water and cook-

ing wine). Despite fog, snow, and freezing temperatures, we all rum-
maged around for shorts and bathing suits and lounged on the deck. I
posed in a swimsuit by the diving board while Lillian took a picture.
Fred proposed a toast to Club Baf. It was hardly Club Med weather but
I guess our giggles kept us warm.

❄

Making the most of what we had was the mark of another mad but
spontaneous dinner party in the wilderness. "Dinner time," yelled
Charlie, the sous-chef, straightening his outsized tin-foil tie and waving
us to the campfire. We emerged sheepishly from our tents and our willow
bush dressing rooms and gathered together on a wide gravel bar of the
South Nahanni River, half an hour's paddle upstream from Nahanni Butte.

Donna, looking like an aerobics-class Tinkerbell in her long underwear, pranced along a driftwood log. Her sister, Laurel, modestly lifted
her green garbage bag skirts clear of the silted pebbles. Heather and I
held hands more for mutual encouragement than in emulation of an
intimate couple going out to dine: she the boy in her shiny thermal
suit; me her partner in a borrowed silver space blanket draped like a
sarong over my naked shoulders and garlanded with willow leaves at
the arms and ankles. In lieu of a rose, I held an alder branch.

We seated ourselves on a gigantic log, roots included, that wiry
Roger Vieux had hauled singleshoulderedly to our raft-plank dining
table. Barry, the head chef and leader of our rafting expedition, tin-
foil-tied himself, welcomed us with wine to our last dinner before the
following day's return to civilization. Barry and Charlie had asked us
to dress for dinner, and it was amazing—and hilarious—how things
grabbed from packsacks and riverbank were fashioned at a moment's
notice into quality attire to match quality dining.

I chuckled at the memory of my Nahanni make-do moose as I
looked at the boys' menu: prime ribs of roast beef with Yorkshire
pudding, steamed-green broccoli, mashed potatoes, succulent gravy;
three Cs salad of cabbage, carrot, and celery; Laurel-made-by-the-
riverbank bread; carrot cake with cream cheese and icing sugar
frosting; coffee with Bailey's Irish Cream liqueur on the side. Such
a dinner would be remarkable at home or in the city. It was almost
incredible as the finale of a ten-day wilderness river trip.

But then all the meals the boys prepared were superlative. We breakfasted on fresh baked breads, muffins, or bannock; on orange or grapefruit sections; on omelette or souffles stuffed with mushrooms, cheese, and tomatoes; on French toast—a source of amusement to our two French cousins, Roger Vieux and Roger Jeune, who had never heard of French toast in Europe. "It must be unique to Quebec," they said, puzzled.

Lunches laid out on gravel bars or sandy beaches were a gourmet's selection of meats, breads, cheeses and fruits, and commonly included oysters, shrimp, crab, cantaloupe, grapes, and tomatoes. Dinners were baked salmon, beef stroganoff, chicken teriyaki, coq au vin, pork tenderloin, Hawaiian glazed ham, and yes, ordinary fare like steak, meat loaf, and lasagne. Always, each dish was accompanied by fresh vegetables and a different salad every night: Greek salad, Caesar salad, Waldorf salad, Coleslaw.

We all helped where we could but woe betide us if we substituted the feta cheese, left out the olives,or sliced the onions too finely. Barry demanded perfection. He almost wept when the grocer hadn't packed the right spices and marauding porcupines ravished the Romaine lettuce destined for the Caesar salad.

Desserts were fresh fruits and whipping cream, apple crisp, peach cobbler, cheese cake, cherries jubilee, and an innovative melange of pies, cakes, and puddings whipped up on the riverbank in minutes. Most desserts were served with a variety of liqueurs.

It was the boys' apparent effortlessness in primitive conditions that I found most amazing. Within minutes of our rafts hitting shore at each scenically selected camp spot, they had a fire going, set up boards from the boat as a preparation cum serving table, collected water, and had gourmet meals underway.

Barry spurned mixes so he did everything from scratch. Some meals were cooked in foil over the campfire, others in a large, old, shallow, heavy metal box that Barry said held a radio during the second world war. But most were prepared in Dutch ovens wrapped in foil with a set number of briquettes underneath and a set number of briquettes on the lid. Our prime ribs came out to medium rare perfection with five briquettes on top and ten on the bottom in an hour and a half.

While dinner and dessert were cooking together in adjacent Dutch ovens, Roger Vieux, tiny but tough, would go off to do his usual Herculean stunt of shouldering in trees for benches and then sawing wood for our campfire, always enough for the next campers' fire as well. The rest of us set up tents, chopped salads, or celebrated the days' floating with cocktails or coffee. Charlie's coffee was voted the best on three continents, and considering we all came from Australia, Europe, and North America, we had to be right.

Irrepressible Roger Vieux, who didn't speak a word of English yet was the life of our party, started a habit in the last days of our float trip by getting up first to see the sunrise (*"fantastique"*), then instead of crawling back into his sleeping bag as some of us in adjacent tents would have preferred, making the morning coffee and bringing it to each of us in bed.

Most of us enjoyed helping, but Barry was definitely the head chef extraordinaire. He had been cooking since childhood. "I had to," he explained simply. "My mother was in a wheelchair."He told us that a French chef with an interest in rafting set the standard for fancy cooking on wild river rafting trips.

In embarrassing contrast to the gargantuan appetites of our group, Barry ate only one small bowl of food at each meal. "It's all you need," he said in his typically understated, laid-back way. Certainly, he had more "won't power" than the rest of us.

❈

Perhaps my most memorable meal in the wilderness was not due to the location, the food, or the attire but to some unexpected guests who came to dinner. It was another of Barry's WhiteWolf Adventure Expeditions.

Our campsite, rimmed by hills and facing a long sandy bank stitched with wildflowers, was exquisite. Our tents were pitched beside the Burnside River in a spectacular natural garden. As usual, George and Jim had their tent up first and were off with their binoculars and field guides to scout the tundra before supper. No sooner had the two naturalists crossed the stream to the esker, than George's head was buried in a patch of purple oxytrope and Jim's eyes were intent on a skitter of plovers. Above them, the undercut bank was riddled with holes, probably *siksik* (ground squirrel) burrows.

Meanwhile, Barry huddled behind a boulder out of the wind to fix one of his gourmet meals. His big black cookpot was sandwiched between charcoal briquettes and stood on a stand for no-impact camping. Every now and then, he zoomed his camera into the mats of flowers that carpeted our camp. Beside him by the rubber rafts drawn up on the beach, two loons swooshed in to land like float planes on the river. Above, a line of white-fronted geese—specklebellies—circled camp in fighter-plane formation. River-polished rocks shone like jewels in the water. We hurried to finish our chores. The world beyond camp was waiting.

"Wolf!"

I looked up from my tent to see George and Jim pointing behind me. I turned quickly and glimpsed a flash of white as the animal disappeared around the nearest bend in the stream. A moment later it reappeared farther upstream. There was no use following, but we all stopped what we were doing to marvel at the sight of a wolf as it climbed effortlessly up the slopes and loped over the rolling hills behind our camp. Stopping occasionally to sit on its haunches and look back at us, the wolf seemed more curious than fearful. We stood entranced as it climbed the last ridge and trotted across the skyline.

Suddenly, a second wolf appeared on the horizon. Through our binoculars, we saw the two wolves merge in some form of greeting. Then one lay down, flopped its front paws over the ridge, and stared down at us. Barry quickly set up the scope and we lined up to look. Into focus through the telescope came the wolf's greyish head, black nose, black ear tips, and white chest. It turned sideways, opened its jaws wide, and yawned. I wished I was close enough to get such a portrait with my camera.

Then the wolf howled. Not the traditional, drawn-out howl heard in the movies, but short choppy sounds that rose high in the air then descended in a series of barks. The wolf sounded surprised as if saying, "What are you doing here?" That wasn't as anthropomorphic as it seemed. In this remote spot along the Burnside river west of Bathurst Inlet, we were possibly the first humans these wolves had encountered.

To my surprise, George howled back and an unforgettable duet began between man and wolf. It lasted an hour. We stood transfixed and listened.

"Supper's ready!" Barry called. The spell was broken.

Eagerly, we gathered round the table to share barbecued steak, baked potatoes, Caesar salad, freshly baked blueberry cobbler with whipping cream, red wine, Bailey's Irish Cream liqueur—and our reactions to the latest wildlife sighting. "Amazing," said Andrea fervently, speaking for all of us, "to dine so elegantly in the wilderness and be serenaded by wolves." The music of the wolves was the only accompaniment needed at this wilderness restaurant.

River trips are famed for sophisticated meals served in unsophisticated conditions, and we were always hungry for our guides' latest offerings. However, these wolves assuaged another hunger: the need in all of us as civilized beings to communicate with things that are still wild. That's why we run rivers, climb mountains, watch birds—and that's why we felt such awe in the company of the wolves that came to dinner.

Perfect Shots—
The Gun or the Camera

THE JET FROM OTTAWA HAD JUST ARRIVED and Iqaluit's terminal building was crowded. Bureaucrats with briefcases hurried off to government offices. Inuit mothers, their babies staring from the hoods of their parkas, sat patiently waiting for smaller planes to take them to other settlements on Baffin Island. Hikers and fishermen, eagerly anticipating trips to the hinterland, checked their packs and fishing rods at First Air's ticket counter.

But where were the hunters?

I was looking for two Houston women who had come to Nunavut to hunt central barren-ground caribou: Linda Young and Charlotte Rothwell, the successful bidders for a hunt donated to the Houston Safari Club by Jerome Knap of Canada North Outfitting. The idea of three single middle-aged women on a hunt was unusual enough for me to book the same trip, although I wondered what they might think of having a non-hunter naturalist/photographer along—and what the men in the rest of our party would think of having women along.

Suddenly, I spotted our outfitter, red-bearded Jerome, who quickly introduced me to the group—John and Gary from Ohio, Chet, Tom and Angelo from New York, Charlotte and Linda from Texas. No wonder I had not recognized the two Houston women. They did not fit my stereotyped image.

Charlotte, dressed fashionably in black, her hair pulled high in a topknot by a matching black bow, looked to me as if she was carrying a musical instrument to a city symphony rather than a gun to a remote tundra tent camp.

Linda, diminutive, grey-haired and in jeans, was making last-minute checks of her luggage. To my astonishment, her suitcases contained popcorn, candy, nuts, chips, crackers, beef jerky, packaged pizzas, Scotch, several liqueurs, various cold and sore throat remedies, a hot water bottle, two pillows, four kinds of footwear, a musical alarm clock, battery-operated video games, even a reading light on a stand. "Everything the well-prepared hunter needs, right?" she grinned. Linda was the teaser of the two but we were all to benefit from her stash when we got to camp.

The two women had taken up sport hunting seriously after the loss of their husbands. Charlotte wanted to hunt with her grownup children to keep doing things as a family, and Linda wanted to prove she could face challenges on her own. The younger set introduced them and they teamed up.

"But when we decided on a trip to the wilds of northern Canada, the kids thought we'd gone too far. Baffin Island seemed like the end of the world," laughed Charlotte. "I'd hunted a lot in Africa so I wanted to experience cold." She added hastily, "But not extreme cold, so I chose a caribou hunt not a polar bear hunt."

More than that, it was an experimental caribou hunt. Usually, sport hunters head to mainland Canada to hunt large herds of barren-ground caribou during their fall migration south to the treeline. On Baffin Island we were breaking trail, hunting small groups of non-migratory animals that remain on the tundra.

"We don't need big herds, just consistently big bulls," said Jerome, a wildlife biologist as well as an outfitter. Jerome hoped to find them in a new hunting location near Kimmirut (Lake Harbour), a small picturesque Inuit community a hundred miles south of Iqaluit. If our experimental week was successful, he would set up a semi-permanent tent-frame camp and bring in guests on a regular basis.

We were the first organized group of tourists to come to Kimmirut, the first clients of the local Hunters' and Trappers' Association. The natives saw hunting as good business to bring dollars to the local economy in a way that suited their lifestyle. And sharing the native lifestyle was seen by all of us as the unique experience of the trip.

It was the last week of August. Our guides were waiting for us in the hamlet's truck parked beside the runway when our Bradley Air charter landed. Quiet, meticulous Padluq in his Greek fisherman's cap, twinkling-eyed Pitseolak ("My friends call me the Pits"), his young brother, the ever-helpful Eyesiak, and an older man, Bee, the hamlet mechanic who brought his family along (wife Katie and children Mailia, Jenny, and baby Joanassie). Katie was delighted to see three women in the group ("I thought I'd be the only one," she smiled shyly).

After a quick visit to the Renewable Resources office to buy twenty-five-dollar caribou tags and to the Co-op store for soft drinks (alcohol is prohibited in this dry community although it is allowed in camp), we bundled up in layers of our warmest clothing and clambered aboard the guides' three boats for the hour-and-a-half ride to camp. Each boat towed a freighter canoe for ferrying us between boat and shore at low tide.

As we twisted through a patchwork of islands along the convoluted coastline, all were on the lookout for caribou. "They calve inland," said Jerome, "but the bulls should be by the water or high on ridges to escape irritating warble flies."

Ironically, we stopped to shoot—not a caribou but an iceberg. Pits and Eyesiak knocked off a block of fresh ice to make tea. Stopping for tea and bannock was to become a regular daily ritual.

Our arrival at camp was pure magic. The sun setting behind white *iglu*-shaped canvas tents on a protected headland turned the sky and sea a fiery orange. The air was full of bird song as loons whickered and gulls from an adjacent cliff colony wheeled and screamed around us. A bull caribou with an immense rack stood silhouetted on the skyline above camp—a good omen for the next day's hunting.

"This place is called *Kunikbiq*, the Place Where Two Men Kissed for Nothing," Pits said in the cook tent during a hastily prepared supper. Inuit are characteristically shy and speak in soft lilting tones, but that comment got him our immediate attention. "Two Inuit came to hunt here and saw two big male caribou. They were so happy they kissed each other but they missed the caribou so they kissed for nothing." We laughed. Such easy exchanges between guides and clients are not common in native hunting camps—at least not so early in the trip—but it was a mark of our instant camaraderie.

Ours was not a plush camp. Temperatures hovered at freezing point; we washed in tidal pools; we slept on the ground on foamies; and that first night we had no source of heat. But we were a jolly and adaptable lot, especially the irrepressible Linda. "How long does it take for your body to rot?" she quipped, thinking of a week without bathing.

Both women were used to more civilized safaris. Linda had hunted stags with jaeger meisters from blinds on royal estates in Europe. Charlotte had stayed in four-star hotels while hunting ibex in Turkey. But here in a tent on the rocks in Canada's Barren Grounds, they were game for anything. "Except next time I hope I'm not parked beside a bird sanctuary," joked Linda, who preferred the music of an alarm clock to the music of nature.

"Now don't take your trophy the first day and be bored for the rest of the week," warned Jerome as we divided ourselves between the boats next morning. "There should be plenty of caribou."

After what the Inuit said had been weeks of cold rainy weather ("We haven't been swimming all summer"), our first day of the hunt was glorious, unexpectedly warm on the land although chilly on the water. Our boats were the open Lake Winnipeg type, but you could always huddle amongst the gear in the forward cabin to be out of the wind. Weather changes rapidly in the North so we were like chameleons, constantly adding and subtracting layers of clothing. "Be prepared to be cold, wet, and hot all in the same hour," warned Jerome.

We marvelled at the Inuit, who stood at the tiller in jeans, down jackets, and baseball caps. Once or twice they stopped to hunt seals. "Seal meat is rich in blood," said Padluq, "Seal meat keeps you warm." The Inuit eat ringed and bearded seals, but the men couldn't explain why they don't eat harp seal meat, the third common seal species of the area.

Shooting seals has a low success rate. You stand, gun in hand, in a slowly circling boat scanning a grey and glassy sea waiting for the round head of the seal to break the surface. Most times before you can fire, the bump has sunk silently out of sight. Your only hope is to chance on the target accidentally or patiently circle till the dives

144

are shorter and you have worn the animal out. After dozens of shots, Pits finally got a small pup of the year. I could well understand why the Inuit do most of their hunting for seal (and caribou) on the ice. As they told us, skidoos get them to their hunting grounds more conveniently than boats do.

Interesting to me as a naturalist were two sightings of something in the water that no-one could identify. It seemed to be swimming on its side making undulating stroking movements. "Don't shoot," said Pits quickly. It was too small to be a whale, too big for a fish. I could think of nothing else it could be but a river otter or a sea otter. If so, it was way out of range.

Later in the day, we spotted a polar bear eating something on the beach. We were all agape at its size and nobody asked to go closer for a second look. Glassing seals, seabirds, and polar bears while threading through the passages between Big Island and Baffin Island was an adventure in itself. But caribou were our main concern.

Collectively, we saw between ten and thirty caribou a day, mostly young bulls. There were enough for us to be selective. Some were seen and shot easily from the shore; some popped up unexpectedly from behind boulders; others were spotted as dots in the distance and required three, four, and five-mile stalks up hills, along talus slopes, around lakes and over rugged, rocky ground that reminded us of minefields. The terrain tested our stamina and the quality of our boots, but it was wide open and the air was clear. "It's the kind of country," said Chet, "that makes you feel insignificant but glad to be alive."

You're always looking down while walking on tundra, adapting your steps to ever-changing rocks, boulder piles, hummocks of moss and grass, sloughs of water and mud. Thawing of the permafrost is brief in an arctic summer and ground water is never far away.

Caribou are drawn to grassy lichen-rich meadows in sheltered valleys and the ends of fiords, or windswept gravel eskers where they can dodge the bugs. Despite their colour camouflage, we saw caribou quite easily while scoping such open terrain. Judging their distance was more difficult. For most hunters, targets on the tundra appear closer than they really are.

The other women and I groaned whenever Jerome pointed to a bull several ridges away on the far horizon and suggested we follow it, but I always found we got there quicker than anticipated, probably because there was always something interesting to see on the way—gaggles of geese, old graves and outpost camps, emergency rock shelters, *inukshuit* (rock cairns to mark travel paths or hunting decoys), a lake or two with landlocked char, plants that elicited comments from the Inuit like Pits telling us that rubbing puffballs healed wounds. As Angelo said, "This Canada's a damn interesting place. It looks simple but you are always running into the unusual."

Once they knew we were interested, the Inuit would always stop to point things out. We were lucky to have guides who were born in outpost camps and still enjoyed living a traditional life. "My grandfather teached me how to hunt and how to read the sky and water," Eyesiak told me. "He died at sixty-one, he was very old. I miss him."

A bonus for the hunters was ambushing additional caribou en route. Charlotte was lucky enough to get her first trophy close to shore with a well-placed shoulder shot at a hundred yards from behind a big boulder at the beach. "A beautiful animal," she said in satisfaction when she came off "automatic pilot" and turned around for a posed picture with Pits. Her smile was almost as wide as the trophy, six inches around the main beam.

Linda got her bull within moments of Charlotte, but she lamented the fact that it took more than one shot to put the animal down. Soft-hearted Linda ate no wild meat and said she didn't care if she took a trophy home or not. My stereotypes were being attacked daily.

Charlotte was eager to stalk a second caribou. The Inuit radioed Kimmirut for Robert, the Renewable Resources officer, to come to camp immediately to sell Charlotte a second tag.

She waited till the last day. But this was no easy hunt like her first. Striving for a better rack, she turned down one bull after another. Then, after a five-mile stalk and a slug up a cliff by Cowboy Hat Mountain, "sucking air till my body screamed," she eventually got her trophy.

"I had my sights on another bull with a bigger rack but when this one appeared out of nowhere behind a rock, I decided to take it because I preferred the palmate shape of its antlers," she said when the rest of our party puffed up to her. The men were impressed by her endurance.

After a patient three-mile stalk, Steve shot a promising bull, but Pits took a quick look at the animal's swollen leg joints, loose hair, black bumps, and glazed, jelly-like eyes and would not put his knife into it. It had brucellosis, a disease that according to local reports appears in "half a dozen animals out of hundreds." With Baffin's caribou population apparently on the increase, hunting is encouraged as one way of culling numbers and curtailing disease. We left Steve's animal for Robert to investigate.

Caribou might have been the focus of our week but for the Inuit it is the focus of their lives. We ate little else. In the field, the guides were quick to snack on pieces of raw liver or hack out fat which they sometimes dipped into the stomach contents. Back at camp, Steve, our gourmet cook, prepared the usual roasts, steaks, and stews, but he also cooked liver, heart, kidneys, and highly popular tongue. Like the Inuit, we wasted nothing.

Well, almost nothing. We did not consume much of what the Inuit relished most—raw eyeballs, tundra oysters (testicles), the fat that lines the eye sockets, or "blue cheese" alias the semi-digested contents of caribou stomach mixed with cubes of fat, put back into the bag formed from the stomach lining and left to ripen overnight. Steve and I tasted such delicacies but I can't say I liked them.

Linda kept to her snack food. "I'm not adventurous," she'd protest.

"Not adventurous?" the men retorted. "Then what are you doing here?"

"When are you going to hunt, Lyn?" asked Eyesiak matter-of-factly.

"Me?" I blurted out in surprise. I had spent my days slugging over the tundra with the hunters but staying in the background to protect their shot whenever they came close to caribou. I had no intention of hunting myself. Up till this trip, I had a stereotyped image of trophy hunters—high rollers who flash into camp one day, put a bullet into the biggest head they can find, and flash out again. But Eyesiak was serious. He expected me to shoot—and not just with a camera.

"I'll lend you my gun," offered Charlotte.

"Mine's lighter," suggested Steve.

There didn't seem any honourable way out. It was hypocritical to slam hunting and then eat meat that had been killed for me. I was a northerner and it made sense to supplement my fly-in, store-bought meat with meat from the land. And, I argued further, I could use the antlers as a Christmas tree and the hide for a blanket, perhaps even a leather dress if I learned how to tan. That would mean lugging everything—meat, hide, and antlers—clear across Canada, but like my Inuit companions, I would show respect to the animal by using every part of it.

Still, I hesitated. Killing was a new concept. I didn't understand my hunting friends when they looked down at every animal they shot and said, "Beautiful!" How could they say that when they'd just killed all that beauty? Steve and Angelo confessed that all hunters have such conflicting feelings.

I had learned a great deal that week about hunters. They cared a lot more for the animals and the land than I expected. For the Inuit, hunting was survival even in these days of settlement living. For the *qallunaat*, hunting was the experience and challenge of being out on the land, sharing a simpler lifestyle than what they'd left behind in the South. Perhaps hunting answered a call from their primeval roots.

I shrugged. With no hunting experience except for a parrot I shot in my uncle's orchard thirty years previously, I would probably miss.

My companions gathered enthusiastically to advise and watch me practise on the beach behind camp. Surprisingly, I remembered everybody's instructions. As the sand flew up around each target, Steve said approvingly, "If that was a caribou, it'd be dead instantly." "Good!" echoed Eyesiak. "Very good!" smiled Pits. Three hours later, we were in the boats scouting for real caribou.

High granite cliffs closed around us as we entered the fiord. As I looked up at the near perpendicular sides and the loose rubble, I groaned at the thought of having to scale the steep slopes. I prayed my guides didn't find caribou there.

Suddenly, Eyesiak in the boat ahead cut the motor and pointed four hundred feet up the cliff to a patch of ice in a shaded gully. A bull caribou looked down nonchalantly. With its back against the overhanging rock wall, the animal probably thought itself safe in its high domain and was pleased to use the ice to escape warble flies.

"Do you want him, Lyn?" asked Steve, looking through his binoculars. "He's got a fair-sized rack, long even beams, palmated on top and a double shovel. Not a bad trophy. Anyway, you're more interested in the meat."

I didn't want to tell my hunting buddies that I was scared of heights, of shooting into the sun, of losing face if I missed. It was too late for excuses. Padluq, my guide for the day, nosed our boat into shore and we started sneaking around the side of the fiord to get downwind of our quarry. Padluq led the way. Steve carried his gun for me. Tom carried my tripod and camera. All I had to do was to stay calm and concentrate on getting into the right position to fire a clean shot. I didn't want to make that caribou suffer.

I was thinking more of taking shots with my camera than a gun. All kinds of good pictures were passing me by—pincushion mats of moss campion, patches of purple saxifrage, lacy patterns of lichens on rock—and when I dared to look away from my boots, gleaming white icebergs sailing down the middle of a turquoise sea.

It was that magic time again when the late afternoon sun gilds the rocks bronze and the landscape is bathed in warm wonderful light. The bull was still hidden from us behind a fold in the hill. I had to hurry before the sun disappeared over the top of the gully and the animal grazed in shade. I needed good light for both my gun and my camera.

Padluq whispered, "Lean down here." Guiltily, I interrupted my wish list for pictures and lay down on the slope. "Take your yellow hat off," cautioned Steve as he folded my vest to cushion the gun. "Okay, Lyn, he's all yours. Be calm."

Surprisingly, I was calm. I was on automatic pilot, just like Charlotte said. I had a job to do. I could have been aiming darts at a dart board. But I wasn't. I was aiming a gun uphill into the sun at something live and moving. Black tunnels and sun spots kept melding in my scope, causing the target to go in and out of focus.

"Pull back from the eyepiece," whispered Steve. "You'll see more clearly."

I did, and for one instant, the caribou stood broadside, clear in the crosshairs, a perfect shot. I breathed in, exhaled halfway out, just as I was told, and aimed for the front shoulder. But before I could squeeze the trigger, the caribou turned to face me and I shot it in the neck, just missing the vital area.

"Fire again," said Steve swiftly, before I could lose my resolve. "Hold high on an uphill shot, otherwise the bullet'll be too low."

After the second shot, the animal dropped to his knees and rolled down the snowbank towards the boat. "Won't have to carry the meat so far," said Steve with a grin.

"You're a hunter," said Padluq with a rare smile as he and Steve loaded everything into the boat.

No, I thought wryly, I'm a photographer. It was 9:00 P.M. and still bright, but the sun had sunk below the fiord slopes and I was thinking of all those pictures it was taking with it.

NOTE

No, I wasn't a hunter, but I did take care of what I hunted. I didn't perform any traditional rituals, pray to animal spirits, or thank the Creator for sending food, as aboriginals do. But I respected the animal in my own way and tried to use it wisely.

This was quite an undertaking. First, I had to process, separate, and package the hide, meat, and antlers. Then, because I was determined to waste nothing, I had to lug the entire animal home. This meant crossing Canada from Lake Harbour in the east to Iqaluit, Ottawa, Yellowknife, and Fort Simpson in the west. The doorman of a downtown hotel in Ottawa was intrigued when I entered the lobby carrying a full set of antlers. Fortunately, airline clerks allowed me to leave my bags containing the meat and the hide in the airport freezer.

Back in my old trailer in the bush at Fort Simpson, I freezer-wrapped the meat, let the antlers bleach by the door, and stretched the hide on a frame. A Dene woman friend taught me how to scrape and tan. My intention was to turn the hide into a leather wedding dress the following summer, but unfortunately the village dogs ate it instead.

At the subsequent two weddings, one for northern friends in Fort Simpson and the other for southern friends on Vancouver Island, I burned the too-fast-thawed caribou stew and few of the guests would eat it, despite my hurried explanation that the taste of Baffin Island caribou was unique. I tried currying the cooked meat to disguise its scorched origins, but my husband still guessed, so I finished up eating almost the entire caribou myself.

The antlers still sit by the door, and I haven't hunted since.

I'll Do Anything But Fish

THE DC-3 THUNDERED ONTO THE GRAVEL AIRSTRIP at Bathurst
Inlet Lodge and rolled to a stop in front of us as we waited to board
our flight home. The doors swung open and a man hollered, "Which
one of you is Lyn Hancock?"

Startled, I stepped forward as he descended the ladder, fishing
rods in hand. "So you're the famous fisherwoman of the North," he
began.

I cringed.

"I heard you were here. I chose this place because of a story of
yours I read back in New York. Where do you think I should fish next
year?"

I was embarrassed. He had read the story of catching my first
fish. It was an accident. Most of my catches are accidents. I don't
even like fishing; in fact, I am terrified of fish. I don't mind mice,
snakes, or spiders. I can take seals, eagles, cougars, and apes in my
stride—and even in my sleeping bag, parka, rubber boat, and hatbox. But it took me six months of grim determination before I could
handle slimy, quivering, goggly-eyed cod. And that was only because
I had to feed it to my pet seal.

151

For me, fishing is a way to get me to places where often the last thing I want to do is fish.

I did not fly to Bathurst Inlet Lodge for the fishing, though some people do. I was intent on more exciting pursuits such as trudging the tundra to film muskox and caribou, climbing the cliffs to watch peregrine falcons, flying the barrenlands to photograph waterfalls.

But one day, on a trip to a creek south of the lodge, my companions—Troy, aged seven, Robbie, aged nine, and Tim, aged eleven—insisted on fishing. They had come north to fish and that was what they were going to do. Their guides were nineteen-year-old Sam Kapolak, an Inuk, and Boyd Warner, the fifteen-year old son of the lodge owner. Along for the ride were Troy's father, George Gibson, a doctor from Yellowknife; Robbie and Tim's grandmother, Nancy Stride from Toronto; Roger, a ski-trip director from Vermont; and me from British Columbia.

Sam and Boyd dropped us off where Fishing Creek entered the inlet. In the lightened boat they negotiated the fast-moving, shallow waters of the river while we meandered to the lake to meet them by the inland route. The boys' rods were in the water almost as soon as they reached their guides.

9:58 A.M.: "Okay, you kids," I said, slinging cameras and binoculars around my neck. "We oldies'll look for wolves and muskox wool while you fish." And to the guides, "What time will we be ba—?"

10:00 A.M.: A scream rent the air. "I've got one!" Before Sam could get to the boat for a landing net, little Troy had managed to land a fish almost as long as he was—a ten-pound lake trout. Dr. George told me later that his son, a veteran of northern fishing trips, was probably the only kindergartener to take a ten-pound arctic char to Show and Tell.

I dived for my camera and, acting like a Hollywood movie director, started shouting instructions. "George, I want to take a picture." Always cooperative, George looked up and grinned cheerfully. "George, not you, I want a picture of your son. Troy, push the cap away from your face. And don't look so pained. It can't be that heavy."

Poor kid, there was no time to click the shutter.

10:01 A.M.: "Robbie's got one!" Nancy yelled. "And it's big."

Everybody rushed to the water. There was Robbie reeling in a

I have winged my way many times to Bathurst Inlet Lodge, one of my favourite stops in the Arctic, and the last place in the North where you can see traditional buildings still in use as a community—the red and white Hudson's Bay Company trading post, the Oblate Missionary Church, and the *iglu*-shaped houses of Inuit who have never abandoned the land for settlement living.

Eric Itoriligak harpoons a seal from an ice floe in Foxe Basin while I mind the boat.

Agnes and Fred Carpenter in Sachs Harbour enjoy my agony in eating *okshuk,* alias rancid seal oil, a highly popular Inuvialuit accompaniment to dry meat. I must admit I have tasted better condiments in my life.

On the street in Hall Beach. Some things are easier for Inuit today. Mrs. Itoriligak uses a sewing machine to repair her tent before returning to her outpost camp in Foxe Basin.

Flat stones piled on top of each other are called *inukshuit* by the Inuit. They build them as beacons, to mark trails, or to decoy caribou. *Inukshuk* means "like a person," although not all *inuk-shuit* resemble people.

George Pratt and Phillip Pitseulak pull carefully on the ropes as Polar Bear rises from the marble of Andrew Gordon Bay.

Carving camp on an idyllic day in Markham Bay.

Annie Michael poses with one of her carvings in the tent we share at soapstone camp on Markham Bay.

Ivy exchanges European culture for Dene culture under Muriel Betsina's moose-drying racks at a traditional camp near Yellowknife.

Winging it to the peace and stillness of the northern wilderness near Little Doctor Lake.

There are no greens or golf clubs on courses at Lake Hazen on Ellesmere Island.

Arctic foxes are frequent visitors to the Astrolab at Eureka on Ellesmere Island where scientists come from around the world to study the atmosphere.

A Twin Otter lands Marek and Wojtek on the frozen Arctic Ocean while a TV film crew records the beginning of their historic trek to the North Pole. I wonder if the cameramen's fingers were frozen to their cameras, too!

My last shot before my fingers froze and my glasses fogged was of two lonely figures pulling for the Pole.

This is my idea of an Arctic Heaven—paddling through the ice floes of Foxe Basin on an idyllic day to look for walrus and polar bears.

When a polar bear suddenly pops its head up from behind an ice floe and stares straight at you, then that's the time for winging it—away.

second lake trout—all twelve pounds of it. "Come and get in the picture," I shouted, ecstatic about two big fish. Sammy grabbed Troy's fish, Boyd grabbed Robbie's fish, and I composed a photo of two little kids struggling to lift their prizes onto a handy set of caribou antlers.

There was no time to focus.

10:02 A.M.: "Tim's got one!" his grandmother called. "And it's even bigger." We turned to look, and there was Nancy's second grand-child straining against what turned out to be a fourteen-pound lake trout.

I could hardly believe it. Three young boys, seven, nine, and eleven years old, with three fish—ten-, twelve-, and fourteen-pound-ers! Staggering under the weight of their fish and spurning the help of their guides, the three youngsters lined up for my camera.

10:03 A.M.: I was focussing when George yelled, "I've got one too!"

The kids dropped their trophies to run to the shoreline and offer verbal support. "Come on, Dad, you can do it!" Troy encouraged.

"Easy, Dr. Gibson, don't reel it in too hard," Tim chimed in.

"Keep your rod tip high," Robbie suggested. The rod tip was high, forming a very tight arc. Crack! The rod snapped under the pressure and the fish swam free.

10:04 A.M.: There was no time for commiseration. Roger had made an ideal cast and was now fighting a ten-pounder. He landed it and decided, "I don't need it; let's put it back." Dr. Gibson gently worked the hook free, moved the fish back and forth to force water over its gills, and we watched it swim away.

"Your turn, Lyn," Boyd said, pushing his rod at me.

"Me! I can't fish. I don't even like fish. I'm scared of them." I fought back childhood memories of squeezing myself deep into the bow to avoid the slithering, flopping piles of snapper my father insisted on bringing into the dinghy. Of running down the street in terror away from gleeful neighbourhood kids chasing me with slimy mackerel. Of forcing myself to axe off those cod heads. I had come to the Arctic for animals, and that didn't include fish. I was trapped. "I don't know what to do," I protested.

"I'll show you," said Boyd. "It's easy."

"Okay," I agreed reluctantly, "but just one cast."

Boyd told me what to do, and with beginner's luck, I flipped the lure out into the river. I started reeling it in. One cast would be enough to show the kids I was a good sport.

"Faster," ordered Troy, the seven-year-old.

I obliged—all the sooner to go birdwatching. "Oh, it's hit bottom. There see what I've done. I've caught the bottom."

"No, you've got a fish," shouted Robbie, the nine-year-old.

"Don't be silly," I answered, sensing a thrill of fear. "It must be an old boot." In these pristine waters?

"No! It's a char!" yelled Tim, the eleven-year-old. A sliver of pink and green knifed the water. "Hold onto it! Don't lose it!"

Suddenly, there were no more awful, fishy memories. I wanted only to hang onto the moment—and the fish. "Nancy! Grab the camera. Take a picture."

The line was heavy with fish; it stopped coming in. I dug in my heels. "Keep winding," commanded Boyd, as Sammy, a smile on his face, stood by with the landing net.

"I can't turn it!" I moaned, enclosing all of the reel's bale in my hand and desperately trying to inch the line around the spool. The pressure was terrific. "It's going to break the rod."

"Keep it high!" That was Dr. George.

"Nancy! Haven't you got a picture yet?" I pleaded, trying to turn to see if she had located my camera among the lake trout, caribou antlers, hiking gear, and other equipment scattered around her feet.

"Which camera?" she asked gallantly.

"Use both of them, the colour and the black and white,"

"Here Roger," Nancy commanded, passing the buck and the camera to him, "you take them. I'm only used to instamatics."

Later Roger was to say I was totally out of control. Nancy was sorting cameras and lenses. Roger and George were clicking shutters as cameras were handed to them. Boyd continued patiently instructing me on how to bring in the fish. And Sammy? Sammy waited quietly, probably quelling internal hysterics at the antics of white people.

The kids pranced up and down, more excited about my fish than their own. And I was straining backwards in an agonizing position with the end of the rod pointing back into the air behind my back.

The char was heavy and fighting strong. I dug in my heels and tried to pull the rod around so I could wedge the butt-end against my chest and take some of the strain off my aching fingers. I felt that at any moment I would lose the rod, the char, and my new-found interest in fishing.

"Have you got a picture?" I yelled at the patient photographers.

"A picture?" Roger yelled. "We've got twenty of them; how many more do you want?"

They say that after I stopped swearing to the entire heavenly family, I babbled: "The rod's going to break. I can't keep it high. It's going. I can't move the bale. It's fixed. The fish's fixed it. The char's still there? My father won't believe this. He came to Canada and said there were no fish. He didn't get one."

"You're not going to either, if you keep your eyes on us," my audience hollered. "Keep your eyes on the fish."

Then at last the reel ran free, and I could wind again. It kept on winding and the ripple far out in the water soon surged into a wave at my feet. Sammy scooped up for my close inspection a sixteen-pound arctic char. My first cast and my first fish—ever!

My Inuit friends carefully wrapped the fish in plastic and heavy cardboard and tied the package with rope so I could carry it on the plane. It did look a bit like a rifle when I boarded the jet to fly south from Yellowknife, but the flight attendants were kind; they kept it in the galley when I found it wouldn't fit under my seat.

I mean, surely they didn't expect my first fish to be that small?

✳

I gatecrashed my next fishing trip. When our Twin Otter left Pond Inlet that afternoon on the flight over the awesome scenery of Baffin Island, I had the feeling that none of the men aboard knew why I was there. They must have been wondering where this woman was going with her huge packsack, bulky cameras, and necklace of pens and notebooks. She was certainly not carrying a fishing rod.

Ironically, each of the two parties aboard thought I belonged to the other one. The nine fishermen thought I was a Greenpeacer, reporter, or scientist going to the secret narwhal research camp at Milne Inlet, and the whale researchers thought I was an angler bound for Koluktoo Bay.

The researchers were much relieved and the fishermen much perplexed when the mystery woman alighted from the plane in Koluktoo Bay. I had taken a chance on wangling a last minute seat (number 13) aboard a Twin Otter chartered by a bunch of city businessmen for their annual "get away from home and office" fishing trip. Happily for me, I couldn't have lucked in on more compatible companions. After the initial shock when I identified myself as a tagalong photojournalist, they insisted I sleep in one of the official tent cabins, not my pup tent.

"You'll probably show us up and catch all the fish," groaned Ian, who'd arranged the charter.

"Don't bet on it," I said modestly and meant it. I didn't care about the fishing; I just wanted to see the scenery.

There's nothing fancy about the Toonoonik Sahoonik Co-op tent camp at Koluktoo Bay, seventy miles west of Pond Inlet, but its setting of snow-packed peaks and towering fiords is spectacular and its camp manager memorable.

Oscar, looking like an oldtime trapper with his grizzled beard, gravelly voice, and bright eyes, welcomed us into his tiny kitchen and regaled us with stories of camp life. His rules were clearly stated on the cabin walls.

> Welcome to the Canadian North. Please enjoy your-
> self. This is Arctic Living. The Ritz is down the street.
> If you have problems adapting to our way of life here,
> please confer with the mirror in the washroom. It will
> most likely be a great help in solving your problems.

"It's either a feast or famine here," Oscar warned as we sat down in front of a huge pile of steaks. "Our radio communication is not always what it should be. One year we ordered eggs but too many came—ninety dozen—so the boys started writing to each other on egg shells. Another year we got too many pancakes but no eggs or syrup. Then too much lettuce but no mayonnaise."

My companions went to their bunks that night hoping to cope with such problems as too many fish.

Next morning, the sun had me up before 5:00 to photograph impeccable reflections in tundra pools. No need for longjohns. I greeted the dawn in a sundress. Tom came by in shorts with a pre-breakfast drink of champagne and orange juice. John Junior joined us with gin and grapefruit. Everybody was up early, impatient to start fishing.

"There's no use in going upriver now," Oscar said in fatherly tones as we all helped to get breakfast. "Go up at the wrong tide and you'll come home cold, with no fish, and disappointed. Go up at the right tide and you'll come home cold but with lots of fish and ecstatic. Wait for high tide at 11:00 o'clock and you can go up in the boats."

There's only one place you need to go fishing at Koluktoo Bay and that's the Robertson River, 2½ miles and a short boat ride (at high tide) from camp. It must be the loveliest fishing hole in the Arctic. A ribbon of clear green water perhaps fifty yards wide surges through rapids to a low waterfall between layers of pancake-like rocks that make handy steps and stairs for convenient angling. The layered rocks are splayed with yellow willow branches, encrusted with orange lichen, and whitewashed with gull droppings. Behind, the tundra rises almost imperceptibly and then abruptly to 900-foot hills on the skyline.

The Inuit chose wisely too. The sunken pits of their semi-subterranean houses, filled with whalebone once used as rafters, line the banks along the river. Farther away, a lone white skull delineating a human grave sits on a sandy mound.

But the fishermen weren't interested in rocks. Their eyes were on the water and their hands on their rods as soon as our Inuit guides, Elizirie and Matthisie, let us out of the boats. The guides hardly had time to dump the lunch boxes on shore when Ron hollered, "I've got one!" Matthisie grabbed the landing net, ran down the rock steps, scooped up a white-bellied char ("They'll be red when they spawn in the lake"), whipped out a scale to weigh it in at seven pounds, (too small to keep when much larger ones lurked), and threw the char back in the water.

And so it continued for hours. Ron, Gerry, Allan, John Senior, and Tom on one side of the river; Ed, Doug, Ian, and John Junior on the other side; Matthisie and Elizirie in boats in the middle of the river, ready to disentangle lines and lures or dash to the side with their landing nets when a fish was caught.

I wanted to go fishing with the boys, but I didn't want to fish—at least I didn't want to catch one. Both Johns and Ian hospitably loaned me their lines, and I tried to look suitably thankful, but I also tried to look busy with my cameras. Fortunately, Matthisie saved me from fishing by saying in no uncertain terms, "You cook!" and then leading me peremptorily to the Coleman stove. This was one time I didn't mind playing the stereotypical female role.

Matthisie sat by my side expertly gutting the "keepers," slicing off the skin as if it was paper, and cutting up fillets into chunks. I watched, mesmerized, when he threw out a heart and it lay on the bare rock still pumping away after I'd cooked the rest of its body.

Lacking cookbooks, lemon, flour, and other trimmings, I just served thick slabs of char, fried in butter on the Coleman, slab after slab after slab, rich, juicy, and bright luscious red—redder than other char, I was told, because of the colourful rock surroundings. I hoped it wasn't due to my inexperience as a shoreside chef, but the fishermen had difficulty leaving their lines to eat.

I like to think it was because the char were so abundant. Gerry threw back thirty char by lunch. He and Ian on opposite sides of the river hooked into one char at the same time. For a while there was an exciting tug-of-war, and we all stopped what we were doing to watch. First Gerry reeled it to his side and removed his lure, then Ian did the same thing on his side. Within seconds, Gerry had caught the fish again and landed it.

By the time we left on the tide, each side had caught about forty char, averaging about nine pounds each in weight. ("Add four or five pounds to that because of fighting them in fast water," said Gerry.) Although the boys could have kept four fish a day, they were allowed only seven overall when they left, so with such abundance, there was no need to take any back to camp. We had a week to go.

I sneaked a look outside next morning—August 23—to see the surrounding mountains covered with the first snowfall of the season. No sundress or shorts today. And no boat to take us upriver. We decided to walk. A vicious north wind blew us sideways into the river as we trudged upstream. The yellow hills were now whitened with snow and migratory snow geese, reminding us that winter was coming. The char would soon be spawning under ice. We decided to catch—and keep—some today.

Yes, we—I—would fish too. I was bored with cooking, and probably not needed. There was a rumour in camp that the boys had asked Oscar for Cheez Whiz sandwiches instead of char. So it seemed a good day to sneak away to a private spot along the river and hope nobody would notice my clumsy efforts at fishing. I dared to hope that nothing would come to my lure.

My first casts were quite respectable. My line went as far upstream and as far across as everybody else's. I reeled it in, trying to emulate a wounded fish, a trick I'd picked up from my companions. Meanwhile, the others were reeling fish in as soon as their lines hit the water. Gerry went by. "Start with your lure closer to the end of the rod," he suggested in passing.

I did—and immediately got a char. It ran, first one way, then the other. I reeled it toward me, kept the tension, and watched nervously as it slurped up the rocks. Gerry came along with a net. "Want to keep it?" he said matter-of-factly. "No, throw it back," I replied. "Sassy," commented Tom with a grin.

Well, that wasn't too bad. I looked at the others and noted their different styles. Gerry started reeling in slowly, then stopped abruptly, alternating speeds. Doug snapped the rod jerkily side to side. John Senior cast casually over his head. Ron wore yellow filters on his glasses to see the fish more clearly, more deeply.

I cast again, letting the line drop deep in the fast water so it didn't bounce on the waves. I felt the pull. "A fish," I announced casually, my heart pounding. The line went taut. It must be a big one. All the fishermen on my side of the river wandered over to watch the action of the cook/photographer turned fisherwoman. Now, Lyn, keep your cool, be blasé, and they'll never notice this is only the third fish you've ever caught. Unfortunately, my public announcement came at the wrong time.

"Have you really got a fish or is it Baffin Island?" John asked with a sly chuckle. The truth dawned. I'd lost the lure and leader he'd loaned me, besides. "He can afford it," Doug laughed.

On the next cast I knew I'd got a char—a big one. The others noticed too. They hurried over again and gave advice. With this audience and my previous *faux pas*, I might as well blow my cover. "I've never really fished much before," I confessed. "I need all the advice I can get."

My companions responded with alacrity. "Tits up," said somebody. "He means keep your rod up," said somebody else.

"That's difficult, it's too heavy," I joshed back, beginning to like this fishing, especially when Matthisie was standing by with the net. At least my crew wouldn't see me in a blue funk if I felt the fish wiggle.

"She does have a big one, a fighter," said Allan, impressed. "Move along the rocks downstream, go down to where Gerry is," said Doug solicitously.

"Just get the cameras and take pictures, will you?" I said earnestly as I followed his instructions. The char was taking me closer to the edge. Tentatively, I took a step down to the next level. The fish pulled away. My next step was water.

"Don't fall in," said Ian. And don't lose his rod, I said to myself. "Grip the rod higher, to the cork," said one of the Johns. I changed my grip very carefully. I did not want to lose this fish. I bent lower to the water. So did Doug with my camera. So did Matthisie with the net. I felt that the hook was set, but with all this attention I couldn't take chances. The char was fighting strongly. I pulled the rod into my thighs, reeled in the fish, tits up as they said, and landed the char at my feet.

"Very good," Tom said admiringly. "You look as if you know what you're doing."

"You've been fishing before—a lot," said Ian accusingly, but with a grin.

I smiled enigmatically. He was wrong but I argued no more. Perhaps I should keep them guessing.

❋

You really have to be creative to avoid fishing in northern wilderness waters. The next time somebody suddenly invited me to go fishing, I decided to be up-front from the start and tell my hosts that I was interested in catching other things rather than fish.

"Lyn Hancock! What are you doing here?"

The voice in the truck behind me as I hiked down the main street of Cambridge Bay belonged to Don Hamilton, owner of the world's most northerly fishing lodge, High Arctic Lodge on Victoria Island. Don is a bluff, genial man with a keen sense of humour. He is also a stickler for precision who has had fifty years' experience flying bush planes in some of the most dangerous conditions on earth. He combines his passion for planes and his love of the northern outdoors by flying fishermen into remote areas.

Don has a permanent camp at Merkley Bay. He chose the lake because when it was test-netted, the fish were so big—thirty-pound lakers on the average—they tore the nets. He also rotates his guests by plane to several outpost camps on other parts of Victoria Island. I knew there would be no way I could avoid fish on Victoria Island. But I hoped to find other attractions.

As if reading my mind, Don continued persuasively. "I've seen lots of muskox on Victoria Island this year. One group is stuck on an island opposite the lodge. They got stranded when the ice went out and now they can't swim off. Arctic foxes are denning near some of the outpost camps. Why don't you come to Merkley with me this afternoon when I fly in with the groceries?"

"Sounds great, Don. I'd like to get some good wildlife photos. Mind you, I've just come off a cruise ship through the Northwest Passage, and I'm supposed to be getting a plane back to Simpson tomorrow. But—"

It didn't take much to persuade me to change my plans. After a few quick phone calls and a re-sorting of my pack, I was soon buckled into Don's Cessna 206 and on my way to High Arctic Lodge, eighty-six miles north of Cambridge Bay.

As well as pointing out caribou and muskox, Don kept up a running commentary on where the fish were, how to catch them, and which were trophy-sized. Most of his clients welcome such information. I was devising strategies to avoid fishing altogether.

I knew I couldn't keep my phobia secret for long when Don's smiling wife, Marlene, showed me my lakefront cabin. Lunkers were thumping so audibly along the edge of Merkley Lake they kept me awake. As the ice around the edge of the lakes broke off in the thaw, fish cruised by with their mouths open, scooping up shrimp and insects that lived in the ice or on bits of vegetation blown there from the tundra.

"Why don't you do the fishing and I'll take the photographs," I suggested breezily to my two guides. Kevin was in his early twenties but a veteran of several fishing seasons at High Arctic Lodge. Bobby was a teenaged Inuit trainee. Normally, guides are not allowed to fish when they're guiding guests. Kevin and Bobby were glad of the opportunity for a change of pace.

Sport fishing was a whole new world for Bobby. Until now, fishing meant taking fish out of his grandfather's nets. He was not used to sitting in a boat watching others catch fish, and certainly not used to releasing fish in the interests of conservation.

Kevin was a patient teacher. "Let your motor warm up, don't go full throttle . . . Set a marker on shore so you travel straight and don't get lost . . . Use different levels of speed for different levels of water . . . Fish are likely to be found along the ice but also in deep holes by the shore . . . Drive up slowly to a fish hole because char spook easily and have good eyesight . . . Good lures for char are colourful Pixies, Devil Dogs, Daredevils and Crocodiles, Potato Bugs and Five of Diamonds . . . Don't handle the fish too much when you're releasing it so you keep the mucus on its body . . . When casting along the ice edge, submerge your rod tip to prevent the line breaking when the fish runs under the ice . . . It is the guide's responsibility to keep the boat away from the ice."

Supposedly, Bobby was taking all this in. But there seemed a slight glaze to his eyes. Suddenly, he hollered, "But when can I catch a fish?"

It was Kevin who promptly cast and got one, a ten-pound char, not trophy-sized but I was impressed. He cast again and got another. Meanwhile, Bobby got a lesson in carefully removing the hook with pliers, rocking the fish back and forth to revive it, and watching it swim away, unharmed. This was not what he really wanted to do.

After a few photographs, we cruised over to Howard's Point, named for a guest who always had good luck fishing there. The guides pulled the boat in to shore, and Kevin, rod in hand, waded back in the water. "Why are you casting so close to shore?" asked Bobby.

Kevin played it straight. "Because that's where the fish are." He was right. They lurked in deep holes close to shore. In quick succession, he had landed—and released—several large lake trout. Obviously, this was not to be Bobby's day for fishing. I wondered if he was thinking of going back to his grandfather's nets.

At Don's second camp farther north at Hadley Bay, my guides Dave and Steve would not listen to my excuses for not fishing. They were determined I would catch a fish myself. Otherwise, they threatened, I'd have hamburger patties for supper.

Trophy anglers fly to the outpost camps in Hadley Bay because the lakes on the river systems flowing into the bay are ideal spawning grounds for arctic char. In this region, the fish are far larger on average than they are in other areas in the Arctic. At the time of my visit in mid-July, the lakes were almost completely iced over. A strong chill wind was blowing. The place felt desolate.

Steve and I stood at the water's edge for an hour, Steve with his fly rod, me with a spinning reel, but no fish, either char or trout, came to the surface—at least not for our lures. Arctic terns, however, plunged into the lake and came up satisfied. Loons looked happy. I must be the only creature at this fishing lodge who was glad she wasn't catching fish. It seemed I could cast my line forever and not worry about dealing with what might be at the end of it.

Meanwhile, Steve, the professional, was holding forth on the finer points of the game. "Less than 5 per cent of fishermen fly-fish for char here because conditions are seldom calm enough . . . A true sportsman uses an eight- to twelve-pound line not a twenty-five-pound one . . . The acme is to catch the biggest fish on the lightest line . . . Work your lure. Let it drop in the water then give it a series of quick twitches. Let a char run initially, or you'll break your line. When you reel the fish in, keep your rod high and your line tight."

I was beginning to feel mesmerized. Steve was talking, the terns plunging, the lines running out, the lines running in. Casting became routine and mindless. Suddenly, "Steve! I've got a fish!" The lithe dark form of a lake trout squirmed up to my feet in the shallow water. I was too surprised to be scared. I did remember Steve's words. I held the rod high. I tried to step back but I was the one who was hooked, not the trout. My borrowed hipwaders sank into a mudhole, one of the hazards of fishing at North Camp. I was transfixed. I tried to lift one boot but stumbled. Fortunately, Steve was there to pull me free as the fish swam away. He laughed. "Don't worry, Lyn, one year we had to pull a guest out by boat."

I was aroused. The sight of that trout at my feet was enough to bring back the memories of Bathurst Inlet. I remembered my initial lethargy, the perfunctory way I had cast that lure, the yells of my companions that I had tied into a large char when I was sure it was a boot or the bottom, the charge of adrenalin as the fish fought, the advice I followed despite the excitement, the guide's glee as he swept it into the net, the laughs back at the lodge when everyone said they had heard my yells for miles.

"Steve," I said dramatically, "I'm going to get serious too. Let's get out on the ice. We need a fish for supper."

"Okay," he smiled as he picked up the gear. "But we'll have to be careful."

Conditions for fishing were far from ideal. The wind had picked up, and waves were tossing against the shore. But I was determined. We walked down the beach to a place where we could hop onto the ice and used it as a platform to get farther out in the lake. It was rotting ice and Don would not be pleased that his guest was taking such chances. Still, Steve spent most of his life hunting and fishing, so I considered myself to be in competent hands. He would be able to get me out of trouble—I hoped.

"Scarcely good conditions for fly-fishing," said Steve ruefully as he stood at the edge of the ice, fly-casting into the wind-torn waves. "You're doing better with a spinning rod. We're relying on you for supper."

"Okay," I replied, trying to sound as if I knew what I was doing. With my luck, I would be making hamburger patties for the evening meal. Steve wasn't taking chances. He set the drag a couple of pounds lower than the test and demonstrated again.

A fish grabbed the lure instantaneously. It was a surprise to both of us. "Here, take the line," Steve said, shoving the rod in my hands. I felt the challenge. I remembered Bathurst Inlet. I remembered Koluktoo Bay. The fish peeled off into open water, a long, long run. "You've got a char," my fishing buddy said. That's what Sam Kapolak had said. How did they know when it was still underwater?

"Concentrate!" Steve broke into my reverie. "Give it line. That's right, you don't want the line to snarl or twist up and break. Now reel it in, keep the pressure constant, you don't want the lure to fall out." He was right. I didn't. I wanted to bring in that fish. I needed another fishing story for the next decade, I thought, lapsing back into reverie for a moment.

"Keep your rod up," Steve interrupted. "The fish are feistier here near Hadley Bay."

It was feisty and yes, beautiful—for a fish. It looked like a giant streamlined bullet, a shiny one with its pink-spotted sides and belly glinting in the clear water. It came up quietly to my ice platform. If it had been a red belly, a spawner later in the season, I would have taken its picture.

Pictures. I suddenly remembered that for me, photography is more important than fishing. "Steve, take a picture." My musings came to an abrupt end as the char turned, thrashed wildly, and fled again to open water. We had to start casting all over again.

This time I concentrated, working the char close and not taking chances. Steve leaned down and picked it up in the net. We *would* have char for supper. I even closed my eyes, gripped the fish under the gills, and started walking towards camp.

A minute later, I gave up my pose as the happy hunter and opened my eyes wide when I realized I might not get to camp that night at all. While we were playing that char, the ice behind us had cracked apart. Dark water now filled the gap. And more leads were opening all the time. They reminded me of miniature Red Seas, and I prayed for divine intervention.

"Follow me," Steve said confidently. "And jump when I say so."

The thought of spending the night on the ice with my fish un-cooked was enough for me to obey at once. I followed nervously as Steve threaded a path through the moving ice. And I jumped—even more nervously—when he said, "Jump!" Fish in hand, I stuck to my guide like a shadow. And we did make it back to the tent for a cooked char supper.

❉

The swivel chairs on Don's dinghies were designed for catching fish but they were perfect for capturing birds in my camera. The yellow bills and crimson eyes of loons glistened in the golden light of the midnight sun, and it seemed a pity to ruffle their perfect reflections. Slowly and carefully, Kevin steered me into the fleet to film them. One pair sang a fantastic duet. What made it more miraculous was its echo under our boat. The duet on the water matched the duet in the boat. The calls were so realistic that it was hard not to believe we had caught the loons on our keel. The sounds must have trav-elled through the water and ricocheted off the boat.

"There's a king eider, sitting at the lake edge," I nudged Kevin quickly. He was excited too. He cut the motor and we nosed silently into the picture. Surprisingly, the eider stayed and we got a field guide look at its spectacular multicoloured head with the orange shield on its bill.

"Do you want to go upriver to look for muskox and caribou?" Kevin suggested when the eider finally flew. It was a rhetorical question. We puttered upstream with binoculars ready.

"What's that pole? Can't be a tree trunk," I laughed.

"It's an arctic fox," Kevin replied. "It may have a den nearby."

Expertly, he manoeuvred the dinghy through the surging current across the ever-changing river bottom to get to shore. I expected to jump, but Kevin, wearing chestwaders, pulled the stern into the bank and I landed dry-shod.

At fifty yards, the fox squatted on the tundra and watched us. It was a male in brindled summer pelage with a long white stripe down its tail and a v-shaped white patch on the upper end.

I fell into line behind Kevin and we slowly stalked the fox, stopping and starting, blending our bodies as one, keeping in the path of the sun, staying upwind. The fox loped away to a patch of willows in the east, where it stood hidden except for a pair of eyes and ears peeping from the foliage.

I kept clicking as we got closer, trying to get in as many shots as possible before it loped out of range. To my amazement, the fox stayed. It lay down in front of the willows, squinted against the sun, curled its thick furry tail around its body, yawned—and went to sleep, at least it looked that way. Kevin and I hurried forward till the fox was in full frame.

At three yards, it stood up and ambled away farther east. Again we followed. Again it lay down, closed its eyes, and looked as if it were sleeping. I put in another roll of film.

For half an hour, we repeated the pattern—fox moving east, Kevin and I following it and taking pictures; fox stopping to lie down till we approached within three yards, fox moving on again. I reached around to get more film from my pack and caught a glimpse of bigger game behind me.

"Kevin, a caribou!" I shouted. Majestically striding down a ridge on the horizon was a bull caribou with the most resplendent rack of antlers I had ever seen. Following closely were three more bulls, then a female and calf.

"Let's follow them to the shore," Kevin responded eagerly.

The bulls kept heading in the direction of the river; the calf gambolled alongside. Only the cow, with the natural protective instincts of a mother, looked up and saw us. No slow stalk this time. We abandoned the fox and dashed towards the caribou. Dashed is a relative word for stumbling across tussocks of dry grass and mud boils with knee-high ravines in between. The tundra looked as if a giant elephant had emerged from a wallow and padded over the land.

I tried to go fast, but the caribou relentlessly got ahead. Crossing rivers, not grazing, was on their minds. No amount of puffing would close the distance. I stopped to rest. I looked behind and THERE, a few yards away, was the FOX.

While we were following the caribou, the fox was following us. It sat on its haunches, whined, yelped, and whined again as if to say, "Don't leave me." Anthropomorphic nonsense, retorted my scientific side. It's lonely, pleaded my emotional side.

"Look!" said Kevin. The caribou had reached the shore and were already swimming across the river, but on a sandy mound at the water's edge where they had begun their crossing were the heads of several little fox pups. In a medley of yelps, they disappeared with their mother down the holes of their den.

Kevin and I hurried to the den. What a glorious location—on a riverbank clothed in lush grasses, sprinkled with rosettes of tundra flowers and lit by late afternoon sun. Footprints and droppings on the sand showed where the family had been playing. Squeaks and growls underneath warned us to leave.

Our friendly male had changed his tune. Seduction having failed, he now circled his den and came nipping at our heels. He snarled, bared his teeth, bounced forward aggressively then snarled again. He was a brave fox. I admired his spirit. We let the family relax and returned to the boat.

Two days later, Kevin dropped me off at the river where we had first seen our friendly fox. It was there again by the same willows, barking at a pair of jaegers that were swooping down. It ran off, long tail streaming behind, first in one direction then in another but always away from the den. Meanwhile, I found other game to follow—or follow me.

A pair of ruddy turnstones emulated the fox and tried to lead me away from their nest—wherever it was—until another turnstone proved a greater threat. Fluttering and screeching, the male parent flew at the interloper in what seemed an attempt to tussle it to the ground.

The jaegers gave up on the fox and turned their attention to me. Then, in what I thought was an uneven battle, they bravely bombarded a cow caribou. And, in what was a hopeless attempt to catch up with it, I strode off after the caribou as it in turn sprang away from the jaegers.

The caribou and I were headed for the same place. I let it maintain the lead not only because it outclassed me in speed but also because the wildlife en route was so engrossing. On an ice-edged blue lake, a tundra swan sailed like a yacht behind a flock of common eiders. Lapland longspurs tending their young twittered in the willows. A black-bellied plover strutted down to the river to drink. I missed seeing snowy owls. Perhaps their nests had been raided by foxes.

By late afternoon I crept up on the den but it seemed nobody was home. Faint whistles could have been birds. Had the parents moved their young to another den? Kevin would not be picking me up for several hours. I found some comfortable tussocks that were contoured to my body, lay down, and dozed.

Three hours later, a woeful squawk burst behind me. It was the mother fox back from the hunt. She sat on her haunches two yards from my knees and screeched as if to say, "Oh no, not you again!" She went through her whole repertoire. Squawks, screeches, yelps, yaps, whines, growls. When those failed to remove me, she tried enticements, she tried attacks. I sat still, talked to her quietly, and took pictures.

And then Kevin came. The fox was down the hole and into her den by the time I boarded the boat.

Next day, I stalked an old bull muskox with Steve. After an hour squeezing and portaging our boat through slivers in the ice pack, we fought the current up Nanuk River to get within a mile of the bull. There was nowhere to hide on the flat tundra, so it was a slow stalk, making use of every mound, melting into Steve's shadow, freezing, bending down when the muskox stared in our direction, walking ahead when it looked away. We walked slowly enough to see a fox catch lemmings and hear wolves howl.

"How close do you want to get?" asked Steve, who hunts big game in Africa. It was another rhetorical question. He was the one who dared to get close. About thirty yards away, the double-humped mammoth strode forcefully towards us, lowered his gleaming horns to the ground, sniffed audibly, and rubbed his head against scent glands in his legs. It was a strategy intended to scare me—and it did.

"Don't run, Lyn, if it charges!" said Steve. No, I thought for one mad facetious moment, I'll do as Don told me another guest did and dodge it like a matador. But then I didn't have Don's plane as a handy getaway. Perhaps I should have gone fishing.

Together, one behind the other (you can guess who was behind), Steve and I did a slow two-step backwards as the bull approached till he deemed us no threat and stopped advancing. Then, with hairy skirts swaying in the wind, he wheeled and galloped away.

I spent my last day at High Arctic Lodge meditating beside twenty-eight starving muskox that had been stranded on a tiny island when the ice went out. Normally, muskox browse on willows, rushes, grasses, and some flowering plants. On this island, there were no willows or grasses left, just dried up dryas and saxifrage and much-trampled moss. Constant pounding from hooves had ripped up the active layer and exposed the permafrost so that the ground was now wet slush.

The animals were desperate. Most had missing teeth from breaking off rocks and biting into the ground to get at roots. One was already dead. Another lay on its side, waiting. Jaegers hovered overhead, waiting to pick holes in eyes and vital organs. Those animals still upright were staggering. Only the calf was perky, probably because of its mother's milk.

Moving the animals was not feasible. There are plenty of muskox on Victoria Island, it costs too much to fly in alternative food, and earlier attempts to rescue stranded muskox on another island by herding them into the water had failed because the animals panicked and drowned. The muskox didn't know it then, but the next day hunters would come to put them out of their misery. It was the only solution.

❖

If I had heeded my mother's advice not to talk to strangers I would have missed out on a lot of memorable experiences. I would have missed the only fishing trip during which I didn't have to fish—a "fly" fishing trip from Taloyoak to Abernethy Bay.

Behind the Boothia Inn in this small Inuit community on the Arctic Coast is a desolate graveyard of piled stones and wooden crosses. There are no names to tell who is buried there, but the biggest pile of rocks marks the grave of Ernie Lyall who helped build the Hudson's Bay Company trading post that began this community in 1949. Ernie, the only white person to rate an "Eskimo" disc number—E1, passed away in 1986, but seven years later I flew into Taloyoak to track down his wife Nipisha and some of their nineteen children for a story on this legendary northern family.

Active movers and shakers in several communities, busy at a variety of projects, the Lyalls were all over the place. I caught flamboyant Charlie on planes flying between Ottawa, Calgary, and Edmonton, at airports in Cambridge Bay, Gjoa Haven, and Pelly Bay, and in his truck or on his four-wheeler in Taloyoak. Whenever I wanted to find someone, I just flagged down Charlie. He knew everything and everyone in the community.

One day while I was photographing the old stone mission, he turned up with a truck full of fishermen, Canadians who worked for six months a year in Saudi Arabia. They'd just flown up from Edmonton in their floatplanes, dropped down to Taloyoak, and of course bumped into Charlie. He'd got them a local guide and mapped out the best fishing spots. Obligingly, they all posed for me at the church then left for their planes parked by a lake on the outskirts of town. Now that's the way, I sighed enviously, to get around the country.

Five minutes later, they were back. "Lyn!" called Doug through the window of Charlie's truck. "Would you like to come flying with us for a couple of days? We're going up to Thom Bay, Abernethy River, and perhaps Fort Ross to do a bit of fishing." Needless to say, I screened out the part about fishing and accepted the rest of their invitation with alacrity.

I almost changed my mind while we were taxiing from the lake, but by then it was too late. For the next two days, heavy cross winds, falling tides, and minefields of rocks and chunks of ice made all takeoffs and landings hazardous, thick fog often obliterated our passage through the stark black rubble hills, and at one point, we flew blind into the setting sun.

Our pilots, Bob and Doug, forgot our headsets were on and kept up a running commentary which they probably didn't want their passengers to hear.

"How are you doing, big guy?"

"Not good. It's a bugger navigating like this."

"The fog's right down to the ground. What'll we do?"

"Go to the left. Beat around it."

"Think it'll get worse than this? Have you got me in sight?"

"Yep. You're a mile ahead of me."

"I've lost you. You're in the clouds."

"What's your heading? Your altitude?"

"I see you straight ahead."

"Good, follow me."

"Did you pick up any ice in there?"

"Yeah, I got some. Where can we land?"

"Remember we have passengers. Don't frighten them. I don't think they want to swim ashore."

"Any idea how we'll get in there amid all that ice, Bob? We may have to wait till it melts. Do we have enough gas for that?"

"A nice fish just jumped in front of you, Doug."

"Well, that's the main thing."

"Yep, let's get our priorities straight."

"There's a seal."

"Where there's seals, there's fish. So what are we waiting for? Let's get down there and get our rods in the water."

Obviously, we'd arrived at Abernethy Bay. From a ravine in the hills on the nearby horizon, the boulder-strewn Abernethy River gurgled over the tundra and emptied into the ice-clogged Gulf of Boothia. At its confluence with the sea, dozens of milling fins churned the water into froth as arctic char prepared to swim upstream to the spawning lakes. It was a good sign—for the anglers amongst us.

Inuit families have camped here for centuries to take advantage of the bay's abundant wildlife—not only char but also ducks, seals, caribou, and polar bears. According to our guide, George Totalik, as many as twenty-five families lived along the river at one time. "It's good because the river doesn't freeze to the bottom. There were no skidoos then. We could get enough fish to feed our dogs all year."

People in Taloyoak relish the taste of the rich red shrimp-eating char from Abernethy Bay and asked us to bring back fish for them. I smiled at the thought of white people fishing for the Inuit. The last Inuit family abandoned Abernethy in 1971, and it was just too far and too difficult now for people to travel back and forth from Taloyoak. Even in float planes, I thought ruefully.

Doug twisted a long and tortuous path through house-high icebergs before he found a suitable stopping place. Emil jumped from pan to pan and boulder to boulder to secure the plane to shore then insisted on gallantly carrying me on his back over the same route. Five minutes later, Bob arrived. He must have taxied a mile through the icy obstacle course before he reached land.

It took another ten minutes of boulder-hopping along the rugged beach to get to the river but the arduous route was worth it. The men must have caught twenty char in twenty minutes. All were thrilled with the abundance and size of the fish. To avoid crossing lines and losing lures to a huge wall of ice offshore, Bob and Emil fished on one side of the river, Marco, Thai, and Doug on the other. Our guide was kept busy running to both sides of the stream, wading into the chilly water and releasing the fish with his bare hands.

It must have been easier in the old days. "I remember as a kid in Abernethy Bay, the people built stone weirs along the river, and when the fish swam by we could just spear them with our *kakivaks* (fish spears)," said George between dashes. "It was the same every year, in May and June when the ice cracked up, the fish would run from the lake to the sea and then in late August and early September, they would start to swim back upriver to the lake."

After a slow start, seventy-three-year-old Marco started catching fish and then there was no stopping him. He reeled in one big char after another, outdoing everyone. His son took video film. "You'll be showing this to your buddies for months," grinned Emil.

"Amazingly wild fish," Bob commented. "They're not hungry at this time of year. They've probably never seen lures before but they're biting them anyway because they're so wild."

"Want to borrow my rod, Lyn?" asked Doug solicitously.

"No, thanks," I replied hastily. "I'm too busy taking shots of you guys against the icebergs. Give me your camera and I'll take some for you too." On this fishing trip I had no need to explain my altruism.

The late evening sun was gilding the ice with alpenglow when Bob signalled us to pack up and return to the planes. The men could have stayed to fish all night, but the ebbing tide and the incoming ice pans were fast working together to block our exit. We hurried to grab our gear, store char for Charlie's smokehouse in the pontoons, and weave our way out of Abernethy Bay.

After so much taxiing, we had too little gas to fly farther north to the abandoned trading post of Fort Ross on Bellot Strait, one of my personal dreams, but we did share a unique highlight the next day on the way to fish Abernethy Bay again.

On George's advice we dropped down to fish Ilaunalik Bay first. I was happy following caribou trails through the rugged terrain, but despite casting for an hour from shore and again from Bob's rubber boat, the men had no bites. We got back into the Cessnas and were just taxiing out of the bay when it happened. "Narwhals!" came Bob's voice over the radio.

"Where? Where?" I said excitedly, tapping Doug's shoulder. I'd take narwhals over fish any time. As I looked down from my side of the plane, several streaked bodies, some with tusks, dived from sight.

"They'll be up again," said Doug, encouragingly, as he taxied in circles, trying to find them. Bob was doing the same.

But where? I was torn between gazing at the water, waiting for the narwhals to reappear and groping for my telephoto lens. I leaned down to sort through the lenses at my feet just as everybody gabbled at the same time. "Over here." "No, over there." "One group's just come up by Bob's plane." "He's getting shots through his window." "Swivel around, Lyn, there's some narwhals surfacing behind our plane now."

Despite the efforts of my companions, looking for whales from taxiing planes was not the best method for capturing them in my camera. The pod had divided underwater into several groups, but they never seemed to surface where my lens was pointing.

It didn't matter really. We were all thrilled just to see these legendary whales. Our Inuit guide was equally excited. To my surprise, George had never seen narwhals before. He didn't share our enthusiasm for getting close to them. "My father says if you wound one, he'll attack the boat."

He said there used to be a lot more narwhals in the old days. "Narwhals come around about every ten to thirteen years, not often. They come in late August till about the end of September. Our community gets ten tags a year, but we don't get to use them much."

Inuit prize narwhals for their *muktuk* (skin), a delicacy in the traditional diet, and for the ivory tusks of the males, which are either sold or used for carving. But George, like us, was content just to look at these narwhals in Ilaunalik Bay.

My fishing companions were no longer strangers. They invited me for a char dinner back at their camp in Taloyoak, and we planned to go fishing again the following year. They were thinking of the best fishing spots. I was thinking of all the other things that fishing trips can bring.

Breezing Into Camp

ALL MORNING KIMMIRUT (LAKE HARBOUR) people on southern Baffin Island had been streaming down to the beach on three-wheelers or on foot: women with babies in their *amautis*, teapot and Bay bags in one hand, buckets of Pampers in the other; men with plastic milk crates stuffed with the usual northern staples—tea, sugar, jam, and pilot biscuits; boys carrying guns, parkas, and blankets.

"What a day! 15 degrees C at the end of September is unbelievable," Mattoo Michael kept saying as we waited in the dinghy for his brother Pitsiulak. Other boats were getting ready to go out on the land—berry picking, clam digging, hunting, and camping—but our destination was Markham Bay, ninety miles to the north, where each summer, carvers from Kimmirut, Cape Dorset, Iqaluit, even Quebec, come to camp, quarry, and carve soapstone.

Pitsiulak arrived with a nut for a friend's broken motor and climbed aboard. Elisapee, Mattoo's daughter, nestled down in the bow amid parkas, sleeping bags, and blankets, intending to sleep for the long seven-hour trip ("six hours if uninterrupted, a week if bad weather"). Mattoo gunned the two seventy-horsepower motors, and passing all others, we skimmed down the inlet over a glassy sea. I could scarcely believe my luck.

The Michael family of Markham Bay were master carvers—all of them—especially Elijah and Annie, and their sons, Mattoo, Pitsiulak, Pauloosie, and Pea. Even their grandchildren carved. The week before in Iqaluit, I had seen a video film of the famous family made for European TV, but it seemed too difficult then to track them down in person at their outpost camp, a hundred miles north of Kimmirut.

A few days later I was strolling along the main street in Kimmirut when I saw three Inuit sitting in armchairs outside a house and carving blocks of soapstone. I asked them to pose for my camera and, by amazing coincidence, found their names were Mattoo, Pitsiulak, and Pauloosie Michael. The brothers were obviously used to being models, and we had fun acting for the photograph as if it were a Hollywood production. Pauloosie, especially, was a natural ham.

Mattoo had come into town that day from Markham Bay to bring his little girl to the nurse. "I am going back to camp tomorrow. Do you want to come?" As simple as that.

So here I was on this idyllic day "climbing the current" en route to meet the rest of the Michael family. Mattoo, who said he wanted to be a guide and outfitter some time, as well as a famous carver, slowed for me to take pictures of icebergs riding like ocean liners and low-slung rocky islands "where we shelter when weather is bad." He stopped to take on water, to shoot seals, to point out the place his father was born, and to show me a bowhead whale beached two years earlier. "My father has the baleen at camp."

At first, I thought the golden brown hump streaked white with bird droppings and draped with seaweed was a rock. Mattoo approached it cautiously. "I hope there are no polar bears feeding on it," he said soberly. "There were six last time." I noticed that Pitsiulak fingered the gun strapped to his back. I looked at the still-juicy white meat oozing over the gravel and suddenly, all the white rocks became polar bears. "I see nothing," Pitsiulak said comfortingly, scoping the near horizon.

Fifteen miles before the carving camp at Aberdeen in Markham Bay, Mattoo pointed out his family's outpost camp and explained why his parents moved there in 1977 from Kimmirut. "They wanted us to learn the way they used to live, to keep to a traditional Inuit life and not grow up bad. We do our own hunting, fishing, cleaning skins, and sewing. We carve when we can. There are not enough jobs unless you go away to other settlements so I must carve to stay in this area."

Mattoo knows exactly what he wants to do and has the talent, confidence, and eloquence to achieve his ambitions. His first trip out of Kimmirut—to demonstrate carving at Expo 86 in Vancouver—was "my thrill of a lifetime." His next thrill, he said, would be to carve in Australia and other places around the world. He wants to carve a ring for Prince Charles. "And one day I'm going to carve like Michelangelo." Meantime, he was looking forward to going to a carving show the following month in Cincinnati.

In contrast to Mattoo's ebullience, Pitsiulak was shy and softspoken. He said he would like to go to school to "get more grades" but added "I couldn't leave my parents alone at the outpost camp." Both boys learned their carving skills by watching their parents.

We arrived at the soapstone camp in Markham Bay just before sunset. I had not expected such beauty or so many people. Over a dozen white *iglu*-shaped canvas tents stood in line along a raised rocky beach against a backdrop of low cliffs and rounded hills. A dozen canoes were pulled up on shore and several schooners were anchored in the narrow little bay. A lot of children, some young women, and a lady who looked like she might be Mattoo's mother, Annie, came down to greet us and help pack our gear to the tents.

I followed Annie through a low plywood door in her tent to meet Elijah Michael, a handsome man lounging on the sleeping platform, smoking a pipe. Neither parent spoke English so smiles and gestures had to suffice.

The boys dug into a big pot of meat. My southern culture prevented me from helping myself, so I offered the staples I brought in my pack. Annie's eyes lit up and she distributed the cookies and candy to several children sprawled over caribou skins. "Do you want anything to eat?" asked Mattoo, gnawing on some ribs. I nodded and pointed to the pot. "Caribou?" "Seal," he said as Annie ladled me a bowl of rich warm soup.

Annie sat tending her tea kettle with her adopted baby, Mosesee, at her breast. What gave poignancy to the scene was a figure about a foot high that sat beside her—another mother with long braided hair and with another baby at her breast. The most beautiful soapstone carving I had ever seen, it would command thousands of dollars in a southern market. I looked at my pack, remembered my pocketbook, and resisted with a sigh. Seeing my interest, Elijah unrolled a blanket beside him and brought out one of his own carvings, just as large, of a falcon with tall upspread wings in the act of killing a rabbit that was pinned by one ear. The two carvings expressed the dual roles of their creators: the strength and vitality of the hunter, the care and fecundity of the mother.

I was anxious to see where the carvings had been born. When would the men go to the quarry? I would have to wait for a signal. It was the kids exploring the rounded hills above camp an hour or so later who alerted me to Mattoo whistling from the boat. It was low tide, time to go dig soapstone, they said. I rushed down to the beach and piled aboard.

Just a few minutes away in a circular cove that was almost a lake at high tide was Soapstone Hill, a smooth, grey, granite-like mound about fifty paces one way and thirty paces the other. How could this nondescript hill looking much like any other of the ubiquitous boulders along the beach be transformed into falcons, rabbits, breastfeeding women, drumdancers, polar bears, caribou and seals— exquisite carvings that the Michael family, and others, produced.

About twenty men and boys standing in tidal pools at the low side of the mound were digging away at the wall of rock. Some were chiselling; some were prying cracks wider with crowbars; some were driving wedges. Some were sloshing buckets of water where the soapstone had broken away. Others—in pairs—were piling chunks of soapstone on pallets and carrying them to the other side of the hill to the boats. They reminded me of men carrying pallets of Dutch cheeses to market.

The Michaels had a different method. Mattoo and Pitsiulak laboriously retrieved a heavy wooden box from higher up the beach and dropped it at the side of the hill opposite to where the other men were working. "These are our tools," Mattoo said simply. All looked up expectantly as he stood above them on a projecting hunk of rock with a pneumatic drill. A few pulls—and then silence. The rest turned to their picks and wedges and mallets and shovels. I wondered who would win, man or machine. Finally, the drill roared into life, and with Pitsiulak guiding it with gloved hand, Mattoo pepper-shakered the rock with holes. Others from our boat, whose names I had not yet learned, hosed away the dust and hammered in wedges to make the cracks as wide as possible.

Mattoo then gestured to two of the boys in our party, who returned a few minutes later from the tents with a box labelled S-Mite. Dynamite? "No, cement," said a girl standing beside me. Mary Akavak had come to Markham Bay for a couple of days with her boyfriend, Nicky, who hoped to get some soapstone for himself by helping the others. Nicky and Pitsiulak filled the holes with S-mite as if it were a brown chocolate cake mix, and Mattoo gave the signal to return to the boat. The tide was now swirling around the ankles of those working at the lower level. Soon it would be dark and much of Soapstone Hill would be under water. One of the boats with a freshly killed caribou on its prow nosed up to the rock face, and the manual workers loaded their soapstone pieces directly aboard.

I returned to camp to find that Annie had shoved aside the boxes in her food tent and laid down a thick foamie for me as an alternative to my lightweight sleeping gear. Mattoo lit a candle and insisted I leave the Coleman stove on all night for heat despite my protestations that my down sleeping bag was enough. "It's colder here than Kimmirut," he warned. I appreciated his concern.

Next day Elijah came with us to the diggings. He checked that the soapstone block was good quality and that the S-mite had set sufficiently, then he wandered off to the side with one of the pieces from the boys' cache. "He's probably going to check the quality of the stone," Mary said.

Meanwhile, I was busy on the land side of the tide pool taking pictures of the workers—and their reflections—as they took turns in slugging away at the tops of the wedges. "We leave in good shape after working here for the summer," smiled Mattoo. They certainly work long hours. Long after I went to bed the night before, Mattoo and Pitsiulak were ferrying soapstone by boat to caches on land where it would be accessible in the winter by skidoo.

Suddenly, a long flat piece sliced off the block and crashed into the little lake that was forming at their feet. Mary said it weighed about ten thousand pounds. "It's dangerous work. A few days ago there were a lot more people and one person hit his hand with a hammer, another was hit on the shin by a chisel, and a big piece of soapstone fell off the carrier onto a man's foot."

Now that the outside layer of the mound was removed, the boys began to chip cement out of the long zebra stripes inside to reveal the glorious green of the soapstone they would soon be carving. They worked past dark, slugging away with sledgehammers and crowbars by the light of lanterns till piece by piece was enticed away from the parent block. Mary brought the ubiquitous Coleman from the boat and prepared tea and bannock.

The quarrying process would be repeated again and again till enough soapstone had been reduced to manageable pieces for taking "to the land." Mattoo said that sixty thousand pounds had been removed in two or three days before my visit. Soapstone Hill used to be twice its present size. "People have been quarrying soapstone here for generations," he added.

Meanwhile, Elijah still kept chipping away at his own soapstone block on the side. Just before Mattoo "called it a night" and packed up his tools, I wandered over to see what Elijah was doing. Incredibly, it seemed to me, a plump mother with two long braids down her back and a baby at her breast had broken out of the lump of stone Elijah had picked from the pool such a short time before. For a carver, Soapstone Hill is not nondescript.

One morning well before the sun peeked over the hill on the opposite side of the bay, I looked out of the tent to see the Michael family breaking camp. Little Mosesee was sick. I knew that we would be leaving for Kimmirut immediately. I looked at the huge pile of gear on the bank outside the family tent and wondered how it could possibly fit into the boat, especially as Annie and Elijah were also going to town. Although there was room for them to stay at a house, Mary told me they preferred to be in their own tent. It seemed that everything was going: bedding in blue Canada Post bags, food in plastic milk cartons, kettles, lanterns, stoves, freshly made bannock from the neighbours, even the baleen from the beached bowhead whale.

I picked up a foamie and nearly dropped it under the unexpected weight. Finished carvings were carefully wrapped in styrofoam and rolled in foamies and mattresses; unpolished ones were strewn around the boat. Annie climbed aboard, casually swinging her mother and child masterpiece into a place by the teakettle. Elijah plunked his carving down by a washbowl of caribou and cans of Klik.

Carvings elegantly displayed on glass in sophisticated city galleries while viewers tiptoe reverentially around them will never be the same for me again. I will always remember their humble origins in camps such as Markham Bay.

❋

Unlike my spur-of-the-moment visit with the Michael family to Markham Bay, my trip to the carving camp in Andrew Gordon Bay was preceded by weeks of preparation. But such is the way of the North that even the best laid plans go awry, and I end up winging it anyway.

Frobisher Bay Jewellery Shop read the sign. A bit pretentious, I thought, for such a drab brown building. But inside this Iqaluit shop, history was being made.

In the display area, Nicki Ishulutak tended to tourists enchanted with muskox-handled *ulus* from Arctic Bay; then he sat down to play his guitar to delighted customers. The strains of Mozart filled the adjoining workshop where two Inuit were quietly working in front of a board that said: "To Do: 5 bear earrings, 5 beluga earrings, 3 ulu earrings, 3 bird earrings."

"Could you do me a pair of beluga whale earrings?" I asked hopefully. I was answered in Inuktitut, a language in which I'm helpless. "What's that mean?" I asked Craig Hall, the arts and crafts supervisor.

"One pair of beluga earrings to go," he quipped. "They'll be ready this afternoon."

Jesse Kakee from Pangnirtung set to work immediately. Beside him, Mosha Michael put down the silver he was cutting and volunteered to mend my watchband. Meanwhile, in the next room, Mozart was being drowned out by the intermittent buzz of a big diamond stone cutter. Craig led me there to see history in the making.

A workshop that would transform Inuit sculpture forever was in progress. George Pratt, a well-known sculptor from Vancouver, was standing at a huge machine cutting a chunk of white marble that was destined to become a polar bear. Crowded around him were Inuit craftsmen from all over Baffin Island.

Craig explained that the workshop had been set up in response to a crisis faced by carving communities across the Arctic: a severe shortage in accessible supplies of soapstone, the medium they have used for decades.

"On Baffin Island, we have an extraordinary and diverse range of carving stone—and large quantities of it. It hasn't been exploited because Inuit have not had the tools or the technology to do so," explained Mark Webber, who was coordinating the project. Craig and Mark were especially delighted about a "river of marble" at Andrew Gordon Bay near Cape Dorset. They said it stretched around the shoreline for more than eight miles and promised a never-ending source of stone for carving. "It's marble that rivals the finest Carrara stone from Italy," said Craig enthusiastically.

George had been brought to Baffin by the territorial government to show Inuit carvers how to use the latest tools: diamond-edged saws and files, power routers, chisels and drills, air-driven hammers—all necessary for Inuit if harder stone was to be carved.

"Inuit have an instant grasp of how to put the new machines together and use them for new effects. This is the beginning of a whole new style in Inuit sculpture," George said fervently. He was struck by the way Inuit carvers could work side by side on the same sculpture "not speaking more than forty words a day," yet be able to communicate so well that each side of a marble face mask matched perfectly.

When I returned to the shop that afternoon, Jesse hung a beautiful pair of machine-carved beluga whale earrings on my ears. I liked them so much I splurged by ordering "a polar bear set to go."

A week later when the workshop ended, the carvers returned to their communities to pass on the new information about the new materials and new technologies to other carvers. More workshops followed, and in 1989 George supervised the carving in marble of a life-sized drum dancer on location in Andrew Gordon Bay.

"This gave me an idea," George explained. "More and more cities across North America are commissioning monumental sculptures which can be worth hundreds of thousands of dollars to the carvers. Inuit are capable of sculpting stone for the 'tall buildings' market like the Indians of the Northwest Coast have done with their totem poles."

He solicited a $250,000 commission from Royal Trust and invited three of his Inuit colleagues—Philip Pitseulak from Pond Inlet, Simata (Sam) Pitsiulak from Kimmirut, and Taqialuk (Tuk) Nuna from Cape Dorset—to help him carve the legend of Sedna, the Sea Goddess. It was to be the largest sculpture ever attempted by Inuit and the first commercially commissioned monument carved in Nunavut. It would be displayed permanently in the lobby of the Hong Kong Bank of Canada building (which Royal Trust owns) in downtown Toronto.

There are many versions of the Sedna story in Inuit mythology. According to the version chosen by the group, Sedna was a poor orphan girl who was mistreated by her tribe. They abandoned her when they were moving to a new camp. As the kayaks pulled away from shore, the little girl pleaded to be taken along. In desperation, she jumped into the freezing water and swam after the boats. As Sedna tried to pull herself to safety inside the boat, a cruel member of the tribe took an axe and chopped off her fingers. Sedna drowned.

Her severed fingers became the creatures of the land and sea, and she became their mistress, the goddess of them all. Now, when people are wicked to each other and fail to show respect for their land, she withholds the creatures so that the people starve. The sins of the people become tangles in her long black hair, and only when the Shaman descends into the depths and combs the evil from her tresses does she allow the creatures to roam once more and the land to be bountiful again.

I arranged to fly to Cape Dorset, the take-off point for the Sedna carving camp in Andrew Gordon Bay. It was agreed that I would fly into the community in the morning and in the afternoon scrounge a ride to the camp by boat with Jimmy Manning, the assistant general manager of the West Baffin Co-op, who was coordinating supplies and logistics. "If you have any trouble, I'll come in and get you myself in the rubber raft," George promised over the phone.

I should have known better. I arrived at the airport at the pre-arranged time, but there was no-one to meet me. I hitched a ride downtown and learned that Jimmy had already left for Andrew Gordon Bay a few hours earlier on the high tide. "He forgot about you," said Tuq Nuna's wife matter-of-factly; then she added, "but they know you're here." That was all. No apologies. No instructions. No alternative plans. It was the Inuit way. They think it impolite to say no so they say nothing—or invent some face-saving excuse. Later, Jimmy told me that he couldn't wait because he had to get emergency gas to the carvers to fuel their tools and that he couldn't let me know because radio reception between camp and town was poor. It was a case of time and tide wait for no woman.

The informal way of the North has its advantages. I dropped my pack and camera bags in the porch of Jimmy's big, new two-storey house on the beach and cleared a space beside the hot water heater for my sleeping bag. The house was always full of people, coming and going at different times of the day or night, helping themselves to anything in the cupboards or refrigerator, slicing off chunks of raw caribou on the floor, playing video games on the TV, sleeping wherever and whenever they felt tired. I woke up one morning to find two kids squeezed behind the chesterfield while upstairs, beds and mattresses remained empty. Nobody thought it strange that I should doss down without a formal invitation. Sharing, yet at the same time minding your own business, are worthwhile Inuit traits.

Next afternoon, there was much excitement in the community when Jimmy returned in his boat with his brother, Sam Pitsiulak, and two of Sam's partly-finished Sedna carvings—life-sized Seal and Shaman. A real seal hung over the bow attested to the men's hunting success on the way home. There would be a seal feast tonight.

Originally, carvings were to be suspended in nets supported by oil drums and towed behind Zodiacs for the minimum eight-hour journey through the often wind-tossed, freezing seas between Andrew Gordon Bay and Cape Dorset. Knowing the local conditions, the Inuit were sceptical and preferred to transport them in their own boats. Jimmy lost no time in rounding up a front-end loader to lift Seal and Shaman out of his boat and move them to where they would stay until a way was found to get them to Toronto.

But when would a boat be returning to the carving camp? I tried to curb my impatience over the next few days and refrained from asking. Instead, I welcomed the opportunity to join in family life with Jimmy and Sam and Sam's wife, Gila. Both brothers are famous in their own right: Jimmy for photography and art promotion, and Sam for whatever he turns his mind to, whether it's carving or flying his homemade Ultralight. Both are charming and eloquent as well as talented. Time passed quickly, but I was still anxious to get to Andrew Gordon Bay to see the other carvers and the birthplace of the Sedna ensemble.

Time was running out for the project. Sam and Jimmy told me of the problems that had plagued it from the beginning and were still threatening its successful conclusion.

The worst ice pack in forty years stranded the carvers, their families, and their equipment in Cape Dorset and delayed their arrival in Andrew Gordon Bay. The helicopter that eventually rescued them was stalled by weather and breakdowns. Gales blew down their tents. The ice persisted most of the summer, and boats couldn't get through to deliver gasoline for stoves, tools, and machines. The carvers had to carry heavy cans of gas to camp, a distance of several miles over rough tundra terrain that George called the Hoh Chi Minh Trail.

Unable to bring modern machines to Andrew Gordon Bay, they had to extract the enormous blocks of marble by hand, much as Michelangelo did more than four hundred years ago at Italy's famous Carrara deposit—drilling holes, hammering in shims and wedges, levering, prying, lifting, jacking—and to contrive ingenious ways to move the marble into position for carving. It took three men all day to move one eight-thousand-pound block sixty feet.

Then followed weeks of monotonous labour in the rain, wind, fog, and snow of one of the worst summers on record to remove thousands of pounds of rubble before the life in the stone could, in Sam's words, "pop out." They had to improvise. When water dripping over the marble was needed to cool the diamond blades of their mini-grinders and slice the rock more easily, Sam set up a hose and plastic bucket and Tuk scrounged a gas tank from a dead snowmobile.

There were lots of near misses. One time, Phillip's mini-grinder caught fire. Another time, a full moon, high tide, and howling gale combined to drive the waters of the bay a record two feet higher than normal, washing away tools, generators, and gas cans. Sam rushed wild-eyed into George's tent at midnight, yelling, "We're finished, we're finished!"

In the middle of the storm, Sam and George launched the rubber raft and plunged through the waves to try to fish out equipment that was spread over a mile of rough, freezing seas. And then they had to spend more days stripping down what they had retrieved, removing salt water and getting their tools to work again.

Death comes easily in such seas. There was another time their apprentice, Luke, pitched into the numbing waters while seal-hunting alone in the rubber raft. Seeing a seal poke its head up, Luke jumped for his rifle, jerked the tiller too hard at high speed, and fell overboard. Miraculously, he grabbed a safety line and hung on as the boat kept going. Somehow, he pulled himself back into the boat and steered for camp, frozen and almost drowned.

Ice continued to cause problems. George was to tell me later, "Ice looks gorgeous but it's frustrating. It goes away and you get to work, then the wind changes and it comes in again. Once an iceberg landed right on top of the marble block we were sculpting and stayed there for days."

Finally, five days after I arrived in Cape Dorset, Jimmy said he could take me to Andrew Gordon Bay after work. An apprentice, Simeonie, came with us to help George carve Sedna, the largest figure in the tableau, and hunt food for the camp. To my surprise, Sam chose to stay behind in Dorset with his family and to help Tuq Nuna who was carving Walrus from a big block of gneiss (granite). Sam and Tuq would return to camp at the weekend with a film crew—weather willing.

Once the decision was made, our departure had to be timed precisely, not only for the tide at Cape Dorset but also for the tide in Andrew Gordon Bay. If we didn't arrive at Alariak Island with enough water under us to negotiate the narrow passage into the bay, we would have to detour around the island and add two more hours to our journey. Or hike the Hoh Chi Minh Trail.

We left the stark black rock of Cape Dorset's Kingnait Mountain behind and threaded through a chain of flat, pink, rocky islands. Jimmie pointed to the camp where his grandfather Peter Pitseolak, one of the first Inuit photographers, lived in the 1940s. "I used to visit him there. My grandfather did his own developing. For me, seeing images coming from ordinary paper was magic. I started taking pictures myself."

We would have landed briefly at Pitseolak's camp, but Jimmy was worried about a wall of grey fog that blocked our passage ahead. He kept closely to the shoreline where a line of *inukshuit* (stone men) on the highest ridge afforded us some comfort as they had done for Inuit over several generations. *Inukshuit* surrounded us as we beat our way through the narrow passage by Alariak Island and slammed into the oncoming tide. Jimmy twisted the wheel continuously left and right to seek the deepest water.

We swirled through the fog into a different world. I looked down through the transparent water to see our boat skimming over a multicoloured carpet of polished marble. It was a magic carpet that swept us into the carvers' camp. Polar Bear lay on its back, half-submerged in the misty sea. Sedna the Sea Goddess with her arm around Narwhal waited nearby, both still imprisoned in their stone tomb. The tools that were bringing them life lay on rocks above the high tide line. Jimmy cut the motor and we slipped quietly into shore. The absence of people added to the eeriness of the scene.

The carvers had set up their tents on the bare rock beyond the marble slabs. Brooding granite cliffs and a dark sky provided a dramatic backdrop. Obviously, the camp ate well on country food. Dozens of arctic char were splayed and hung on the drying racks. Carcasses of seal and caribou, easy smorgasbord snacks, lay on the ground outside the tents.

Inside the main tent, Phillip Pitseulak sat on an S-mite can, carving a pink marble beluga whale. George lay stretched out on a cot reading *King Lear*, and Phillip's wife, Searnaq, bent over the Coleman stirring an inviting caribou stew. I dropped my gear on one of the cots that lined the back wall of the tent. Budget-conscious George had decided that we would all sleep together to save on fuel. Searnaq poured tea and we talked of weather and hunting. Phillip had shot a duck that morning on a small lake on the other side of the granite cliffs.

"It'll be some hours before the tide is low enough to resume carving," George said. "Do you want to see the marble, Lyn?" I grabbed my cameras and we left the tent.

From the boat, the band of marble under our boat had looked like carpet. Now as I stood on land watching it roll along the beach in front of me, it looked more like a river, a highway, a runway. This geological phenomenon is not unique in the north, but it is unusual because it is so extensive, so well exposed, and so pleasantly coloured. "If it was just white, it wouldn't be so valuable," Sam had told me enthusiastically, "but it has such patterns, such colours—every colour in the rainbow—and some of the finest grain in the world."

George explained how in ancient times particles of calcium carbonite called oolites settled on the ocean floor and over zillions of years cemented themselves into what he loosely termed lime-stone. When it crystallized under the pressure of the earth's over-burden, it became marble. "Marble is the ultimate sculptural stone because unlike soapstone, it comes in pastel colours that cast shad-ows on itself. Marble portrays moodiness. The great sculptures of the world are done in light-coloured marble."

From a distance, the rolling rock river looked smooth in texture and uniform in colour. Closeup, smooth pink and white slabs alter-nated with buff and yellow bands that were pitted and pockmarked like granulated sugar. In some places where the rock was eroded into rubble, black and orange lichen made lacy patterns. We walked over a gallery of natural sculpture.

Originally, Sedna the mermaid Sea Goddess was to be white, but the elders who claimed they had seen her insisted that Sedna was "flesh-coloured like char." Fortunately, there were thick slabs of pink marble right by the carvers' campsite where boats could come in later to collect the sculptures. Blocks of marble chosen for the other figures were not so convenient. To share generators for the power tools, Shaman had to be moved the length of a city block, Seal two city blocks. With carving time limited to five or six daylight hours at low tide when the seam of marble was most exposed, Polar Bear had to be moved to higher ground where Phillip could work on it, then be moved back again to the water's edge when ready for pickup.

In the days that followed, I spent low tide silently watching George as he worked on Sedna. Skeins of snow geese honked overhead streaming south but he didn't hear them. A barren-ground caribou bull rubbed the velvet from its antlers against a boulder on the ridge behind, but he didn't see it. The tide crept slowly, imperceptibly at first, along the slab of marble at his feet till the water lapped around his ankles, but he didn't feel it. Fog, wind, sleet, and sometimes snow swirled around him, but he didn't notice.

He was alone with his vision. For six hours at a time, he stood there beside the massive pink marble block, fretting furrows into the rock face, slicing off the ridges. Every few minutes he stopped to sharpen his diamond-bladed mini-grinder on nearby rock. Always the artist, he didn't waste a stroke but carved a *qulliq* in the rock at the same time. Gradually, his face, his clothes, the sculpture itself, grew white with dust under the perpetual rattle of his tools. The pink chips flew and piled around his feet.

He washed the marble and a black quartzite slash appeared across what was to be Sedna's head. Black streaks can be left alone in the fins and tail, but not across a face. Would it become a headband or a necklace? There was still time to raise or lower the mermaid's head. George beckoned Philip, who had been finishing Polar Bear's paws, to come over and give advice. The Inuk spoke little English but by gesture and gesticulation, consensus was achieved. The black slash would become a necklace of seaweed. Philip remained to create a smile for Narwhal's face.

As the men worked, the sea advanced inexorably, lapping at their ankles and creeping up their legs. Once the carvers were standing in water, it took only minutes for Sedna to claim her own. It was an eerie feeling watching the marble entourage sink beneath the sea. While they waited the hours for the figures to reappear, the carvers moved up the beach to their tents. They carved smaller pieces for themselves: Philip, a pink beluga whale; George, a white halibut. The radio crackled ceaselessly in static or Inuktitut. Sometimes, Philip left the tent to hunt. George stayed to read or play his guitar.

At high tide, I went exploring with Simeonie. We followed the marble highway east to a grassy meadow which was once a Thule campsite. The heavy lichen cover on the sunken tent rings, stone gravesites, and remains of human skulls attested to its age. Old vats of oil left over from boiling whale fat were scattered on the beach. According to Sam, a whaling ship was wrecked here in 1847.

While my thoughts were occupied with past history, Simeonie's thoughts were constantly on the sky, the land, and the water. Always the hunter as I am always the photographer, he watched for any slight change of shape or movement that would bring food to his gun. We climbed the high ridge behind camp and made a wide circle to the south and west over the brilliant fall-coloured tundra. The fog was rolling in again, blotting out the sky. We took the marble highway home.

Other hunters had arrived. Pee Meekeega, one of Cape Dorset's well-known print makers, and his friends and relatives were to stay the night. They laid their caribou skin blankets on the ground in the warehouse tent and came to the main tent for tea. As each hunter entered, he hacked off a chunk of raw caribou with his knife and found a seat on a cot or S-mite can. Meekeega told me that the wind was too strong for Jimmy to come and get me. I was stuck, I suppose, but time and schedules dimmed in importance as the days passed. I had almost forgotten that Air Baffin was going to take me to Sanikiluaq, that I would be late for an appointment in Ottawa. Only the present seemed to matter in this timeless land. Like the Inuit, I shrugged. "*Ayorama*," I said, "it can't be helped."

Next day, Simeonie said that Ahota, the project's ferryman, was arriving in the big boat with Tuq and the film crew. They couldn't come into the bay by the shortcut: they had to walk the Hoh Chi Minh Trail.

When the six newcomers reached camp there was scarcely time for introductions. Simeonie burst into the cook tent and shouted, "Caribou! Caribou!" Apparently, he had shot a caribou by the Thule camp. Its leg was broken but somehow he had forgotten his hunting knife so he had to let it swim away. The film crew dropped their tea and pilot biscuits, grabbed their cameras from still-locked cases, hurried down to the water, and set up their tripods. I followed hastily but tried to keep out of the scene.

Oblivious to cameras, Simeonie and Ahota launched the rubber raft and, despite fog and heavy swells, took off after the caribou. The wounded animal was only a blimp in the screen-wide sea. Within minutes, we heard a shot, a sudden gunning of the motor, and through our lenses, we saw they had gaffed their prey. The cameras rolled as they dragged the caribou onto the beach. That night, Sharon, Ellen, and I roasted caribou tenders for those who preferred cooked meat. When the stove blew up, I threw it out through the door just in time to save the tent. Perhaps it would be safer to eat the Inuit way.

"Will Jimmy be coming tomorrow?" I asked Ahota.

"*Imaka*," he shrugged. "Maybe."

It was cold, windy and wet next morning, but Jimmy arrived in his boat with Sam. Drenched, they were as irrepressible as ever. Meekeega's group had gone, but the rest of us crowded into the cooktent, knelt on the pebbles or squeezed onto the cots. Versatile Sam, who once had led his own band, took over George's guitar and improvised personal songs for us all. George retreated into reading Shakespeare. Until low tide.

I wanted to stay but winter was coming fast. Soon the carvers would be spending more time trying to survive than carving. Nobody knew yet how Polar Bear, Sedna, and Narwhal would be transported back to Dorset or even how they would get to Toronto. The weather told us that it wouldn't be in nets behind oil drums and rubber rafts.

My last day at Andrew Gordon Bay dawned clear and cold. It was a perfect day for photography, but I was not surprised when Jimmy told me we must take advantage of the weather and leave within two hours.

I ran to ask George if Polar Bear could be raised before I left. All week I had been watching the tidal pools, waiting for the wind to die down and the sun to come out so that when Polar Bear stood tall on the beach for Philip to finish, I could picture its image in the tidal pool's reflection.

"Let's wake up the film crew so they can use the opportunity too," said George.

The next hour raced past as I waited in my chosen spot and anxiously watched the sky. Fog and cloud were never far away in Andrew Gordon Bay. I needed bright sun in the right place for the best image.

Fortunately for me, the men worked quickly. Simeonie bored a hole in the marble and set up the come-along which would act as an anchor and also provide the basic power to raise the statue. George and Sam slid 4 x 4 blocks of wood under the back of the bear, which was tied in ropes and lying prone on a narrow peninsula of land between the tidal pool and the sea. Philip attached the wire rope from the hackle of the come-along to the bear. When all was in place, the men and the film crew took their positions: Sam at the come-along, George by the body of the bear to keep it from edging sideways, Philip at the end of a stretch rope to steady the statue, the film crew close to the action, me behind them.

Above the whine of the generator and the click of the come-along, the men called to each other with anxious instructions. "Tighten the choke . . . The bear's swinging sideways, hook the rope . . . Push it two feet your way . . . Slide another 4 x 4 behind it . . . Get another rope from the Zodiac . . . Easy now."

Slowly, the big white bear inched upward. In the deteriorating light, I clicked shot after shot as it rose to its feet and stood towering over the carvers at the edge of the sea. Polar Bear is Lord of the Arctic. Nobody denies its title. Its size and might attest to that—but Philip had made Sedna's Polar Bear almost cuddly with oversize paws crossing its heart like some friendly Boy Scout. The carvers loosened its ropes then wedged the massive statue tight on all sides to keep it upright to withstand the tides.

It was time for me to go.

A month later, Sedna, Narwhal, and Polar Bear were lifted from Andrew Gordon Bay by landing barge from the Canadian coastguard ship *John A. Macdonald* to join Seal, Shaman, and Walrus in Cape Dorset. Then as ice and snow reclaimed the land and sea for another year, the *Aivuk*, the last cargo ship of the season, took the Sedna ensemble down Davis Strait and through the St. Lawrence Seaway to Montreal; from there, a truck transported the sculptures to their final resting place in Toronto.

As busy shoppers and office workers now hurry past Sedna standing with her friends in the lobby of a big southern bank, few are aware of Sedna's birth pains on a lonely northern beach.

Winging It with Ivy

"I'M COMING TO VISIT," said my best friend Ivy over the phone.

I was horrified, not because I didn't want to see her but because of the time and the place. For more then ten years I had asked her to visit the Northwest Territories, a part—a large part—of Canada that very few southerners appreciate because they haven't been there. I wanted her to stalk polar bears, muskox, and walrus; to drive a dogteam, raft a river, or camp on an ice floe.

But she had always protested. "I don't like cold, mosquitoes, barrenness, or primitive living. I like comfortable beds, good food and wine, and culture." With that she'd gone off to museums, art galleries, and theatres in Europe, luxury ski resorts in the United States, tropical paradises in the South Pacific. No amount of persuasion could convince her that we had culture in the north.

So now that she wanted to give the Northwest Territories a try, why was I horrified? Because at the time she wanted to come I was committed to staying home for a while. Home was Fort Simpson, a pretty settlement overlooking the Mackenzie River, a place with great historical significance but in my opinion not spectacular enough to warrant a once-in-a-lifetime trip for a reluctant tourist.

Moreover, Ivy gave me no time to pre-plan an itinerary. Okay, I told myself, we'll wing it, that's part of the North's appeal. "You have to be flexible up here and go with the flow," I warned her over the phone. "Take Canadian Airlines' milk run flight from Edmonton to Fort Smith, Hay River and Yellowknife. Talk to the passengers. I'll meet you in Yellowknife and we'll go from there."

She confessed she didn't really know where Yellowknife was, or for that matter, that Yellowknife wasn't Whitehorse. Nor did she know that the Northwest Territories had nothing to do with the Yukon. "But I'll learn," she said blithely.

At least, I told myself, we would start the two weeks in grand style on the weekend of the Canadian Airlines Yellowknife Midnight Golf Tournament, an annual event each June in which golfers from across Canada gather under the midnight sun at the Yellowknife Golf Club to play golf—northern style. "And you don't need your furs. It can be quite hot in June."

Trouble was, it rained. I slogged through the muck and mud of the Mackenzie Highway, taking twice the usual time to drive from Fort Simpson to Yellowknife. Ivy slithered across the sodden tarmac of Yellowknife Airport in her expensive Italian sandals and tropical walking shorts. Together, we climbed into my pickup truck and drove to town to check in to the Explorer Hotel. This iceberg-in-the-sky that dominates the Yellowknife skyline is grand and luxurious but at the time of Ivy's visit, it was under renovation.

Despite such an introduction, Ivy was glad she came. At least, that's the impression I get when I read her diary of our eventful two weeks winging it through the North close to home.

❊

If I was given only one word to describe what I thought of the NWT as the days progressed, that word would be "contradiction." It suggests itself even before the plane has landed. Either the Subarctic is a large lake networked with clumps of land or it is a large land mass shot through with puddles and lakes. The landscape set up echoes in my mind of a childhood spent on the Canadian Shield. The same scrubby trees and rock, the same flat terrain, and the same down home feeling between people.

194

Our hotel, built to resemble a giant iceberg, becomes for me a microcosm of what is taking place in Yellowknife itself. Construction and reconstruction with a vengeance. But, in spite of the plastic sheets hanging from the ceiling, and the entrance and foyer reduced to a shambles of boards and nails, people smile and joke their way around bits and pieces of renovation as if inconvenience was the best thing that has happened to them. Forward motion should not be checked, and I sense that forward motion is what Yellowknife is all about.

And yet from my room on the eighth floor, nothing but peace and repose meet the eye. Old Town and Latham's Island in the fine misty rain of early evening—a wonderful study in greens and browns and shimmering water. No forward motion here: more like a postcard set in time. Which is the real Yellowknife?

❋

The unusually dreary weather does not affect the warmth of the welcome awaiting us at the golf club. Ivy is unused to balls bouncing off rocks, burying themselves in sand, being stolen by ravens or having to be washed. She has never before tee-ed off from platforms festooned by flower pots and pop bottles, nor has she dragged mats behind her to smooth the "greens" of sand not grass. We take three times longer than our companions to do the course, but in typical Yellowknife style they maintain their sense of humour and are patience personified. She appreciates the small bottle of warming fluid her golf mates give her to be taken internally.

❋

I haven't been up this late since New Year's Eve, yet here I am in a clubhouse which was once the fuselage of a DC3 with mud streaks all over my white and aqua designer rain gear, hair dripping into my beer and soggy feet keeping time to the music, feeling like I'd just conquered Everest. All around me are people laughing, comparing scores, swapping mosquito/rain/golf jokes and vowing to be back next year. I raise my glass. Yes, I'll drink to that.

❊

Next day we take a tour of Yellowknife.

❊

Stemware of champagne and orange juice on a starched linen table in the Factor's Lounge of the Explorer Hotel greets me for breakfast. Did I expect chipped pottery and oil cloth?

Contradiction and contrast are everywhere. In New Town mansions sit cheek-by-jowl beside one-room log cabins and two-room trailers. In Old Town there is no well-defined lot line or nicely set out city street. Yellowknifers have elected to preserve shacks in the name of heritage that any other city would have bulldozed decades ago.

But people still live in them! People with a sense of humour. Model airplanes, plywood flowers, and grinning beavers decorate the outside walls of historic edifices. A hand-lettered sign proclaims that here once resided Slim Campbell who died on this site in the olden days (1962). Outhouses are built as add-ons to outhouses.

As I look around this unlikely piece of real estate and chuckle at the Ragged Ass Road sign, I suddenly become aware that Yellowknife is very little older than I am. What kind of history is this? The shack where the ladies of the night once plied their trade isn't exactly the Cathedral at Chartres but it is being trotted out as a fine example of Yellowknife's past. Perhaps Yellowknifers have learned from others' mistakes that by the time society gets around to valuing something it is often gone. They may have no Sistine Ceiling but what they have is where they've been.

Evening. I throw off the rubber boots that Lyn insists I wear all day and I feel almost elegant in my New York silk original as I descend for dinner. It is the golf tournament's awards banquet. Even my gourmet palate finds nothing to complain about during the five-course meal: every mouthful is superb. I had feared being met with blubber al dente or something unrecognizable in moose but find instead a quite civilized filet de boeuf. My dinner companion turns out to be Bryan Pearson, a former MLA and our conversation quickly turns to opera and the season at Bayreuth.

196

Just as I am feeling that I might be in any of the great cities of the world—London, Paris, Rome—Lyn interrupts to inform me that I must change immediately into jeans and dash over to Petitot Park for caribou stew with some canoeists who are paddling to the Arctic Ocean. Just before dessert?

I adamantly refuse to change into jeans. This is unfortunate as at the swampy end of Petitot Park I have my first major skirmish with the animal life for which I understand the North is famous. Forget about muskox and polar bear. The fauna that sets its stamp here (in blood) is none other than the lowly mosquito. Never have I been so popular. Open-toed sandals and bare legs that stretch on into bikini panties, decolletage and short puffed sleeves. I have it all. And how they appreciate me! I leave Lyn waving her arms in what is to become for me the Territories salute and I beat an unceremonious retreat back to the protection of the Explorer Hotel.

❄

At last the rain stops and the midnight sun starts shining. It's 3:00 A.M. so I decide not to wake Ivy because at 6:00 A.M. Chummy Plummer is taking us on an hour-long flight to Taltheilei Narrows on Great Slave Lake for the opening of fishing season. A wolf bounds across the airstrip as we land at Plummer's Fishing Lodge. I am impressed.

But Ivy is more impressed with the fishing—forty-pound lake trout are common here. Ice still covers much of the lake. "We can catch our fish already frozen," she quips as we pile in the boat with companion Graham Mann and guide Dennis Fontaine. Despite the ice all around our boat, it feels hot, and Graham catches a couple of respectable eighteen-pounders.

He generously gives us his fish to take home, but back in Yellowknife, Ivy yearns shamelessly for Kentucky Fried Chicken. I am determined to get her used to northern culture. I want her to eat country foods like caribou, muskox, and char the way aboriginals eat them—raw, boiled, or dry. She doesn't look keen at all.

She insists on eating conventional food, but I entice her to eat in unconventional places. We climb to the roof of a shoebox house that slants up a rock for a barbecue in the sky. We exchange yarns with

Dene, Inuit, and other longtime northerners over coffee at the Miners' Mess. We eat Chinese food at the Strange Range in the company of belly dancers. We chat to the cook in the kitchen of the Wildcat Cafe, one of Yellowknife's original log buildings.

❄

Those days in Yellowknife become something of a haze. Lyn is inexhaustible in her attempts to flag down a suitable itinerary. "You have to be flexible," she keeps telling me, but she didn't say anything about training for the decathlon. We run from one end of Yellowknife to the other, toting bags, gulping meals, considering and discarding ideas faster than Ben Jonson can get out of the blocks. Through all of this, Lyn insists I wear rubber boots even after the rain has long ceased. "Be prepared for everything," she says, determinedly.

I am wearing the boots when she takes me upstairs to have lunch at Our Place, Yellowknife's most elegant cocktail lounge on the main street. The minute we enter I'm wishing I am some other place than Our Place. If only my backpack blended better with the brocade. Gorgeous Grace, the owner hostess, leads us past dark-suited business types as if we were visiting royalty. Maybe in the North anything goes.

Lunch over, we get the word Lyn says she's been waiting for. "Head for Muriel Betsina's, she's ready to take you." Then follows another four-minute-mile to local tourism operator Bill Tait's office, where we engage in a little power-waiting for all of the pieces to come together. Again I am struck by the contrasts—quick flurried starts followed by retrenchment and consideration. Of what? I'm never entirely clear. It's a bit like waiting for Godot—what you expect never quite takes place. Next thing I know I'm standing on a rickety dock in Ndilo confronted with a brand-new power boat. It belongs to Muriel's brother George Blondin who has just had it trucked up from Edmonton. George is used to canoes and kickers (outboard motors), I am told, not big power cruisers. As a long time boat owner down in Vancouver, I am expected to get this new boat started and then take it over to his sister's island where we are going for another lunch.

I try to tell Lyn that I know nothing whatever about outboard motors: that our twenty-eight-foot Uniflite is driven from a command bridge which affords a splendid view of everything except the machinery. I can't even find the key—or where to put it. George can, however. And, as I rummage through the glovebox looking for instructions and entertaining visions of pushing Lyn overboard strapped to an anchor, we are silently cut loose and paddled out into deeper water.

Somehow through trial and error I get the leg down and we are off at breakneck speed with a strong wind coming up. George takes the wheel and, like any male with a new toy, ups the speed to full throttle.

Muriel, screaming against the wind, cautions him about breaking in the new motor. George roars on. After a few moments I start to relax a little. Although a low cloud sits over us, the scenery from well down in the water is superb: Yellowknife fading into the distance, the native village of Dettah looming on our left, and our destination—a little island that is suddenly becoming larger and larger. Surely we are going around it. But no. Without warning and without slowing down or deviating from his dead-ahead course, George leaps out of the captain's chair, yelling as he leaves the wheel, "How do you stop this thing?"

We do stop. In eight inches of water. Later when George goes out to practise he finds that the first item on his shopping list in town will be a new prop. In fact, he wonders if he should get a case lot while he's at it. I encourage him to go for the quantity discount.

Our little troupe struggles on to Muriel's Island. Here I see how hides are tanned, how fish and meat are dried, how the native people set up camp and I hear from both her and George something of the history of their people as well as something of their own personal philosophies. No-one could fail to be moved by the quiet dignity and strong sense of purpose of these two. In my mind, George and Muriel should be declared national treasures.

A late sun appears. Muriel sets out the meal. I approach the table with some apprehension having already tried the smoked fish appetizer produced from a fifty-year-old dried meat bag made of caribou skin. (From the taste of it, the fish might be even older.) But my surprise is matched only by my enjoyment of the meal itself. Potatoes, carrots and braised moose, the secret of which, Muriel tells me, lies in soaking the meat overnight in onion water. Simple but delicious, I have to admit.

As the smoke from the birch fire drifts over the camp, George adds to my sense of having gone back in time by singing some of the songs of his ancestors. The insistent beat of the caribou hide drum sends images through my mind of some simpler elemental past when man and nature were one. The sound is not a melody as the white man defines it: it does not speak to the ear. It speaks instead to the blood. And for those few moments as the sun casts its rosiness all around us, I feel that I am with people I have known all my life and even before that. I am with the wise ones in a world that can only momentarily be revisited.

With this mood still on me, I want to get back to my room and just sit. But sitting is not on Lyn's list. I doubt she has any real grasp of the concept at all. Instead we fly down the streets again—a three-mile walk, a one-mile midnight paddle (with the mayor), a hitch-hike back to town, a quick drink at the Strange Range where some of the white man's culture sheds both clothes and inhibitions, and so to bed. Just another day in the NWT—or at least Lyn's version of it.

The next day, Lyn takes me to her home in Fort Simpson. I have given up wondering what to expect so it does not surprise me that one of my first excursions there is a trip to the dump. You haven't seen a town until you've seen its garbage. Acres and acres of it. Gazing over the rubble of bottles and cans and old building materials, I wonder why no bottle deposit law has been encouraged. I want to warn these people about litter, about their environment, about the need to act now to preserve the beauties of the land. How can they be sure that a land so flat and empty will not be looked at one day as an excellent dumping ground for the waste products of the entire nation, or for that matter, the world. If today Vancouver can truck its garbage to Cache Creek, who knows what twenty years will bring? If people here can act to conserve their fish stocks—and they have—surely they can find a way to get all those beer cans off the roadsides and back for recycling.

Lyn is busy so I am left on my own. A stroll down the main drag of Fort Simpson doesn't remind me in the least of the Champs Élysée.

In fact, it doesn't remind me of any other main street that I have ever encountered. The buildings are all widely dispersed—here the Bay (now called the Northern), another block away the liquor store (open for only two hours a day), and somewhere over yonder a gas station. Land is obviously not at a premium here. Vancouver developers would kill for empty spaces like this on the Lower Mainland. I wonder what the next fifty years will bring.

I wander down to the river with the bag lunch I have brought from Lyn's. The Liard, brown and slow, rolls right along this stretch and joins the Mackenzie just at the head of the town where it receives an infusion of bright blue water. After the hustle and bustle of downtown Fort Simpson (I joke), I am happy to sit with my feet in the river and watch the blowflies swarm around an old black lab who has befriended me and with whom I share my lunch.

I wander along the spring-eroded banks to see the Papal Site. A scene of vast and unlimited space, symbolic perhaps of the gulf between man and God, greets me and I try to envision the crowds that must have thronged here under this marvellous Cross to receive the Pope's blessing. All is still and empty now and I cherish this chance (to paraphrase Keats) to gaze silent upon a field in Fort Simpson.

For the walk home I have been given directions which will allow me to stay close to the river most of the way. The only hitch comes when the small stream I'm to wade across turns out to be a mini-river in its own right—at least fifty feet wide. What to do? Knowing that much of the water in the Territories (at least in this region) is fairly shallow, I decide to go the wading route rather than backtrack. I mean I'd look pretty foolish if I walked all the way back to town and the "stream" turned out to be only six inches deep.

Aries are seldom daunted by adversity, in fact they are often encouraged by it. So off with the shoes and socks, roll up the knee-length shorts, and plunge in. After the first few tentative steps I begin to wonder if I haven't made a mistake of the serious kind. The soft grey mud underfoot becomes even softer until I am being sucked in up to my knees—and there's at least a foot of water on top of that. The water is surprisingly warm, and I wonder if when it reaches my armpits I should try swimming. The fact that I must look ridiculous causes only a passing thought; my main concern is for the camera in my backpack.

I look even more ridiculous when I stagger onto the opposite shore, pulling each mud-laden leg with great difficulty from the primal ooze. I am wet to the waist, my legs are streaked with fine silt mud, my clothes are a mess, and I have nothing to dry my feet with. Lyn thinks I've been assaulted when I finally return to her trailer, but no, I assure her, it's just your average sightseeing trip in Fort Simpson.

Not the least average is my flight by Twin Otter over the Ram and Nahanni rivers the following day. Incredible mountain peaks, deep canyons and plunging valleys, another world entirely. We circle Virginia Falls, twice as high as Niagara, and I marvel at the thought of prospector and trapper Albert Faille, a legend in this country, taking his scow apart at the base of the falls, carrying his lumber, his motor, and the rest of his gear to the top of the falls, then putting it all together again for the continuance of his journey upstream to look for the motherlode. This he did nearly every year till he was an old man. Yes, if I return to Fort Simpson, I will take a trip by boat down the South Nahanni.

After two days of high living in Fort Simpson, we are off along the Liard Highway, more aptly called the Liard Trail, bound for the Blackstone River where it meets the Liard. Here I meet the Lindberg family, old friends of Lyn's who have homesteaded here for decades. What a variety of new experiences: helping to cook a meal without electricity and running water; driving an ATV along a trapline; sharing Happy Hour with an affectionate goat on a deck overhanging the Liard river; visiting the sagging remains of Anna Lindberg's home cabin in which the blue wallpaper is still intact. The matching delphiniums she planted long ago must love this spot. They have multiplied throughout the fern forest and, paradoxically, seem both incongruous and natural at the same time.

But it is in talking with neighbouring trapper John Turner that the theme of contradiction returns to haunt me. I don't know what I thought a trapper ought to sound like but certainly not like John. A raconteur, a philosopher, a wit. From John, I who work with words every day, learn a new one (one I swore did not exist)— "parsing" which means to break up a sentence into its component parts of speech. How did a man who has spent most of his adult life on a trapline learn these things? And how can a man who shows every evidence of being sensitive and kind continue to use leg-hold traps without apology? I can see I have a lot to learn about the North.

❄

I am determined to give Ivy a sample of everything the Subarctic has to offer. Fortunately, days are almost twenty-four hours long, and without too much complaint we get to use them all. Yellowknife, as the capital of the Northwest Territories, is a great place to take advantage of the extemporaneous. Yellowknifers are always going places, doing things. Before Ivy catches her flight home, we return to the capital and I make an impromptu decision to go fishing in Lac La Martre. "It's only a forty-minute scheduled flight northwest of Yellowknife and they say the lake is packed with fish," I urge. "Also you get to see another small Dene community, Lac La Martre, or as they call it now, Wha Ti."

There are more lakes in Canada than in all other countries put together, and most of Canada's lakes are in the Northwest Territories. Flying over them, they all look pretty much the same. "A kid's finger painting of reed-lined sludgy soup, most of them," says Ivy, looking down from the plane.

And then there's Lac La Martre. It comes at you suddenly, different from all the others, a shining emerald jewel framed by golden beaches and streaked with islands like strings of pearls. Somehow misplaced in the subarctic muskeg, it looks like a tropical lagoon.

The Dogribs call the lake Choti, which means "rainwater," and perhaps this name refers to its mirror-like surface in which the sky is reflected. Explanations for the French name are not as simple. Some say the explorer Mackenzie or his crew named the lake for the abundance of marten found there. Others think that the lake was associated in earlier times with deaths by epidemics and massacres and so it was given a name which meant "excrement." This perhaps explains why French explorers and traders called it Lac de la Meurtre which means "lake of the dead." Then it was changed to Lac de la Martre to sound more inviting.

It is certainly inviting the day Ivy and I land in town. The door of Ptarmigan Air's Twin Otter opens onto a sea of expectant faces and a line of pickup trucks. Just like it was all over the Territories in the old days, not so long ago, everybody comes to meet the plane—men, women, children, dogs. A plane is the lifeline to the outside world.

"I feel like Stanley coming to Livingston," Ivy grins as the pilots drop our gear on the airstrip and we lug it to the back of the nearest truck. Scrounging rides is common in small northern communities, and we haven't seen any taxi van or truck that says Meni Dene Lodge, the only one at the time located right in a Dene community.

Not that it matters. Wha Ti, the village of four hundred Dogribs peppering the pie-shaped slice of land that thrusts into Lac La Martre, is small enough that we could have walked. Our truck heads to the town centre, a mere hundred yards away. We scramble on with the groceries and get out with them at the Co-op. In the huddle around the store is the hotel Meni Khon, and behind a red picket stockade, a neat and freshly painted Meni Dene Lodge.

Our room is small, more like a bunkhouse or a trailer, but it is private and abuts the beach. It seems we have the lake to ourselves. The manager, Ray Bourke, has forgotten we are coming, but he says he'll arrange a boat and guide for us the following morning. The lodge is deserted.

"Everybody's out fishing at an outpost camp in the middle of the lake. The lake trout here are huge. Last week nobody got less than thirty-eight-pounders and the biggest was fifty-eight pounds."

Ray tells us that the Dene see nothing extraordinary about their monstrous fish because the fish are always there. In fact, they regard them as a nuisance because the fish rip up their nets. Trophy lake trout, they say, are not as tasty as smaller trout, whitefish, walleye, and grayling which are also available in the lake.

The fisherman from Chicago who comes struggling up the steps with a forty-pounder doesn't share the village opinion. He is positively beaming. "There's plenty more out there," he says as he poses for our cameras. "This is the best lake trout fishing in North America."

"Whoopee! I can take some south to smoke," chortles Ivy as we leave the stockade for a tour of the town.

Considering Wha Ti was settled back in 1783 when a fur trading post was established in the area, it is surprisingly traditional. The main activities are still hunting, fishing, and trapping, and many people are out now camping around the lake and drying their meat and fish for winter. Most of the houses (and other buildings) are still log cabins with log or plywood teepee smokehouses beside them. We are told that as recently as ten years ago many people lived in tents.

The well-kept cemetery behind a stockade overlooking the lake is the most picturesque part of the community. Each grave is surrounded by its own white picket fence and decorated with plastic flowers, rosary beads, cups, kettles, fresh greeting cards—even money. It is traditional to leave some of the dead person's possessions on the grave to be used in the afterlife.

Everybody is friendly, open, and unsophisticated, especially the smiling kids who soon tag along as we troop to the Co-op, the nursing station, the school, the dog compounds, and the plywood teepees where fish are being smoked. "Picture me?" they ask as they crawl over boxes of construction materials and ham it up for our cameras.

Life in Wha Ti is a whole different world away from southern cities and suburbia. I can see its appeal for anglers who want something different. I remember the blind New York fisherman who had recommended it to me. "I've been fishing the big lodges up north for years," he said, "but last year I wanted something more than a Howard Johnson-type holiday transplanted to the Arctic so I took the advice of Bill Tait from Canada North Outfitting and checked out all the people he'd sent to Meni Dene. They all raved about the good fishing and we got that, but we also got something more memorable—an immersion into native culture, congenial native guides who invited us into their homes and took us to archeological sites. We had wonderful outdoor experiences but we also felt part of the community."

Taking things in stride and being prepared for anything are desirable characteristics in travellers to the North. Next morning when the cook doesn't show up for breakfast, Ivy and I are happy when Ray turns us loose in the kitchen and we cook a meal ourselves. Working in the lodge kitchen and dining room give us further opportunities to meet the locals. Archie Beaverho, one of the hamlet's notable artists, delivers the water in the water truck then takes us to the community hall to show his latest murals.

"Jeremy, your guide, will cook you a shore lunch," says Ray later as he points us to the boats. "As you're only staying today, there's no time to take you to the outpost camps where most of the guys are but you should find plenty of fish around here and when you're tired of lake trout you can try for grayling in the river close to the lodge. You can get them on spinners or on a fly."

Ray is used to serious fishermen. Ivy is a salmon angler of note down south but I don't consider myself an angler anywhere. Ours is a spontaneous trip and I haven't even brought a rod. No worries, Jeremy, our nineteen-year-old Dogrib guide goes home to get his.

I don't know if it is his rod or his lake full of fish, but with little knowledge other than Jeremy's instructions, I spend my morning reeling in one lake trout after another. Fishing is getting in the way of my note- and picture-taking. While fish keep rising to my bait, all sorts of words and photos are getting away from me: bald eagles landing on nests and swooping down on fish, loons sailing serenely by low, picturesque, red rocky islands, and everywhere, swallows, sparrows, ducks, and arctic terns.

But most compelling is the lake itself. Sometimes I feel I am floating in sky, not water, as the clear emerald waters of the lake reflect back the rocks, the trees, the puffy cumulus clouds. Often there's not even a thin line across the horizon to remind me we are still connected to land: we have become the air and water ourselves. Big Sky is an appropriate name for the outpost camp somewhere to the north.

I'm told that Lac La Martre is large (eighty-five miles long by forty-five miles wide), that it has holes a hundred feet deep, but for me its most significant feature is colour, a wonderfully luminescent emerald colour that shimmers in the sunlight and seems tropical rather than subarctic. The lake alone is worth the trip. And it is always changing as weather patterns swirl constantly around us. I am enthralled.

"Lyn, stop daydreaming and catch fish," Ivy breaks into my reverie. "We need some for lunch."

We have been catching fish all right, but much to Ivy's chagrin, Jeremy has been throwing them all back. "We've got lots of fish up here, we can get them any time," Jeremy insists. Ivy looks at her watch. It is half past noon. Lunch time. And no fish in the boat.

Just then, the clouds above—or are they below?—darken, the sky splits, and a sudden rain squall pelts down. I think Jeremy wants to head back to the lodge. Perhaps he is disgusted that he had to leave the guys fishing the big ones at the outpost camp for the sake of two zany old ladies, one of whom doesn't even have a fishing rod and neither of whom has caught more than a ten-pounder all morning. Ivy and I are flexible but we can be stubborn. We keep the next three trout, all handy six- or seven- pounders, the right size for good eating. Resigned, Jeremy scours the lake and the sky till he finds a piece of dry, sun-patched beach for lunch.

But rain is never far away. Ivy and I work quickly to bring the grub box ashore and collect dead branches for the campfire. Jeremy has a more simple idea. He merely pulls three twelve-foot-long birch branches together and sets them alight with gas. It isn't our city-bred method but then neither is his style of cooking.

He slices off a small fillet from the fattest part of each of the three trout and leaves the rest on the sand for the eagles. Ivy and I grimace and hope that the afternoon's fishing will be as productive as the morning's. We don't mind leaving the trophies in the lake for the other anglers, we just need our limit.

Ivy watches in fascination as Jeremy heaves half a pound of margarine ("enough to grease a channel swimmer," she whispers) into a frypan and adds onions, including their skins which soon turn black. In goes another half pound of grease and two fistfuls of potatoes, no skins this time. When all is uniformly blackened, our chef sets the pan of onions and potatoes with another pan of canned beans on the outer branches of his grill cum fire and starts the main course on the hottest part of the "range." In goes more margarine then the fillets of lake trout in their batter of egg and flour. Cholesterol is obviously not a word in Jeremy's lexicon.

"Where did you learn to cook?" Ivy asks bemusedly.

"My father was a chef," Jeremy replies "—in Hay River." Ivy wisely refrains from asking where that is.

Jeremy's shore lunch may not be lean cuisine nor his trio of branches a Jenn-air oven, but even Ivy agrees it is a culinary masterpiece. And Lac La Martre sure beats the Cordon Bleu.

With only a few hours before plane time and the rain squall passing to another piece of sky, Ivy starts fishing in earnest, determined to either bring in a big one or catch her limit. With her limit reached in minutes, she at last gets used to throwing fish back. I resume my bird- and water-watching. Jeremy lies down for a snooze.

Suddenly Ivy screams. "Lyn, grab your line. Look at the size of that fish, it's following the smaller one I'm reeling in."

Jeremy jumps up, and, galvanized by the huge grey shadow beside the boat, says, "Don't bring your fish in yet. Leave it. The big ones are staying on the bottom but they'll come up to chase the smaller ones and then you can get your trophy."

I reel in my line, Ivy does as she is told, and all three of us lean over the side in excitement to watch not one, but several huge trout, all of them certainly forty-pounders, lunging, biting, grabbing at our hooks—or the fish on them. One monster leaps at a hook even when it is out of the water. "Watch your hand," warns Jeremy, "you might lose it."

The frenzy of the scene below matches the frenzy of the scene above, and in the clear emerald water we can see every move. I wonder what the trout feel as they return our stares at such close range.

"Lyn, stop taking notes and start fishing," yells Ivy, a confirmed convert now to fishing in the North.

But we have tied into the trout too late. Time has run out and our chartered plane is due too soon. We still want to visit with a family nearby who are in camp drying their fish for the winter; we have to fillet our limit, clean up, pack, and if possible, manage a meal.

Ray has dinner on the table, light in the chandeliers, and a romantic fire in the fireplace as a climax to our impromptu fishing trip. We leave in style—right from our porch door—in a chartered Air Tindi Cessna 185 float plane. Our pilot is a girl, charming and competent Donna Prowse, who patiently circles the settlement two or three times while we take pictures. From the air, Lac La Martre looks even more incredible. Incredible colour. Incredible fishing.

❄

I am delighted to find that in this seemingly macho land the pilot of our float plane is a woman. I muse on this as we fly over some now familiar terrain. What is the place of women in the North? Never have I been referred to as a "girl" so often. Lyn, who enjoys being thought of as a girl (perhaps this aberration is a holdover from her formative years in Australia) obviously overcomes some enormous obstacles in doing the kind of travelling she does in the North. The mayor of Yellowknife is a woman. So, whereas the culture appears to have some rough and tumble frontier edges, I sense that opportunities here are abundant and that women are not only accepted, but expected to make their way. Now if only someone could convince the men that after the age of eighteen, most of us have grown beyond the girl stage.

❄

We fly through a rainbow en route back to Yellowknife. Ivy comments, "I feel I can almost reach out and touch it. In fact, I'm so high I think I can fly over that rainbow without the plane."

Two hours after we leave our bunkhouse on Lac La Martre, we check into the Yellowknife Inn. Like the Explorer Hotel, it is under reconstruction as well, but I hope the Inn's history and reputation for personalized service will alleviate the disadvantages. I have asked the chef to prepare a special farewell dinner and, unknown to Ivy, I have stipulated country food.

We get in late, long after most of the staff of the Mackenzie Dining Lounge have gone home. But within minutes of our Cessna landing at Air Tindi's float base, limousine driver Vic Evoy is there to pick us up. Cheery Vic is invariably helpful and totally dedicated to his job. The YK Inn, as it is locally called, is his "home away from home." He calls his customers "family," and he treats them better than most families treat each other.

Dressed in our jeans, jackets, and rubber boots and toting our packsacks and fish, we dash into the lobby. Vic quickly stashes most of our luggage in the lobby's storage room and our fresh fish in the hotel freezer. The hotel clerks enthusiastically take on the job of extricating Ivy's hooks and lures when in our speed to get registered they get caught in her handbag. We have to hurry. Chef Patrick Kane is waiting in the kitchen with one dedicated helper to serve us supper.

Ivy and I run to the elevator as fast as our rubber boots can take us. The Yellowknife Inn is a meeting place for all in the North, in- and out-of-towners alike, so it is no surprise in the elevator to bump into Nellie Cournoyea, Premier of the Northwest Territories at the time, and Caroline Anawak, wife of our Member of Parliament. We have no time to chat.

Making a time to meet later, we reach the top floor and open the door. What a revelation! I can't believe it! The whole floor is under reconstruction, but we are given the first room to be renovated. In we stagger with our packsacks, camera bags, hiking boots, and rubber boots to a suite all chintz and brass and oak. We sit resplendent amid our camping gear, awe-struck at the plush carpet, the dusky pink and gold decor, the elegant chairs, a brass bed, a basket of fresh fruits and cheeses, and a bathroom that is bigger than most bedrooms, a bathroom that shines with lights and mirrors.

"This is like a movie set," I giggle as we gaze at our many-mirrored reflections in the makeup room.

❋

Chef Patrick Kane whips up a menu that Henry VIII would have divorced for. Smoked char in a creamy wine and cognac sauce. Caribou and Muskox Pâté served with cocktail rye and Tundra Cumberland sauce. Entrecote of Peary Caribou sauce Champignon Sauvage. Holman Island Muskox Rossini. Rankin Inlet Char sealed in parchment with a julienne of vegetables, fine herbs and butter. Now this is how I like my country food.

❋

Ivy may have preferred a longer sleep in the Inn's new brass beds for her final night in Yellowknife, but I enjoy the informality of the North when the wife of our Member of Parliament comes up to the room for a post-midnight visit. Ivy is farewelled in style as she was welcomed in style. I can't say I've spent too many luxury sleeps like this in the North, but up here anything is possible.

❋

It's not until I am on my way south that I realize I have not spoken on the phone in two weeks, haven't seen two minutes of TV or stood in a lineup or waited behind a string of angry traffic. I'll miss this place and its people because in so many ways it is also my place and my people. This is a part of Canada that has been all but forgotten by so many of us in the South. And one day soon I will return. I'll bring both my Italian sandals and my rubber boots because up here you need them both.

On Top of the World

THE GEOGRAPHICAL NORTH POLE is merely an artificial mark at the top of the globe where all time zones converge, every direction is south, and six months of daylight follow six months of darkness. When you're standing on top of the world, the terrain doesn't look much different than a snowscape in Saskatchewan.

Ekaksak, an Inuk guide who drove a snowmobile to the Pole for one expedition, hasn't seen Saskatchewan, but he agrees. "There's nothing there. All you see is just bad ice. So why do so many *qallunaat* want to go?" Imagining the North Pole to be some *qallunaaq* treasure such as a golden spike, Inuit coined a phrase for it that translates roughly as "the big nail." Inuit don't understand non-Inuit who consider the North Pole their "horizontal Everest" and go there for challenge, competition, or psychological contentment.

The Geographical North Pole has long attracted adventurers: Dr. Frederick Cook in 1908 and Commodore Peary in 1909 by dogsled; Commander Byrd in 1926 by airplane; Roald Amundsen the same year by dirigible; American submarine crews in 1958 and 1959; Ralph Plaisted by snowmobile in 1968; Wally Herbert by dogsled in 1969; and a Russian nuclear icebreaker crew in 1977.

On Top of the World

Weldy Phipps, a veteran Canadian bush pilot, flew to the Pole twice by Twin Otter: first in 1967 and again in 1971 when his wife became the first woman to land at the Pole. However, without the advantage of today's satellite-oriented navigation instruments, some of those early adventurers couldn't prove they actually got to the right spot. One of Weldy's customers who brought along his own instruments accused the pilot of not landing exactly at 90 degrees north. Other travellers to whom one ice ridge looks much like another couldn't have cared less if they landed five, ten, even fifteen miles from the magic number. For them, telling the folks back home they had reached 90 degrees north was all that mattered.

The Great Pole Rush intensified in the spring of 1978. A bevy of adventurers from around the world flocked to the polar staging base of Resolute Bay in the High Arctic Islands to tackle the Pole by a variety of methods.

From Japan came Kenochie Horie to sail an iceboat and, in separate expeditions, Naomi Uemura and a group from Nihon University to drive dog teams. From England came Sir Ranulph Twistleton-Wykeman-Fiennes and Lady Virginia to try by rubber-skirted skidoos. From Hawaii, Iowa, and other parts of the United States came tourists in Twin Otters on what was billed a Playboy Tour of the Pole—although these Playboy Bunnies from the first organized commercial tour group looked more like Silver Threads Seniors to the people from Resolute Bay. And, from Canada by Twin Otter came an elite group of Toronto businessmen with a yen to explore and help Canadian sovereignty.

Horie's iceboat—at least thirty-five feet long with a forty-foot mast and weighing over 1,500 pounds—caused much consternation in Resolute. Nobody could fathom how such a big and unwieldy craft could be sailed six hundred miles through a maze of pressure ridges and ice heaves forty feet high. Eventually, after many rehearsals in the bay and a scouting trip by DC3 to their intended starting point north of the Mould Bay weather station, Horie's crew came to the same conclusion. One of the locals quipped that the closest the ice boat got to the Pole was when a Resolute resident of Polish descent stood by it to have his picture taken. The other Japanese teams were more successful and Naomi Uemura earned the special distinction of being the first dog-sledder to get to the Pole alone. Insufficient fuel, inadequate planes, and poor weather conditions thwarted the Canadian attempt.

Although some polar adventurers start their journey from Siberia, most choose Canada. They arrive in Resolute via regularly scheduled flights, then hire a local aircraft charter company to fly them to a starting point at Ward Hunt Island on northern Ellesmere Island which, except for Cape Morris Jessup in Greenland, is the most northerly point of land in the world. In wind-chilled temperatures that can reach minus 70 degrees Celsius, they take off over more than five hundred miles of cracked, heaped, and drifting sea-ice by the method of their choice.

They do it between February and May when days are lengthening and the ice is still hard. But if the ice melts, dogs, people, and machines must find a way to cross the leads of widening water; detour around them, which may add hundreds of frustrating miles to their journey; or wait till the ice freezes together again, which lessens the time they have to get to the Pole—and back. Sometimes, they zigzag back and forth on the moving ice, losing more distance in a day than they gained.

There are other problems to face: deep snow conditions which may hide hazards, towering pressure ridges, blizzards, white-outs, frostbite, and polar bears. One adventurer quit simply because he tired of the daily drudgery of pulling a heavy sled. "I felt like a sled dog or a pack horse," he told reporters back home.

Even travellers who take the easier way and fly 290 miles to the Pole from a staging base at Lake Hazen on northern Ellesmere Island can have problems. Sometimes, howling blizzards, flat light, or thin ice prevent tourists landing even when their plane reaches the correct coordinates. "Sometimes, passengers see all those forty-foot-high pressure ridges and shifting ice floes whizzing by their windows and decide they don't want to land after all," admits polar pilot Mike Brown.

Landings on the ice are limited to less than an hour during which tourists do such things as lunch on smoked arctic char and caviar, drink champagne, dress up as Santa Claus, raise their country's flag, or just stroll around the frozen top of the world. One year, tourists got more for their money than intended. The pilot landed on a thinly disguised lead, the plane sank through the newly frozen ice, and the passengers spent six hours at the Pole waiting for a reserve Twin Otter from Lake Hazen to come to their rescue.

I have been invited on two North Pole expeditions: one with Pam Flowers, a pint-sized but determined young Alaskan woman whom I met in Gjoa Haven when she ran out of ice after crossing the continent by dogsled from Anchorage; and the other with a wealthy Texas tycoon who asked me to plan a fly-in dinner for him at the Pole in August. I hastened to explain that our dinner date would have to be delayed till the following spring. In summer, our dinner table could be under water.

Although I thrive on adventure, I declined both invitations. I don't have the talent or the stamina to walk with Pam, who has tried twice to be the first woman to get to the top of the world on foot, and I don't have the money to join a fly-in tourist trip (about $10,000). Scrounging a fam trip (familiarization trip for writers to promote a destination) isn't feasible for travel to the Pole because every seat on the plane is needed for cash-paying customers to recover the high cost of fuel.

I have never actually landed at the Pole, but I have come close. In the summer of 1978, the year of the first Great Pole Rush, I had commitments in the South, and I intended to spend only a week in the North. In contrast to my usual chaotic May-to-September wanderings, I spent an organized week at Bathurst Inlet Lodge, a proven destination that provides the essence of an arctic experience in one spot. I left behind the customary accoutrements of random travel—packsack, sleeping bag, and other camp gear—and revelled in the luxury of the lodge and its regular daily itinerary. I even packed high heels and a floor-length Hawaiian muumuu to pose for pictures in the midnight sun. That was the plan.

However, the day I got back to Yellowknife from Bathurst Inlet, I was offered an air ticket to Iqaluit (Frobisher Bay) on Baffin Island via Resolute and $300 for three days' room and board in a hotel. Northern hotels have their quirky attractions, but I find far more grist for life and the writing mill by winging it. Even the bureaucrat agreed. "There's no point in giving you a planned itinerary. You know how it is in the North, Lyn, everything can change. We'll get you started and you can take it from there."

With a tent, packsack, and sleeping bag, and time and flexibility to wait for weather, people, and planes, I hoped to make that $300 last three months, not three days, and to ferret out a more satisfying itinerary than the one planned by officialdom.

A chance cup of tea and scones with a Yellowknife pioneer, John Anderson-Thomson, provided me with impromptu camping gear. Mr. Anderson-Thomson ("Spelled without the 'p', lassie!") was a crusty, meticulous but beloved old Scot who had surveyed almost every road, mining claim, and city lot in the North—and his forty-year-old packsack proved it. It was a simple Trapper Nelson, basically one big bag roped to a green masonite board."You don't need all those fancy pockets they sell you nowadays," he snorted. His packsack was perfect for carrying rocks and survey gear, but my body would have enjoyed a few hip-bearing, shoulder-softening modern luxuries. I turfed out the stones and strings that still lurked in the corners and piled clothes and freeze-dried food around my camera lenses. I knifed an extra hole in the strap for a bit more comfort and hoped my benefactor wouldn't notice. He'd told me to be careful with his treasured Trapper Nelson.

I could make no such compromises with his huge and heavy Woods Four-Star sleeping bag, which the ads maintained was fit for fifty below. Fortunately, taxis in the North are often pickup trucks or sleds and toboggans pulled by fat-wheeled all-terrain-vehicles, and sturdy enough to handle my heavier-than-usual camping gear, at least at airports. As events turned out that summer, I scrounged enough free sleeps that I didn't need my benefactor's sleeping bag, even near the North Pole.

Such were transportation routes in 1978 that to get east to Baffin Island, I first had to fly north to Resolute. Although this small community of fewer than two hundred people is situated in the High Arctic Islands, 596 miles north of the Arctic Circle and only 994 miles from the North Pole, it is one of the most easily accessible parts of the Arctic. Resolute's strategic position and importance as a transportation crossroad came about by accident.

In 1947, the Canadian and U.S. governments sent ships with people and supplies to build a Joint Arctic Weather Station (J.A.W.S.) at Winter Harbour on Melville Island, one of ten planned across the North. However, heavy ice conditions prevented the ships from reaching Winter Harbour, and the station was built on the beach at Resolute Bay instead. Two years later, the Royal Canadian Air Force established a base and built an airstrip and other facilities on higher land nearby. In 1953, the weather station was moved from the beach to the airport, and the expanded complex became known as the Base.

The Base was a powerhouse in the 1960s and early 1970s when dozens of exploration companies and scientific groups used it as a logistics centre for their field research. Transportation, construction, and fuel companies proliferated. Atlas Aviation (Weldy Phipps), Kenn Borek Air, and Bradley Air Services pioneered flights to the Pole. The Department of Transport opened up an accommodation complex of prefab trailers which looked like a sprawling rabbit warren and painted them a bright orange. The Base's nerve centre was the Arctic Circle Club Bar, a popular watering spot, and the place where people who went to the Pole were inducted into the exclusive Order of Arctic Adventurers.

At a busy time such as the annual sea lift, as many as a thousand people lived and worked in Resolute—and devised their own fun to combat Resolute's isolation. Maurice Cloughly, the local school principal whose sailboat was in Ireland at the time, established the Resolute Bay Yacht Club in his house and ran regattas in water-filled school sand trays. Yachtsmen constructed their own boats and propelled them down the sand tray with electric fans.

With its location as a crucial stopover on the way to somewhere else, Resolute attracted a lot of visitors. Even Queen Elizabeth visited Resolute. The Resolute name has royal connections. HMS *Resolute* was one of dozens of ships that searched for signs of the ill-fated Franklin expedition. In 1854, the *Resolute* became frozen in ice, was abandoned, and eventually drifted twelve hundred miles before being rescued by an American whaler. Fully restored by the U.S. government, the ship was sent back to England as a gift to Queen Victoria. In 1880, Queen Victoria presented a desk made from the *Resolute*'s oak timbers to U.S. President Hayes, and the "Resolute desk" is still being used in the White House today.

At the time of my visit in 1978, there were three separate communities in Resolute: the Base at the airport where most of the *qallunaat* lived; the Old Village at the beach which had been created in 1953 and 1955 when Inuit families were moved there from

Port Harrison and Pond Inlet; and a just-completed New Village destined for everyone. Architects had designed a futuristic dome, a plastic bubble, to enclose the new buildings and keep in the heat. Workers were constructing an underground utilidor to support it. (The dome idea died but the underground insulated pipes that transported running water, steam heat, and sewage lived on; the utilidor is now the only one in the North.) Cameras were set up on a hill above the town to document the move from the Old Village to the New Village.

Its detractors often refer to Resolute as Desolate Resolute, sometimes even Dissolute Resolute. High winds, blizzards, whiteouts, and ice fog are common. The dark season lasts four months, and when the snow eventually melts in July there is little to be seen on the land but gravel and rock. Resolute's Inuktitut name is Qausuittuq, which various people translate as "tomorrow never comes," "darkness," or "never has light." (Obviously, it is winter darkness that people remember most, not the continuous summer light of the other four months.)

"Cornwallis Island is perhaps one of the most dreary and desolate spots that can well be conceived," wrote a crew member on an icebound ship that in 1854 wintered in the vicinity of Resolute Bay while searching for the lost Franklin expedition. "It was like landing on the moon," John Amagoalik told a royal commission investigating complaints of Inuit who moved there. "I've called it 'desolate' ever since I was a teenager," said Minnie Nungaq, who was five in 1953 when her family and three other families pitched their tents on Resolute Bay's gravel beach to start the new community.

Resolute was living up to its reputation when I dropped down for what was intended to be an overnight stay en route to Baffin Island. I crossed the tarmac quickly to escape the raw July wind and entered the tiny terminal building to get warm and claim my luggage. Having no particular contacts or plans, I made a nest out of Mr. Anderson-Thomson's sleeping bag, got out my notebook, and just looked around to see what was happening.

Although Resolute's boom years were coming to an end and most oil companies had pulled out, "plane time" had filled the terminal with people and the accoutrements of their professions. I tried to guess what they were doing. Prospectors and geologists changing planes to look for minerals in the High Arctic Islands. A government land use inspector going to Rae Point, where Panarctic Oil had two drilling sites. Researchers in a variety of disciplines on their way to field camps supported by the Polar Continental Shelf Project. Scientists shuttling in and out of the Eureka weather station. A federal administrator planning a national park for Ellesmere Island. A biologist from the Canadian Wildlife Service collecting caribou stomachs on a government-sponsored native hunt. Pilots, cooks, and construction workers making regular crew changes. A wildlife artist going to Grise Fiord, which, except for the military base of Alert and the weather station of Eureka, is Canada's northernmost community. Their clothes and their equipment gave them away, but the gentleman dressed so incongruously in a striped business suit had me stumped. Except for polar adventurers who came in spring, very few tourists had discovered Resolute. I never saw him again.

Everyone, it seemed, had someone to meet them except me. Suddenly, my reverie was interrupted by a young blond-haired man dressed casually in an open T-shirt, a thin cardigan, and yellow Adidas. "Are you the media?" he asked cheerfully, in more of a statement than a question.

"We-e-ll . . . ," I started to explain. "I write and take pictures but . . ."

"Good! How would you like to play golf at the North Pole tomorrow?" The stranger paused. "Well, close enough to the North Pole. I invited the Prime Minister, the CBC, and other media for the First Annual Ellesmere Island Invitational Golf Tournament and Fishing Derby at the top of the world, but nobody replied. Perhaps they didn't think I was serious."

Tom Frook, flamboyant base manager for Kenn Borek Air, gave a quick rundown on the next day's plans. "Nobody official's turned up except for a Seattle couple who plan to run tourist trips to the Pole, but I've rounded up some of the locals and we'll take off tomorrow in the Twin Otter at 9:15 P.M. We should be teeing off at Lake Hazen about one or two o'clock in the morning."

According to Frook, fewer than a hundred people had been to Lake Hazen, the northernmost lake in the world. This flight would be Kenn Borek Air's third trip there—ever—and its first golf tournament and fishing derby. We would be landing on a tundra strip that had never been landed on before.

"Last week we dropped off a couple of grunts [guys] with a Bobcat and a shovel to scrape out an airstrip and lay out a golf course. They've probably not finished it yet but we're going anyway."

I could scarcely believe my luck.

He strode off, turned abruptly, then asked, "Where are you staying?"

"Well, I have a tent and . . ."

"No, we can put you up at the staffhouse. Bring your stuff to the truck."

The next twenty-four hours passed in a blur. There was too much going on and too many people to meet to waste time in sleep, and when I finally attached blinders to my eyes to keep out the light and dozed off for a couple of hours, I dreamed of playing golf with giant Hawaiian salad servers—perhaps because of visiting homes with murals of Hawaii spanning the walls. Dreaming of the South was one way locals survived the long winter, they said. I was dreaming of the North.

In between hitching rides around the three communities with plumbers, biologists, the Bay man, and the Settlement Manager, climbing the bluffs behind town to look for flowers in the gravel, checking with scientists at Polar Shelf, and taking in some liquid conviviality at the Arctic Circle Bar in the Airport Hotel, I managed to find conversation time with my eccentric but accommodating host.

To Tom, Resolute was anything but desolate. "I've been here three years and I really like it. I've only had four weeks back home in Edmonton since Christmas. Guess I'll have to take time off soon, else I'll have no wife and family."

Tom's sense of humour and laid-back attitude to life have helped him handle the whims of would-be polar adventurers. The Great Pole Rush of 1978 was over for the season, but because of the Pole's high press profile that year, Tom was getting a lot of enquiries from people planning to travel there the following year. Some had requests that he either couldn't or wouldn't fulfil.

One tourist wanted to fly to the Pole on New Year's Day despite the difficulty of finding a landing spot in the middle of the six-month-long arctic night. Another asked to stand at the Pole in civilized manner, not in parka and windpants, but in formal jacket and tie. A third wanted to do it alone and was prepared to pay $30,000 in U.S. dollars for the privilege, five times the going rate. A fourth, a woman, intended to go safari-style in a Hercules four-engine transport plane with a backup complement of tracked vehicles inside. A fifth wanted to be photographed at the Pole sipping champagne while being chauffeured around the ice cap in her own limousine.

One group posed a particular problem. The Hollow Earth Society from Nebraska didn't want to go to the Pole (it doesn't believe there is one). It rejects the theory that the Earth has a molten core and was preparing for a four-month journey to its "hollow interior." Society spokesman Richard Harp requested a quote for a flight from Resolute, north over Ellesmere Island, across an open Polar Sea, over the edge of the "1,400-mile-wide polar aperture" and "down through the subterranean world to the earth's central sun."

Tom replied politely that Kenn Borek Air would take anybody anywhere, even to the ends of the earth, but it was a bit difficult to estimate exactly because the particular ends the Hollow Earth Society had in mind were endless. He suggested a flying time of twenty-five hours for a total of $18,000 Canadian. However, he added a warning. "The expeditions we have supported in years past have had us flying latitudes between 70 North and 90 North between longitudes of 50 West and 150 West. We have covered nearly every inch with projects that have included explorers Herbert, Uemura, and Horie. I cannot admit to having seen any trace of an opening, or any of the warm temperatures, plant or animal life, or forest-covered mountains that you say are there."

Mr. Richard Harp of the Hollow Earth Society had sent Tom copies of his correspondence with the U.S. Senate, the Subcommittee on Science, Technology, and Space, and the Government of the Northwest Territories. He included a manifesto entitled "Nine Proofs that the Earth is Hollow." He pointed out that all explorers venturing upwards of 80 degrees north latitude are astonished by improving climatic conditions, fields of vegetation, even butterflies; that Greenland supports a thriving mosquito population; that millions of birds and assorted arctic animals migrate north at the onset of winter; and that the aurora (northern lights) is not a magnetic or electrical disturbance but a dazzling reflection from the rays of the central sun which shines through the polar orifice into the night sky. In a postscript he noted that polar gear should include insecticide and suntan oil.

In a letter to the U.S. Naval Research Laboratory, another member of the Hollow Earth Society, Clarence L. Davis, accused both U.S. and Canadian governments of covering up the fact that the chief purpose of Eureka and Alert was not weather or warring, but gathering information about the earth's subterranean world and its true physical structure.

Mr. Harp was less than amused when he received Tom's reply (and a similar one from Kenn Borek's competition at Bradley Air). He took his business elsewhere. At last word, he and nine other members of the Hollow Earth Society were booking with a Norwegian company for a flight to the centre of the Earth by balloon.

The evening we climbed aboard a Twin Otter bound for Eureka and Lake Hazen on Ellesmere Island was idyllic. With the midnight sun blazing through the window at my left shoulder and the sun's reflection at my right, I felt warm enough to see some of the truth that underlay Mr. Harp's arguments. At these latitudes, low precipitation (mostly snow) and constant northerly winds which blow away the snow from surrounding mountain slopes give the land (in summer) its brown and arid appearance. Scientists, as well as Mr. Harp, label this terrain a polar desert.

Scientists and technicians who live for six months at a time at the High Arctic weather station of Eureka on the west side of Ellesmere Island at 80 degrees north call it "The Garden Spot of the Arctic." Cooks take advantage of the twenty-four-hour-a-day sunlight to grow tubs of flowers and vegetables on window sills or in greenhouses. Eureka is Canada's most northerly postal facility and an official customs entry point (for the few who come into the country via Alert, Greenland, and the North Pole). Visitors treasure their passports which are flamboyantly stamped *Eureka: Garden Spot of the Arctic.*

Eureka was named by Scandinavian explorer Ivar Forsheim, who was trying out fiords on a cross-country trek of Ellesmere Island from east to west. He was hoping one would lead him to the Northwest Passage. Forsheim was so relieved to find a deep fresh-water sound after stumbling through icy mountains from one side of the island to the other that he named it Eureka, Greek for "I found it" and wrote in his journal, "We looked into the promised land."

We stopped down at the Eureka weather station to take on cached fuel. The cook was tending her tomatoes. One of the technicians was standing in a T-shirt outside the kitchen, feeding jaegers as the birds swooped down to take food from her hands. It was hot inside and a surprisingly warm plus 8 degrees Celsius outside.

Leaving my companions to study the weather station, I accepted a quick, impromptu trip by grader along Eureka's Scenic Drive to the Garbage Dump, the Quarry, and the recently-discovered Fossil Beds. Our route was a bumpy one over gravel beds and through barren hills, but Cliff, my friendly Newfie guide, proudly pointed out signs that read Panoramic Place, Scenic Lookout, Lovers' Lane, and Lemming Crossing. Benches were placed at strategic viewpoints. At the Fossil Beds we picked up clams, snails, and petrified wood. It was near here on Axel Heiberg Island that scientists seven years later (1985) were to find tree stumps from the time when ancient forests thrived in these High Arctic Islands. Much of the wood was so well preserved that it burned like fresh firewood.

There was no time to look for arctic hares or the biologist studying their diet preferences, or to look at any of the other Polar Continental Shelf projects which use Eureka's facilities. Our pilot was anxious to continue on to Lake Hazen. As usual, I tried to crowd as much as I could into each moment, right up to the last, and I kept the plane waiting.

Lake Hazen is a thermal oasis. The way the surrounding land slopes toward the sun provides an oasis-like ecosystem with a frost-free season whose temperatures in some years rival those of places thousands of miles to the south. In 1882, Lieutenant Greeley described the weather at Lake Hazen as "excessively hot . . . we suffered extremely." The explorer's thermometer registered an incredible plus 23.3 degrees Celsius at latitude 81 degrees north.

As we flew north along the deeply-incised coast of Ellesmere Island, glacier after glacier spilled over bowls of ice and snow at mountain-top level and spread like pancake batter down dun-coloured slopes to an iceberg-dotted sea. All was brown and blue and white, except for rivers of milky turquoise that dribbled down the middle of each furrowed tongue of ice. Each glacier looked more spectacular than the one before. Totally absorbed, I pressed my nose against the window glass and clicked one picture after another.

Many years later, those first images of Ellesmere Island remain cemented in my mind. But I wonder if my companions share the same memories now. No sooner had our pilot, Harry Hanlan, turned off the seatbelt sign than Tom called, "Party time." Instantly, everybody made their seats flat, gathered into groups and turned the Twin Otter into an outpost of the Arctic Circle Club Bar. Bottles were opened and hors-d'oeuvres were passed around. Fudpucker Air, Tom announced, was now in command.

I could lose myself in the landscape but my companions seemed to need the hospitality of Fudpucker Air to prepare them for landing. None of us, not even Harry, knew if we could land at all.

"Lake Hazen in five minutes," the pilot called from the cockpit.

"In preparation for landing, will you please drain your cans and observe the no-smoking signs," said Tom solemnly as passengers scurried to turn the Arctic Circle Club Bar back to an airplane. "Welcome to the First Annual Ellesmere Island Invitational Golf Tournament. Time is irrelevant here at Lake Hazen. When you look at your watch, you won't know what the time is anyway. So play golf, catch char, hike the tundra. Go to bed if you have to, but we hope you don't. Have fun."

Suddenly, Harry called, "Muskox!" and banked abruptly to show a lone bull fearlessly looking up to face the plane. Winging it to a golf tournament had got me to Lake Hazen and I was grateful, but the chance to see unspoiled wildlife had a higher placement on my personal agenda than golfing and fishing.

As our plane resumed its horizontal position, Tom continued. "Everybody get ready to drag your feet. This strip is only seven hundred feet long."

We all held our breaths and fingered our seatbelts as Harry began the descent. I looked nervously out the window. Most of the northern end of the lake was still covered by ice. A wall of ice-capped mountains with peaks over 1,600 feet high lined the western edge of the lake and a vast brown tundra carpet rolled by its eastern side. The only sign of civilization was the immaculate orange trailer and green Quonset-type tents of Kenn Borek's camp—and the four fuel drums which marked the corners of the "strip." I could see no sign of any golf course, but the "greenskeepers," two tiny figures standing by a Bobcat, looked up and waved. Harry made two low passes over the tundra "bumpway" outlined by the barrels, then came around for a third try. "He's going to give it a go," Tom said jubilantly.

Our De Havilland turbo-prop Twin Otter had short take-off and landing (STOL) capabilities and extra large tires designed for bouncing over rough hummocky tundra, but our pilot wasn't the kind to take chances. Pilots who do don't last long in the North. Nevertheless, I cringed as boulders rushed past my window. Making the most of the pick-and-shovelled part of the tundra, Harry touched down at the very edge of the strip. The engines roared as he pushed the propellers into full reverse and pulled back on the brakes. We sped towards the other end of the strip at alarming speed. I closed my eyes. Please, God, don't let us run out of runway.

A scant ten yards short of the fuel drums the plane shuddered to a stop. Everybody burst into spontaneous applause—then dashed to camp to look for honey-bags, those euphemistically named drums lined with green garbage bags and topped by toilet seats. Whether my companions' reaction was due to our tricky landing or their liberal imbibing, I do not know.

"What's the time?" I said to anyone who would listen.

"One A.M.," Tom replied. "And that's the last time you're allowed to ask that question."

We dumped our gear on our bunks and divested ourselves of our heavy parkas. Susan from Seattle was surprised to feel so warm. Don marvelled at the mosquitoes. Neale remarked on the width of the willow leaves. The Resolute contingent expressed amazement that, unlike Resolute, the Lake Hazen tundra was so richly vegetated. Lyle pointed to a weasel darting from its hole. We had already seen a muskox.

"This is the first day it's clouded over," said Doug, one of the pair who'd helped to dig the strip. "Today is the coldest day we've had—10 degrees above. It's been shirt-sleeve weather up till now."

"Yeah," added Ian, "and this is the first day the wolves haven't come into camp."

Wolves! Wolves were the only large mammal I hadn't seen in the Arctic in the previous two weeks.

"Yeah, a couple wander up to the door every day. A pilot flew in here yesterday and asked if we'd brought our dogs with us. He sure took lots of pictures. I bet we're the first humans these wolves have seen."

It was 2:00 A.M., but you'd never know that meant the middle of the night. The sun hung steady in a baked-blue sky. "We'll golf tomorrow," Tom said, "I'll let you know when tomorrow comes. Meantime, let's catch some char. There's only one canoe, but choose a buddy and take turns."

At the edge of the ice pack a few yards from shore, the water was so still, so clear, that you could see a char charge out from under the ice, nose the lure, nibble a bit, then strike. It happened over and over again. But as you reeled in, you found you were not the only hunter. Release one fish and a bigger one followed. Lake Hazen char are not large; they only occasionally weigh twelve pounds, but what they lacked in size they made up for in sport and abundance.

If ever we got bored reeling and releasing or reeling and eating, we could sit entranced in the canoe—listening to the tinkling music of the candled ice, watching the char as they hung in shadows in the aquamarine water—and be serene in the knowledge that this fishing hole was literally, as well as figuratively, out of this world.

By 5:00 A.M. I couldn't keep awake any longer and retreated to my cot in one of the custom-made canvas parcoll tents built originally by pioneer pilot Weldy Phipps. I slept till 7:00 A.M. curled inside the thickest sleeping bag I have ever encountered (even bulkier than the one I borrowed). Kenn Borek's camp was neat, clean, even luxurious. Tents were furnished with lamps, coffee tables, chesterfields, and beds with double-spring mattresses. They were reinforced with steel ribs and protected from the cold by four inches of insulation. Heat, light, fridges, and stoves were fuelled with propane. Comfort is costly this far north. Everything had to be flown in—and landed.

"Time for golf," announced Tom after our next meal of char. "Doug and Ian have flagged nine holes between camp and the lake. It's a Par 10 course which takes into consideration both terrain and the state of the participants. Take your parkas, mitts, cameras, mosquito repellent, glasses—and don't forget your Scotch. Let's go."

The First Annual Ellesmere Island Golf Tourney was unique. Balls were made of big, superbouncy, fluorescent-orange rubber. Clubs were hockey sticks, broom sticks, conduit pipes, or anything you could scrounge. Holes were marked by prospectors' stakes and honey-bags. Divets were any handy rocks or mud clumps. Hazards were many and varied: glacial erratics (boulders), dry creek beds (gullies), drainage ditches, ice islands, polygon ponds, jaegers, fresh caribou dung, the wind sock, the airplane, and inebriated golfers. Our only caddy—if we needed one—was the Bobcat. Our golf pro, Tom Frook, rode around in it to fill in holes after we swung our "clubs," missed the ball, and uprooted hummocks. Sometimes, he gleefully added hazards by building mounds in front of holes to make shots harder. Sometimes, Tom himself was a hazard.

The nature of the course required special arctic rules. If your ball landed on the ice in the lake, you were allowed to retrieve it by canoe (you lost points if you stayed to fish). If your ball bounced off a boulder and another player caught it, the catcher was allowed to throw it anywhere on the course he or she liked, and the hitter had to continue the game from there. If the distance between hitter and catcher warranted, the hitter was allowed, even encouraged, to tackle the catcher and throw the ball (not the catcher) into the nearest hole. We devised other rules. In our tournament, golfers didn't wait for other golfers to have their turn: they took off after their own balls whenever they wanted. Some took shortcuts back to their Scotch.

My ignorance of the game precluded me from understanding much of my companions' conversation. They were constantly making jokes about such things as "birdies," "eagles," "arctic turns" [sic], and "handicaps, both mental and physical." I was more attuned to photo opportunities, such as the time Ian hit the ball and his club flew into the air but his ball stayed behind; or when Susan hit her ball into the lake and, wielding her broomstick, jumped from ice pan to ice pan, trying to retrieve it; or when Don leaped into the air to hit a flying ball baseball-style with his hockey stick.

I can't remember who won the First Annual Invitational Ellesmere Island Golf Tournament at Lake Hazen. Perhaps memories were clouded by an alcoholic fog which persisted over the course and the clubhouse for the entire duration of our stay. Our golf pro insisted that imbibing liquids was necessary to prevent dehydration from the polar desert air, and he had plenty of supporters for this theory.

He was already drumming up business for another expedition to the top of the world, this time to seek *Horribilis Slitherisis* or Snow Snake, a fur-bearing reptile native to Canada's Arctic Islands. This elusive creature, he said, was easily recognizable by its ear muffs and elf-like snowshoes. My companions were signing up to join Tom's Snow Snake Mutual Benevolent Society when I slipped away on an expedition of my own.

I followed the shoreline of the lake south for about three miles till I reached the Ruggles River. Ice-free all year, this river was a popular fishing spot for personnel from the neighbouring military base at Alert. The army had built an *inukshuk* at the river's mouth, and I picked up some old green tin cans of army rations that I believe were bully beef and biscuits.

Jaegers and arctic terns hovered above, arctic hares hopped beside me, and tracks and droppings showed that muskox, even caribou, walked this way. But my mind was on wolves. I trudged up the Ruggles River and circled, hoping to find wolf dens in the sand banks or along the ridge that looked down upon camp.

Away from the river, the land looked dead. I sat cross-legged on the tundra and scoped the hills with my binoculars. Just rocks. I thought of the visitor to Bathurst Inlet Lodge who wrote in the guest book, "May all your black rocks be muskox and all your brown rocks be caribou." All my rocks were white. The most I could expect from them here were jaegers or snowy owls.

I was wrong.

It was only a dot at first, a white dot, but a dot that got bigger the longer I looked. A hare? No, too big. A wolf! A pure white tundra wolf! And then more dots, more wolves. One, two, three. I put down my binoculars and picked up my camera, cursing the fact that I had not brought my biggest lens and a tripod. Four, five, six, seven. I intoned the words like a chant, at first slowly, softly, then as the certainty sank in, loudly, exultantly. Eight, nine, ten. TEN tundra wolves heading towards me on the hunt. The thrill of fear shot through the joy of discovery. Head down, unaware, the wolves trotted across my screen in single file. I wanted to freeze them in my frame. I howled.

My cry was spontaneous and probably unlike any this pack had heard before, but the wolves stopped instantly. For one heart-stopping moment, ten pairs of eyes were riveted on me and mine on them. I clicked the shutter automatically, but the image was seared more permanently in my brain. Spellbound, I watched.

Abruptly, the leader turned away, and the pack followed obediently to the skyline. The spell was broken. One by one, the wolves cleared the ridge and disappeared.

Overwhelmed by the urge to tell my companions about the wolves, I stumbled back to camp as fast as the ankle-wrenching tundra would allow and burst into the kitchen.

"Wolves! Almost a dozen wolves! If you're quick, you might see them from the ridge. Bring your binoculars."

Silence. Nobody even looked up. The women had gone to bed, but the men were still huddling around the table playing poker and drinking Scotch. They were not impressed by my enthusiasm.

"So? What's the big deal about wolves?"

"They'll be back tomorrow and probably at the door."

I babbled on but nobody noticed. Here I was at the top of the world with wild wolves, but nobody to share my joy. "Please, Tom, is there any way I can phone home?" He didn't answer right away.

I waited anxiously while the next set of cards was shuffled and the next round of drinks was poured. "We could try, I guess, radio reception's not bad at the moment," he said eventually. "But I've only got enough spare gas for a minute's call." Up here near the North Pole, you fuel your phone with gas and batteries, not with coins and credit cards. "Great, let's do it," I replied. "And thanks."

Our first attempt at radio-phoning from the top of the world was stymied by busy signals, our second attempt by interference at Resolute Bay, but on our third attempt, I left the following message: "I have gas only for a minute's call but here at Lake Hazen on northern Ellesmere Island, a few hundred miles from the North Pole, it is the middle of the night, warm, and the sun is shining brightly. I have just played golf on the world's most northerly course and ten white arctic wolves have just passed right by me. Weather willing, I'll be back in Resolute on Tuesday then will head over to Pond Inlet on Baffin Island to see what happens there. Am winging it as usual. Over now for a short comment."

There was no reply, but the ache to share my enthusiasm was assuaged. I was beginning to understand why some people had such an obsession to get to the North Pole.

It would be seventeen years before I passed that way again. In the interim, the Great Pole Rush intensified. Each year, more and more people flocked to Resolute to attempt a polar expedition. Most wanted to work their way there over the ice. Some flew there direct but devised individual ways of celebrating their position. They came from Italy, Norway, Finland, France, Great Britain, Belgium, Russia, Korea, Japan, Australia, United States, and Canada. They used skis, dogs, snow machines, motorcycles, canoe-sleds, balloons, ultralights, parachutes, or helicopters. Eleven got there on foot or skis, four by motorbike or snowmobile, two with dogs. All but one were resupplied by plane with extra food, fuel, and equipment. And all booked a charter flight back. As each season passed, it became increasingly difficult to devise unique ways to do the Pole. Most people wanted the distinction of being first—the first to get there alone, the first to get there by their own power, the first to get there without resupply, the first to get there and back. In 1997 Pam Flowers hopes to be the first woman to get to the Geographical North Pole alone.

Some polar adventurers have become legends in Resolute but more by their failures than their successes. Take Ernest O'Gaffney from California who tried by motorcycle. O'Gaffney's wheels were specially adapted for ice and his handlebars were filled with nuts, raisins, and granola, but he managed only a mile before turning back. According to press reports, he expected flat roads and sled trails, not mountains of moving pressure ice.

O'Gaffney was followed by a couple of Calgary shop owners who cruised above the Pole for half an hour in a twenty-metre blue-and-yellow hot-air balloon. They tried to celebrate their success with a bottle of champagne, the traditional drink of balloons and polar adventurers, but it had frozen in the minus 30 degree temperatures.

Sir Ranulph succeeded in his second snowmobile attempt to the Pole. To get across leads and slushy ice, he and his partner used three-foot-long fibreglass water shoes that resembled canoes with flippers. Rumour had it that one of Sir Ranulph's sponsors was a major cereal company and that the aristocrat had to haul seventy cases of Weetabix to the North Pole. Prince Charles, another sponsor, said that the journey was "a refreshingly mad idea in the best

tradition of British exploration." There are many who would agree
with at least part of that statement.

The safest way to get to the Pole and back is by organized tour in
a Twin Otter from either Eureka or Lake Hazen. Passengers still
need to be adventurous. One problem that is not often discussed in
the annals of polar exploration is the difficulty of "going to the bathroom" when there is no bathroom, either at the Pole or in the plane
taking people there. Adding to the difficulty are the many layers of
clothing which passengers have to wear to survive the unaccustomed cold. Baring one's buttocks to potential blizzards is inconven-
ient as well as extremely uncomfortable.

One experienced polar pilot tells of taking some elderly Americans on a Twin Otter flight to the Pole. "Potty time came after seven
hours of drinking champagne. Everybody got down from the plane
and looked for a large pressure ridge or small snow bank but it's still
a real hassle when you're wearing so many clothes. The husband of
one very large lady in her seventies came to me as I was refuelling
the aircraft and asked me to provide a five-gallon bucket for his
wife, who refused to come out of the plane like everybody else. I
didn't have a bucket. The next thing I saw was him standing at the
door of the plane being a one-man styrofoam cup brigade. His wife
must have had a strong sphincter muscle."

Terry Jesudason, who with her late husband, Bezal, has been or-
ganizing and expediting trips to the Pole from Resolute since 1978,
has no patience with those who poke fun at polar adventurers. She
admits that some who come don't know what they are getting themselves into; however, most are very serious and dedicated to their
cause. "Some have tested themselves in the jungle and the desert
and now they want to challenge themselves on the ice." She says
that some are professional adventurers but most are ordinary people with dreams. "There'll always be dreamers, but the people who
come up here are actively doing something about their dreams."

In 1978, the year of my first blow-in visit to Resolute, Terry and
Bezal had bought some surplus houses, transformed them into a
cosy tourist accommodation called the High Arctic International
Tourist Home, and outfitted their first polar explorer, Naomi Uemura,
who was the first person to get to the Pole alone.

Almost every expedition that has attempted the Pole from then on has relied on the Jesudasons' arctic oasis in Resolute for its base and on the young couple for advice. Polar adventurers eat and sleep there, train, test their equipment, rent survival gear, and compare notes with other expeditionists. While Terry keeps guests comfortable inside, Bezal ensures that they are as comfortable as possible outside. And when their guests leave for the Pole, Bezal keeps in regular contact with them by radio and satellite. One polar explorer said he relied on his nightly chat with Bezal to give him the courage to face each arduous day.

I had kept in periodic contact with the Jesudasons over the years by phone and mail, but it was not till March 1995 that I spent any time with them, and then it was by accident. The reason that I winged my way to Resolute on March 2nd was not to join polar adventurers in prime time, but to surprise my husband for his fiftieth birthday. Frank had been living there for six months, working around the clock in temperatures that got to 60 below during the long arctic night and baching in a bunkhouse with the construction crew of the complex he was building.

He didn't know I was coming. Nor did I till the last minute.

Frank says he hates surprises, but I believe they are a good way to combat SAD or Seasonal Affective Disorder, a depression brought on partly by lack of sunlight and by confinement indoors. Ironically, SAD symptoms often show themselves more at the end of winter when increasing light makes people want to get out but increasing cold and wind-blown snow keeps them in. In the High Arctic, for instance, the coldest months are often February and March just when it's getting light. It's a time that looks like spring but feels like winter.

I have followed sudden impulses before in the pursuit of romance—getting engaged above an eagle's nest on my first date, marrying ten days later in Australia on the other side of the world, flying across the Northwest Passage in a teddy (under my parka), kidnapping a husband by float plane for a tryst at a lonely lake, spending Christmas in a semi-subterranean sod hut and draping Christmas lights on an iceberg. Women's magazines call it adding spice to a relationship or bringing magic to a marriage. The aim is the same even when some of the methods are unorthodox.

So it was entirely in character on the morning of March 1, 1995 that I made a sudden decision to fly from Fort Simpson to Yellowknife to shop and the next day to fly from Yellowknife to Resolute to carry out the surprise. I even had the blessing of the Church. "It's a wonderful idea," laughed Blanche, the wife of the Anglican Bishop of the Arctic, when she picked me up to shop for goodies not found in Resolute. I filled my cart with such delicacies as imported cheeses, gourmet sausages, fancy breads, exotic fresh fruits, nuts, chocolates, oysters, candles, wine—and a giant, luscious-looking, personally inscribed Black Forest birthday cake.

Even the First Air flight attendants grinned as they turned a blind eye to the scales at the check-in counter and helped stash my stuff— pizzas under this passenger, muffins under that one, daffodils in the overhead bin, Black Forest cake in the galley. I was especially lucky, as government bigwigs were aboard that day doing their annual airline inspection check. They overlooked my cargo but the flight attendant confiscated my point-and-shoot camera when I tried to take a photo of Resolute from the air. Why, I still can't fathom. Unfortunately for photography, the community was having a rare, bright, blue-sky day, providing a photo opportunity that might not come again.

The first thing I saw after landing was the sign Staffhouse peeking through snow banked to the rooftops of buildings by Resolute's most recent blizzard. Nearby, at Bradley Air, pilots were digging out a Twin Otter from under a mountain of snow; their truck was still buried, and only the handbars showed on a couple of Hondas parked high on a platform beside them. The March wind was a bit chillier than it had been during my earlier visit in July. Welcome to Resolute in spring.

I hurried into the terminal and this time in the crowd there was a familiar face.

"Frank doesn't know you're coming," Aziz greeted me with a wink. In 1978, Aziz (pronounced Aussie) had been a mechanic and later the base manager for Kenn Borek Air. He now owned Kheraj Enterprises, the company for which Frank was building a community complex. Aziz and his assistant, Wayne, helped get back my birthday goodies from the passengers (the pizzas and Black Forest cake caused some difficulty); then we gathered together my numerous bags and drove the four-mile road to the now consolidated community. Only a cemetery on the beach revealed where the old village had been.

"I've arranged for you to spend the next few days in a house in town where the Queen once stayed. It'll be a change for Frank to get out of the bunkhouse and you'll have more privacy," said Aziz. "But stay inside. Don't let anybody see you till I get Frank to the house to meet you so you can surprise him. We told him to pick up some machinery from there today. Wayne will try to hurry him up."

I was grateful for Aziz's kindness, but it must have been a long time ago that the Queen overnighted in his thinly insulated aluminum-sided house, a bungalow that had once been at the Base. I guess the Queen must have been winging it, too. Although drifting snow obscured the view from the kitchen, wooden tulips in a vase on the table by the window stimulated thoughts of spring. A southern spring, I thought ruefully as I prepared the appetizers, marinated the steaks, and pulled on an extra sweater. The house hadn't been heated since Christmas when Aziz and his family moved in temporarily after their family house froze.

Suddenly I heard a truck pulling up at the door and then footsteps crunching on the snow. Time to put the rest of my plan into action. I slipped quickly into a long black negligee, turned on a tape of "Waltzing Matilda" to give my husband a hint to my identity, and slinked to the door with a goblet of wine. "Happy birthday," I breathed, trying to sound sexy.

But it wasn't Frank. It was Wayne come to tell me that my workaholic husband insisted on drywalling the hamlet office before he responded to Aziz's request to pick up the generator from the Queen's house. My peculiar sense of humour overcame any sense of embarrassment, but I can't say the same for Wayne. He left, red-faced, promising to think of another excuse to entice Frank to the house.

My enthusiasm for playing the vamp waned a little during the rest of the afternoon. Three times someone came to the door and three times I started into my seduction scene before realizing it was for the wrong person. The idea of Frank's wife flying from Fort Simpson to surprise him for his birthday appealed to the construction crew, and they were making mighty efforts to keep me informed.

It was seven o'clock before Aziz finally succeeded in bringing Frank to the door. By that time, Matilda was no longer waltzing. She was huddled on the sofa in a parka trying to keep her negligee warm. Her husband, however, made a grand entrance—he was unrecognizable in a skidoo suit, with an old towel wrapped around his neck as a balaclava, goggles, mitts, and covered from head to toe in whitewash and paint.

Next day, Frank was late for work but he brought back his buddies for a luncheon birthday bash. The menu was an eclectic mix of pizza, oysters, and Black Forest cake. Coincidentally, it was Pizza Day at the school, a day when the senior class makes pizzas for the whole community. I could have left pizza off my shopping list if I had known.

As many as a thousand people lived and worked in Resolute at the time of the boom. After the oil companies and their associated services pulled out, the population dwindled to the present 190 permanent residents (179 in the Hamlet and 11 at the Base).

Resolute is a compact little community that starts at the beach and slopes uphill to the bluffs and its main landmark, Signal Hill. From the window of Aziz's house (when the view was not obliterated by ice fog, blowing snow, or chimney smoke), I could see almost all of the town at once—an assortment of snow-banked one-or-two-storey houses, the modest grey-green Anglican church, the Co-op store, the familiar boat-shaped Nursing Station, Qarmatalik School, and if I took a short walk to the end of town, an ugly block of uneconomic row-housing which had been abandoned soon after being built. Handily, right next door to me, was Bezal and Terry's High Arctic International Tourist Home and a signpost pointing to the North Pole.

As soon as Frank headed into the usual bi-weekly blizzard to go to work, I pulled on the many layers of clothing I needed to negotiate the short distance to the Jesudasons' house.

Bezal had just arrived back from Korea where he was advising the Koreans who were about to launch their assault on the Pole from the Russian side. In the 1995 season, Bezal and Terry were supporting one Korean, three Japanese, one French, and one Polish expedition. All were aiming to get there on foot while lugging sleds. Most had decided against aerial resupply either because of expense or the desire for a more physical challenge.

I tracked down the British team at the Narwhal Hotel at the Base.

Sergeant Richard Mackenzie (Mac), sparked by Sir Ranulph's earlier expeditions, was being sponsored by the British Army on an unsupported solo trip to the Pole from the Canadian side. Fearing that I might affect Mac's concentration on his goal, Bronco, the officer in charge of the British expedition, forbade me to talk to his contender. I did learn that Mac was trying out a "revolutionary" double sledge that bent like a snake over pressure ridges and became a boat over open water. He wore a full immersion survival suit and used snowshoes with crampons to get a grip on rough rubble ice. If snow drifted over his "bombproof" tent, the Brit could still lift one corner to get ice for water and another corner to get rid of his pee bottle. To keep sane while solo, he played his flute.

Already trekking from Russia to Canada via the Pole was a team of explorers led by veteran polar expeditionist, Will Steger. Members of this International Arctic Project came from the United States, Japan, Russia, Denmark, and the United Kingdom. In the first twenty-four hours of their journey, they had been turned back by shifting ice pans and open water, their dogs had plunged through thin ice, two men had fallen into the freezing water trying to save the dogs, and next day the whole team was pinned down in their tents by an eight-day blizzard.

Reluctantly, they had to use a helicopter to get them over 375 miles of slushy ice on the Siberian side, but they slogged on with their dogs to reach the Pole on Earth Day, a day chosen to draw worldwide attention to southern-caused pollution in the north. This team finished the rest of the trip from the Pole to Canada on foot.

World famous Italian mountaineer Reinhold Messner and his brother Hubert started their trip in the same way as Will Steger's team, but the Messners were not so lucky. The Brits heard of the Italian disaster by radio in Resolute, and Bezal and I confirmed it by fax. Only twenty-four hours and eleven miles from the start of their ten-week expedition, the Messners were forced to abandon their mission and return to their starting point in Siberia. As they had probably spent $100,000 and a couple of years of their time, it was an expensive day in their life.

Although some details were probably lost in the translation from Italian and German to English, it appeared that the brothers were first followed and attacked by polar bears; then, two hours later, they lost their sledge and most of their gear.

"That night was the worst night of my life," Reinhold reported after a frantic SOS call finally got through and they were rescued by a Russian helicopter.

On the first day of their expedition, in temperatures of minus 42 degrees Celsius and strong northerly winds, the men had fastened their tent into the ice and were inside melting ice to thaw their first meal when they heard crashing sounds in the darkness outside. They ran from the tent and were appalled to see huge masses of ice smashing around them on three sides.

They managed to pull their tent free of the colliding pressure ridges, but their sleds and most of their gear disappeared into a deep crevasse. In trying to save their precious sleds, Hubert fell into the numbing water. Despite his frozen fingers, he managed to pull himself out in the nick of time.

With their way back to the Russian coast cut off, their boots lost under the ice and only flimsy slippers to protect their feet, their trip came to an end. The brothers were lucky to make contact with a Russian helicopter by an emergency transmitter, and fourteen hours later they were flown to a weather station in Siberia.

Later, I learned that Mac, the British Army sergeant, managed to get to 84 degrees north after forty-one days on the ice, but he had to abort his trip after he sprained his back while trying to pull his sled over a pressure ridge.

When I arrived in Resolute, Canada's Richard Weber and Russia's Mikhail Malakhov were already two weeks into their expedition, ferrying their food caches between Ward Hunt Island and camps on the icepack. They had to start earlier than the other adventurers because they were trying to trek to the Pole and back in the one season without being resupplied. Nobody had done this since Cook and Peary's attempts at the turn of the century.

There would have been no argument as to who got to the Pole first if Cook and Peary had been hooked into a satellite. In 1995, Weber-Malakhov and the Will Steger team not only communicated their exact position on a daily basis but they relayed their adventures and misadventures to millions of children around the world via e-mail and the Internet.

Not all the year's polar adventurers were headed for the Geographical North Pole. One morning I blew (literally) into the

Jesudasons' outfitting room to find Bezal putting sheepskin *mungwas* on Hyoichi Kono's feet. (*Mungwa*s are like sleeping bags for the feet; they are made of two layers of sheepskin and are meant to be worn over boots of caribou- or seal-skin called *kamik*s.)

Hyoichi was doing a solo sled trip to the Magnetic North Pole, but his dream was to walk from the Geographic North Pole to his home town of Tokyo. He hoped to complete the journey, he said, before the end of the twentieth century. Hyoichi's "prospectus" was a gem. He wrote that he was "surprised" that winter temperatures "in Yukon in Alaska" [sic] were minus 58 degrees Celsius and was "astonished" by a polar bear in Resolute. He sounded naive but his list of physical achievements was impressive. He had travelled around the world by bicycle, walked across the United States, climbed the highest peaks in North and South America, run through Mongolia and Patagonia, and rafted the Yukon River.

The cover of Hyoichi's self-produced brochure showed him pulling a heavy sled over the ice and the words *Mamat Kono 95*. "It means I would make delicious polar bear meat," he explained enthusiastically. When I looked a little stunned, he added, "That's a joke." He laughed. So I laughed too.

I found my next polar adventurers by accident but they were the ones who finally got me to the Pole—nearly.

Resolute in March is not the place for a casual stroll. Wind often determines where you will go. You don't walk around as much as you blow around. A notice on the Hamlet Office warned Extreme Wind Chills. 40 KPH. Minus 44 Celsius. You Can Get Frost Bite In Less Than A Minute. So when I wanted to jaw with the pilots at the Base I had to hitch a ride on a truck or snowmobile.

Karl Zberg of Bradley Air is one of the most experienced polar pilots in the business. Since he went north in 1967, he has made more than twenty-five landings at the Pole and many more in between. Karl was entertaining me with stories of sixty parachutists jumping to the Pole from ten thousand feet, when two unassuming men walked into the office to study the map on the wall.

Naturally, I soon started a conversation with the strangers. "So where do you come from?" I asked brashly, oblivious to the fact they might not speak English—and they didn't.

"From Poland," the taller of the two said after my question surfaced through filters of French, English, and Polish.

"And where are you going?" I pressed on with my shameless interrogation.

"To the Pole," answered the other.

WITH TWO POLES TO THE POLE. The headline jumped immediately to my mind. I just couldn't resist. "Can I come with you?" was my knee-jerk reaction.

"Sure," I think somebody said.

And so it came about that after seventeen years of reading about and talking to other people trekking to the North Pole, I was about to wing my way there myself. Well, TO THE NORTH POLE—NEARLY was more correct. But then what can you expect after one minute's preparation? All the way?

On the surface, Marek Kaminski and Wojtek Moskal, from Gdansk, were unlikely contenders for the Holy Grail. On a slim budget, they were camped out at the back of one of Bradley Air's warehouses. They were sponsored by the Bank of Gdansk, but they had money only for one flight to drop them at the traditional starting point of Ward Hunt Island and one more to bring them back—preferably after they reached the Pole. They were travelling lighter than most. Unlike the Weber-Malakhov expedition, who dined on whipping cream and chocolate truffles, the Poles had no specially developed meals. (Their diet of simple freeze-dried milk and nuts and power bars would run out in seventy days.) "We're trying to eat as much as possible before we go," Wojtek explained.

They had few sponsors to supply the high tech state-of-the-art equipment that other expeditionists had. "We're relying on traditional Norwegian gear. We use canvas boots because Amundsen did," Marek said simply. The men would limit their fuel by making weekly, not nightly, radio contact with Bezal back in Resolute. To defend themselves from polar bears, they intended to wrap their tent in rope rather than use flares or guns.

Compared to some of the other expeditionists, their polar experience was limited. "We met five years ago on a glacier in Spitzbergen," Wojtek said as he checked the weight of his gear on Bradley's scales. "It was like Stanley and Livingstone. A few years later, we decided to go to the Pole."

Neither could tell you why. Yes, they had a dream. They were my kind of people.

One of my personal frustrations in travelling around the North is that there are too many things to do, and given the complications that can arise, too little time to do them. Winging it is like a Pandora's Box: easy to open but what do you do with all the things that fly out? In the week I was able to spend in Resolute, I had opportunities to fly to Grise Fiord, the most northerly and arguably the most picturesque community in Canada; to Polaris Mine; and to Ward Hunt Island with the Poles. In theory, there was time to do all three; there was even time to be back in Resolute most days to cook dinner for my husband. Practice was another matter.

First, the Poles had to wait for their "lost-in-transit" snowshoes. Then "something strange that's never happened before" downed our plane. Then the mechanic had to wait for new brake parts. Then a succession of blizzards obliterated the road so I couldn't get a lift to the airport. For three days, I got up at 5:00 A.M., put on a roomful of clothes, stuffed cameras, batteries, and film in every pocket, and waited breathless at the window. A series of phone calls later, I had to repeat the procedure in reverse.

"Only a fool would go out in this weather," said Frank, grumpily. "Why don't you stay home for a day and be domestic!"

Believe me, you don't have to go all the way to the Pole for adventure, you can find it on a domestic day in Resolute. As the front and only door of our house opened right into the face of the blizzard, I couldn't venture in and out without help even had I wanted to. So I had to try a day at home.

To keep the door shut against the face of the wind, I wedged a broom between it and the furnace, the first object inside the house. Outside, Frank roped it to the porch railing. But what to do about the snow that kept coming in through the cracks, snow that was piled knee-high by afternoon? "Shovel it into the bathtub and melt it under the hot water tap," Frank suggested by phone from the job site.

In between trips shovelling snow to the bathroom, I put a load of clothes into the washing machine and turned it on. It roared into action with a life of its own and thundered through the cycles as if it was about to blow up. Suddenly, it did. As the machine erupted, water gushed onto the cold porch floor and turned instantly to ice. I had my own skating rink. I wrung out the clothes by hand and threw them into the adjacent dryer. When I returned much later to take them out, the machine had stopped and the clothes were as hard as bricks. I couldn't wait to compare notes with the Queen.

Finally, on the fourth day, the wind stopped and the sky cleared. I leapt to the phone. It was Greg from Bradley Air. "Get out here as quick as you can. This storm's over but another's on its way. I can't pick you up because my truck's buried to the roof and I have to help dig out the plane." I phoned Frank. "I'll be back for dinner, okay?" Fortunately, the jet from the south was due so I hitched a ride to the Base with Canadian Airlines.

At the Bradley hangar, a Herman Nelson heater was piping hot air to the blanket-wrapped propeller to warm the oil, the Poles were taking photos of each other on the snow-moving machines and giggling as if they were kids going on a sightseeing spin, and our pilot, Russ Bomberry, a Mohawk Indian, was checking the controls. "Where's Karl?" I asked nervously. "Don't worry, Lyn, they don't come any better than Russ," Greg answered. "The Japanese on the last flight called him 'The Man Who Parts Clouds.' It was foul weather all the way up Ellesmere Island, then as soon as they cleared Canada and got to Ward Hunt Island, the sun came out just as Russ said."

Well, that was our plan, too. It was good weather at the Pole but we couldn't get there because of bad weather to the south. Two hours from Resolute, our narrow window of opportunity slammed shut, and like so many others before us, we were forced to land at Eureka. And we would stay there, said Russ, till the weather cleared. After I heard it cost $300 a night to stay at the trailer complex of Eureka, I prayed that would be soon. I could scarcely go down the street to find another motel. But, I told myself cheerfully, if I had to spend that kind of money for overnight accommodation, I'd rather spend it on a once-in-a-lifetime trip such as this than the best Hilton in the world.

We stayed at Eureka three days. Marek and Wojtek spent their time writing final postcards and eating everything in sight in a determined bid to fill up and put on weight before facing their sparse freeze-dried polar diet. As we were always on standby for departure if the weather cleared, every meal was declared their Last Supper.

Now that the sun had been peeping over the horizon for a couple of weeks and the long winter night was ending, most of the scientists at the new Astrolab were winding down their studies of the atmosphere and the night sky and were waiting to leave. Dr. John Bird—atmospheric scientist as well as marathon runner, photographer, mountain climber, balloonist, and pilot—drove me up the road with the night shift to see the colourful Astrolab perched on the summit of a 1900-foot mountain, nine miles from the Eureka base camp.

Despite its isolation, most people like Eureka. "I'm so glad to see a woman," were the cook's first words when I entered the dining room, but Bernadette Allen, who puts in four- to six-month shifts at Eureka, loves her job. Her laughter in the kitchen at dawn sets the tone for the rest of the day. She keeps busy and takes on extra chores such as growing vegetables under lights in the lounge. "And I try to maintain the tradition of a Sunday barbecue despite the dark, blizzards, and fifty below. You have to keep interested." Just for fun, she donned her chef's hat and cotton uniform, and we hammed a picture-taking session on the picnic benches outside the dining room window at fifty below. The Poles took the pictures but from the inside. They would be outside long enough.

Not everybody likes working for months in the dark at Eureka. Karl told me that he had to haul out a mechanic affected by Seasonal Affective Disorder. "He went bananas," Karl said simply, then added, "He wanted to sit on the wing."

Marek and Wojtek were glad we were forced down at Eureka. They were delightfully candid. "Maybe tomorrow I'll be a little scared but I'm glad I have got this far," Wojtek confided.

Finally, Russ said we could go. I put on as many clothes as would allow me to stagger to the plane—thermal underwear, down-filled pants, wind pants, turtleneck wool sweater, fleece shirt, down-filled vest, Bezal's outsize parka, gloves AND mitts, ear muffs, a woollen scarf from the nurse in Resolute, down-filled cap with ear flaps, two pairs of socks, and felt-lined plastic Sorel boots (next time, if there is a next time, those Sorels will not be plastic).

My two problems in keeping warm and taking photos in the wind on the arctic ice were the two areas of my body that I couldn't cover with multi-layers of clothing—my eyes and my hands. Glasses fog and fingers freeze. I used various methods to cope. Dr. John lit the charcoal burner inside a little case I carried in one pocket and Bernadette gave me a stock of extra matches. In other pockets, I stashed a variety of handwarmers, some I brought myself and others left over from previous polar expeditions. You are supposed to scrunch them in your hands for an emergency fillip of heat but invariably, they have never worked for me, except back home in my heated living room.

At 10:00 A.M. we were ready, and Jim drove us over Lemming Crossing to the Eureka Airport with its cardboard cut-out Christmas trees and sheds labelled McDonald's, Pizza Hut, and Canadian Tire. I had to keep my sense of humour because as soon as we lifted into the air, all else was lost in cloud. The glaciers, icecaps, mountains, and fiords of Ellesmere Island are scenically superb, but we could neither see nor photograph them during the one hour and forty-minute flight to Ward Hunt Island.

And then, just as we came to the end of Canada, the clouds cleared and the sun appeared briefly from the fog. Ahead, the path to the Holy Grail was bathed in light.

Canada ended in a dramatic crescendo of mountain peaks, jumbled glaciers, pyramidal islands, and steep bluffs: a symphonic landscape well worth waiting for. The land dropped down to an ice shelf offshore, but almost immediately, Ward Hunt Island reared like a volcano to be Canada's final statement before the no-man's-land of the Pole.

Before we touched down, Russ took the Poles on a reconnaissance flight over the frozen ocean to show them the terrain. From the air, the sea-ice looked flat, a swirling pattern of white silk crinkled here and there by creases and folds, and pleated by dark stripes. Down among them, those crinkles were walls of ice that had to be climbed, those stripes were leads of open water that had to be crossed. Previous expeditionists had reported that there were only five miles of "really bad stuff" before the terrain smoothed out. You could do one or two miles a day, they said, if you were lucky.

Marek and Wojtek were to cover only twenty-five miles in their first month. They nearly gave up after Wojtek fell into icy water, but they persevered and made it to the Pole before their food ran out by covering 435 miles in their second month. Terry told me that they lost a lot of weight.

After a couple of trials to find the best landing spot, Russ brought us down. A big swoosh as snow obliterated our window view, a lot of bumps as we careered along the ice, a final engine roar, and then we stopped.

This would be my furthest north.

We had only forty minutes. Any longer and the instruments could freeze. One of our engines had to be kept running. No Herman Nelsons on the ice pack. Clutching the cameras that were strung from my neck, I clambered down from the plane and teetered onto the ice to take a picture of the Poles taking their gear from the plane. Almost immediately, the scene disappeared as my breath and the warm air from the engine hit the cold arctic air and condensed.

While the Poles assembled their gear, took their pictures, and checked their positions, I struggled with taking pictures in the cold. Not known for keeping things simple by doing only one thing at once, I tried to take movies, colour slides, and black and white prints. I didn't know which camera would survive in the extreme conditions, so I brought them all—Sony, Pentax, Nikon, and Canon. I had tried to prepare myself so well that I had too much stuff hanging around my neck and too many things in too many pockets. I probably looked comic trying to reach through a tangle of scarves, idiot-stringed mitts, and layers of arctic clothing to locate a new battery or my emergency point-and-shoot. Things had to be done by feel as my glasses fogged, but after half an hour on the ice, I didn't have much feeling left anyway.

Russ, his eyebrows covered in ice, stood by watching the action and counting the minutes to take-off. I gave him my video camera to keep warm in his parka, but the cold had already frozen the shutter button. One by one, the cameras and the batteries died. With the wind chill, the temperature could have been sixty below.

My last shot was of two lonely figures trudging away from the plane on their way to the Pole. "Do you want to go with them?" asked Russ with a smile.

No, I didn't want to go with them. I was cold and tired. I could go back to the plane and eventually a heated house. For the next couple of months, they would be always cold, always tired. As they strained forward like dogs, pulling their heavy survival gear, their world would be restricted to one tent, two sleds, and many, many steps.

Why do so many polar adventurers want to do that? For the challenge they say. I don't need to trudge all the way to the Pole. Nearly going there was challenge enough. For me the North Pole is not a golden spike or the Holy Grail; although I don't rule out the possibility of going there one day, I don't see it as my ultimate destination.

As Robert Louis Stevenson once said, "to travel hopefully is a better thing than to arrive." The journey is the adventure—being alone, taking chances, finding energy in strange situations, not knowing if or how they will turn out. My fascination is not in what is planned but in what is unplanned. For me, the discoveries are made along the way.

Tourist Information

Dear Readers:

If you would like to follow in my tracks or wing your way to your own adventure in the North, then I encourage you to contact the following friendly offices for further information. I hope to see you up here sometime.

—Lyn

Information on tourism opportunities in the Northwest Territories may be obtained from:

Eastern NWT   Nunavut Tourism
P.O. Box 1450
Suite 277
Iqaluit, Northwest Territories
X0A 0H0

Toll-Free Tourism Enquiry Number (North America only)
1-800-491-7910 (Operator #277)
E-Mail address:
nunatour@nunanet.com

Western NWT   NWT Arctic Tourism
Suite 277
Government of the Northwest Territories
P.O. Box 1320
Yellowknife, NT Canada X1A 2L9

Toll-Free Tourism Enquiry Number (North America only)
1-800-661-0788 (Operator #277)
E-Mail address:
tourist@edt.gov.nt.ca

Other books by Lyn Hancock

Yukon, Hello Canada series, Lerner Publications, 1996

Nunavut, Hello Canada series, Lerner Publications, 1995

Northwest Territories, Discover Canada series, Grolier, 1993

There's a Seal in My Sleeping Bag, HarperCollins reprint 1992, original publisher Collins, 1972

Looking for the Wild, Doubleday, 1986 (illustrated by Robert Bateman)

Alaska Highway, Road to Adventure, Autumn Images, 1988

Tell Me, Grandmother, McClelland and Stewart, 1985 (co-authored with Marion Dowler)

Northwest Territories, Canada's Last Frontier, Autumn Images, 1986

An Ape Came Out of My Hatbox, McClelland and Stewart, 1979

Vanderhoof, the Town that Wouldn't Wait, Nechako Valley Historical Society, 1979. (Editor)

Love Affair With a Cougar, Doubleday, 1978

There's a Raccoon in My Parka, Doubleday, 1977

Pacific Wilderness, Hancock House, 1974

The Mighty Mackenzie, Hancock House, 1974